Mastering Microsoft® Works

A Self-Teaching Guide

Related Titles of Interest from Wiley

QuickPascal: A Self-Teaching Guide, Weiskamp and Aguiar
PC DOS: A Self-Teaching Guide, 3rd edition, Ashley and Fernandez
PC DOS 4: A Self-Teaching Guide, Ashley and Fernandez
Mastering Enable /OA: Office Automation Software, Spezzano
The New DOS 4.0, Christopher, Feigenbaum, and Saliga
DOS 4.0 Reference, Christopher, Feigenbaum, and Saliga
Using dBASE IV: Basics for Business, Brownstein
R:BASE for DOS: A Business User's Guide, Condliffe
Parodox: A Business User's Guide, Condliffe
Ventura Publisher 2.0: Mastering Desktop Publishing, Jantz
Hard Disk Smarts: Everything You Need to Choose and Use Your Hard Disk, Bosshardt
Using Lotus Agenda, Goodman
Desktop Publishing with Pagemaker 3.02 for the Macintosh, Bove and Rhodes
Desktop Publishing with Pagemaker 3.0 for the IBM PC and Compatibles, Bove and Rhodes
Lotus 1-2-3 Release 3, Williams
Lotus 1-2-3 Release 2.2, Williams

Mastering Microsoft® Works

A Self-Teaching Guide

David Sachs
Babette Kronstadt
Judith Van Wormer
Barbara Farrell

WILEY

John Wiley & Sons, Inc.

New York • Chichester • Brisbane • Toronto • Singapore

Editor: Therese Zak
Managing Editor: Ruth Greif
Typesetting and Production Services: Northeastern Graphic Services, Inc.

Library of Congress Cataloging-in-Publication Data

Mastering Microsoft Works : a self teaching guide / David Sachs . . .
[et al.].
p. cm.
Includes bibliographical references.
ISBN 0-471-51944-8
1. Intergrated software. 2. Microsoft Works (Computer program)
I. Sachs, David, 1947–
QA76.76.I57M37 1990
652.5'536—dc20

89-24902
CIP

Printed in the United States of America

90 91 10 9 8 7 6 5 4 3 2

For Eric, Gabriel, and Jessica	B.K.
For Linda, Emily, Susannah, and Matthew	D.S.
For Dan, Timothy, and Devin	J.V.W.
For Jim	B.F.

Contents

Preface

Welcome to the wonderful world of personal computing! The technology that you are about to encounter is the result of enormous progress that has occurred during the past ten years. Today's hardware and software offer power that is awesome, for a price that is amazingly inexpensive.

The Purpose/Orientation of this Book

This book provides a comfortable introduction to the world of personal computing in general, and to the world of Microsoft Works for the PC in particular. The emphasis is on learning by doing and on learning skills in context. Therefore, after an introduction, you will learn the relevant skills by actually creating a document, a spreadsheet, and a database. Each new chapter reinforces previously learned skills as well as introduces new ones. Throughout each chapter there are Self-Check sections that allow you to test yourself on the skills you have learned.

What Is Microsoft Works?

Works is a software program for IBM and IBM-compatible computers that provides the most popular computer applications—word processing, a spreadsheet with graphics capabilities, database management, and telecommunications—all for little more than the cost of a ticket to a concert or a compact disk. In the computer industry, Works is known as an "integrated software package." This means that while the four separate components, or tools—word processor, spreadsheet, database, and communications—are capable of performing well on their own, they interact with each other more easily than do stand-alone programs that are purchased separately. With Works it's possible to move from one task to another directly, without exiting from one program and starting another. Also, information may be moved easily from one tool to another.

Equally important is the fact that learning to use the individual Works tools is much easier than learning several unrelated packages. Many of the commands in each tool are similar, the screens are alike, and methods of communicating with the program are consistent.

By the time you have finished learning Works, you will be able to do your writing in a faster, more effective fashion, by using the **Word Processor** tool.

The **Spreadsheet** tool is wonderful if you work with financial information or any numeric data requiring calculations. If you need to compare and contrast the prices for office equipment, a spreadsheet is your answer. If you need to prepare the budget for a project or monthly expenses, a spreadsheet is indispensable. What's more, you may use the spreadsheet's graphics capabilities to create charts so that you can easily see the trends or relationships among your data.

The **Database Manager** tool is the answer if you have a lot of data in your life, such as the names and addresses of friends or clients. You will be able to store this information in an orderly fashion, modify it when necessary, and print it, whenever it is needed.

The **Communications** tool of Works allows your computer to communicate with other computers, a growing need in today's advanced technology.

Microsoft Works Version 2

Microsoft has improved an already excellent product this year with it's new release of Microsoft Works Version 2. Works Version 2 has had its menus and screens revamped so they are consistent from one tool to the next. Several functions have been simplified without compromising the quality of the product and several options that classically have only been available in expensive and complex packages have been added.

Overview of Things to Come

For the most part, the world of personal computing with Works is a friendly and inviting one. You will have to learn some new vocabulary words, as it does have its own language. The jargon is kept to a minimum, but there will be some terms and concepts that are new and are perhaps a little unusual at first. Key terms are highlighted in order to help you become familiar with them.

In Chapter 1, our first order of business will be to acquaint you with the elements of **computer hardware.** Without the hardware, of course, you would be unable to run the software, so it is important that you have some basic ideas about the various components and how they work. After that, we introduce you to what is known as the **Disk Operating System,** or **DOS.** This program is vital for using any computer software, now or in the future. We provide you with the fundamentals of the Disk Operating System, so that you can prepare all of your disks for use, make copies of your files, and keep track of all of the files that you will prepare with your word processor, spreadsheet, or database manager.

This book introduces the special world of Works. This guide gives you experience with the basics of the word processor (Chapter 2), spreadsheet (Chapter 3), and database tools (Chapter 4). Equally important, your explorations should provide an overall feeling for what the computer can do for you.

An integrated program such as Works is perfect for an introductory journey through four of the main applications of personal computing. Since the interface is consistent, you will find that learning Works is a pleasant, comfortable experience. Creating a spreadsheet requires different skills than writing a letter, but once you've seen the word processing screen, the spreadsheet screen will look familiar. Having "opened," "saved," or printed a spreadsheet, you'll have a cursory idea of how to do the same with the database.

Chapters 5 to 7 will give you a second look at each tool which provides the adventuresome user with some more challenging skills. What you will find is that even the more advanced skills in Works are simple and easy to use.

Chapter 8 will show you how the separate tools in Works can be "integrated." Each of the component parts has been carefully designed to work comfortably with the others. This ability greatly enhances the power and usefulness of each individual tool.

Finally, in Chapter 9 we discuss the Communications tool. You may or may not have the necessary equipment to actually try the exercises. However, in today's world, knowing and understanding the communication concepts will give you an advantage over those who are still "in the dark."

White Plains, New York
November 1989

Acknowledgments

Mastering Microsoft Works was written by four of us, but it truly represents the work of many more individuals and organizations. We have received enormous institutional support from Pace University and the School of Computer Science and Information Systems at Pace. In particular, much personal and professional support for our work has come from the Dean, Dr. Susan Merritt.

From another perspective, this book also is a product of the **Pace Computer Learning Center,** a loose affiliation of approximately 15 professors and staff, who have provided over 2,500 days of instruction to over 15,000 individuals in corporate settings throughout the United States and around the world during the past four years. Many of these people have become good personal and professional friends, and our shared experiences in the development and teaching of these courses was ideal preparation for writing this book.

Access to state-of-the-art hardware and software made an enormous difference in the production of this text. In addition, we were assisted with some of the actual writing (and rewriting) by Henry H. Gaylord III for the Communications Chapter and Bettie Williams for the Introductory Chapter. Christopher Emberley, Lynne Bacon, and Alice Cronin provided a tremendous amount of work testing exercises and editing text.

Our work with John Wiley & Sons, Inc. has been made wonderfully smooth by all of the support provided by our editors, Therese A. Zak, Ruth Greif, and Ellen B. Greenberg. They were able to provide us with assistance when we asked for it, quick answers when we needed them, and responsiveness to our needs and concerns.

1

Introducing Microsoft Works

If you are like other new computer users, your natural tendency will be to skip this chapter and turn to the chapter that most interests you. There are very few technical terms and concepts that are necessary for you to use Microsoft Works. However, if you take the time to read this chapter, you will learn the basic computer terms and skills that will make your life easier in the long run. Along with generic computer skills, this chapter specifically describes the basics of Microsoft Works. Even if you are familiar with computers, the last half of this chapter is a keystone to the rest of the book. In this chapter the following will be explained:

- What is Microsoft Works?
- Terminology used to describe computer hardware
- Functions of the special keys on the keyboard
- What **DOS** is, how to use **DOS** commands to prepare a disk for use, and how to copy entire disks or parts of disks
- How to get ready to use Works
- How to start Works
- How to create, open, and save Works files
- How to use the Works menu and Dialog Boxes

What Is Microsoft Works?

The computer is a complex system, comprised of two major elements: the hardware and the software. The hardware is the physical equipment and the software consists of programs or sets of instructions to the computer.

Works is a software program for IBM and IBM-compatible computers that provides the most popular computer applications—word processing, database management, a spreadsheet with graphics capabilities, and telecommunications. In the computer industry, Works is known as an "integrated software package." This means that while the four separate components, or *tools*, are capable of performing well on their own, they also interact well with each other. The menu system in Version 2 of Works has been altered so the menus and screens of each tool are very similar. This will help you learn Works quickly and easily.

The *Word Processor* is the tool to use to enter documents or letters. The *Database Manager* is the tool that handles volumes of data such as the names and addresses of friends or clients. The *Spreadsheet* tool is used for numeric data which may require calculations. The spreadsheet's graphics capabilities may be used to create charts so that the trends or relationships among the data can be seen. Charting is also a great way to actually see the mathematical equations you're learning or to create a model illustrating a basic engineering concept. The *Communications* tool of Works allows your computer to communicate with other computers.

The Hardware

The computer hardware most commonly encountered is the *system unit*, which contains the *CPU* (central processing unit), the *keyboard*, the *mouse*, the *monitor* or *CRT* (cathode ray tube), one or more *disk drives*, and the *printer*. These components allow the user to *input*, or enter information; process the information; *output*, or display, the information; and store the information for future use. While your particular configuration may differ slightly, the common configuration found on an IBM PC is described in the following sections.

The System Unit and the Central Processing Unit

The System Unit is the heart of the computer. It contains the Central Processing Unit (CPU), which controls the processing of the data; the main memory, which stores the commands and data being used; and the circuitry needed to control the rest of the hardware.

The Monitor or CRT

The monitor is one of the principal output devices. It displays information you enter from the keyboard, responses that are generated by the software that you are using, and the results of the commands you use. It is important to know what kind of screen display your computer has. The two basic types of screens are color and monochrome. Along with the actual screen there are monitor *cards* (intricate circuitry) which must be installed in your computer. These cards determine whether the screen will display text and graphics or just text. The Install procedure in Works will ask you questions about the type of monitor card installed in your computer.

If you have a graphics card, you can select the *screen mode*. You can choose between two different modes: Text Mode and Graphics Mode. The appearance of the mouse cursor and formatting options such as bold, underline, and italics will be different depending on the mode you choose. See the Mouse section in this chapter or Chapter 5, on advanced word processing, for futher information.

The Keyboard

The computer keyboard (Figure 1.1) is the main input device of the computer. In many ways the computer keyboard resembles a typewriter keyboard. The traditional typing keys remain in the same position on all keyboards. However, the location of the extra computer keys may be different on your keyboard. There are some additional keys that are used to help give

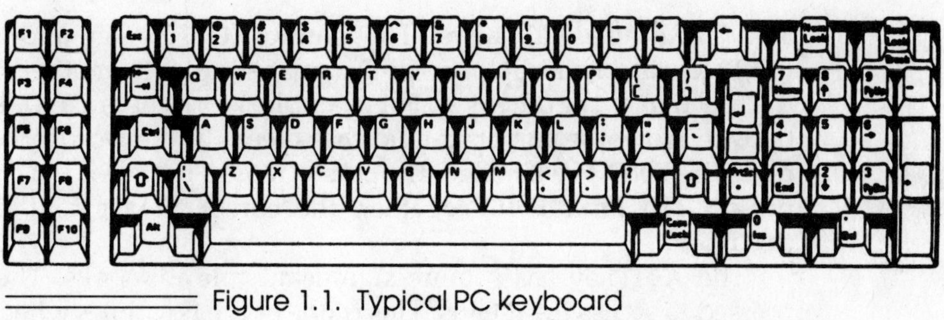

Figure 1.1. Typical PC keyboard

the computer instructions. Some of the keys on the keyboard are described here.

The TAB Key and SPACE BAR: The **TAB** and **SPACE BAR** are typical typewriter keys. On some computer keyboards the **TAB** key may be hard to recognize because it is indicated by an arrow pointing left over an arrow pointing right. The specific effect of the **TAB** key is different in each tool (i.e., word processor, database, spreadsheet, communications) of Works, but in general it moves the cursor a greater distance than one space at a time. The **SPACE BAR** is the big key in the middle of the bottom row of the keyboard, and it is used to create a space.

The *cursor* is the blinking line on the computer screen. It indicates where the next typed character will appear or which item on a menu will be selected.

The SHIFT and CAPS LOCK Keys: **SHIFT** and **CAPS LOCK** are also found on typewriter keyboards. On some computer keyboards the **SHIFT** key is indicated by an outline of an upward arrow; other keyboards also include the word Shift. To type a single capital letter, press the **SHIFT** key and hold it down while typing the letter.

CAPS LOCK is used to type multiple capital letters. It is a *toggle* key, which means that each time you press the key it changes from off to on or vice versa. When **CAPS LOCK** is on, or activated, all letters typed will be capitalized. **CAPS LOCK** only affects the letters A–Z; press **SHIFT** in order to type the top characters on keys that print two characters. The letters **CL** appear on the Works screen when **CAPS LOCK** has been activated.

In Works the **SHIFT** key can also be used in conjunction with nonletter keys to change the effect of those keys. These key combinations typically are used as shortcuts for tasks that can be accomplished in a variety of ways.

The CTRL and ALT Keys: The Control (**CTRL**) key and the Alternate (**ALT**) key are typically pressed in conjunction with another key to change the function of the other key. For example, Works uses **CTRL** key combinations to move the cursor around the screen. In the word processor, if you press the **END** key by itself, the cursor moves to the end of the line. If you press **CTRL** and **END** together, the cursor moves to the end of the document.

The **ALT** key has a more significant role in Works. The **ALT** key is pressed to access the menus. This is one of the few times when the **ALT** key can be used alone. It also is used in conjunction with other keys to provide information necessary to carry out commands.

When using key combinations, always depress the **CTRL** or **ALT** key first and keep it depressed while you press the other key.

The BACKSPACE Key: The **BACKSPACE** key, as it is used in Works, is a destructive backspace. It moves the cursor to the left and it erases any characters that are there. The **BACKSPACE** key is usually located on the top row of the main part of the keyboard. On some keyboards it is represented only by an arrow pointing to the left, while on others it has an arrow and the word Backspace.

The ESC Key: The **ESC** key is used to back out of, or escape from, the current situation. Its uses in Works are to leave a menu, cancel a Dialog Box, cancel a command, quit from Extend, cancel editing changes, stop printing, or erase material from the Formula Bar. (These concepts will be clearer by the end of this book.) The general rule is that **ESC** can be used to escape from an operation before it is completed.

The ENTER Key: In DOS, the **ENTER** key is used to indicate that you have finished typing a command and are ready for DOS to execute it. In Works, **ENTER** has several different functions. It can be used to make selections from a menu or to tell Works that you have finished providing the information it needs to carry out a command. **ENTER** also has specific uses in each of the tools which will be explained in later chapters.

The Function Keys: The function keys are located at the top or left-hand side of most keyboards and are labeled with the letter F followed by a number. Although some keyboards contain additional function keys, Works only uses keys **F1** through **F10**. Some software programs use the function keys as the primary way of giving commands. Works typically uses the function keys alone, or in conjunction with the **CTRL** or **SHIFT** keys, as shortcuts or alternative methods of issuing commands.

The Numeric Keypad: The numeric keypad is an extra set of numeric keys arranged in a square on the right-hand side of most keyboards. It resembles the keypad on calculators and many people find it more efficient for entering numeric data than the row of numbers at the top of the keyboard. Since the numerals share the keys with **arrows** or other functions, a numeral is produced only if **NUM LOCK** is activated or if the key is depressed in conjunction with **SHIFT**.

The ARROW, PGUP (PAGEUP), PGDN (PAGEDOWN), HOME, and END Keys: These keys are called the cursor movement keys, because they are used to control the movement of the cursor around the screen. The **ARROW** keys move the cursor one space, line, or row in the direction of the arrow. The other keys cause bigger jumps in the cursor movement. The specific effects of these keys in each of the tools will be discussed in the appropriate chapters.

On most IBM or IBM-compatible keyboards, these keys are located on the numeric keypad at the right of the keyboard. Some models also contain an additional set of cursor control keys between the alphanumeric keyboard and the numeric keypad.

The NUM LOCK Key: Sometimes you press a cursor control key and nothing happens or a numeral appears on the screen. That is because **NUM LOCK** has been activated. **NUM LOCK**, like **CAPS LOCK**, is a toggle key. Works indicates that **NUM LOCK** has been activated by placing the letters **NL** at the bottom of the screen. When **NUM LOCK** is activated and you press a key on the numeric keypad, the number is typed, or, if the cursor is on a menu where the number has no meaning, nothing happens. To correct this problem, press **NUM LOCK** to deactivate it, and try the cursor control key again. If your keyboard only contains one set of cursor control keys, it is generally advisable to leave **NUM LOCK** deactivated and type numbers using the top row of the alphanumeric keyboard. If you have a second set of cursor control keys, you may want to keep **NUM LOCK** activated and use the numeric keypad to type numbers.

The Mouse

The mouse, like the keyboard, is an input device. It can be used as an alternative to the keyboard to issue commands. If you do not have a graphics screen, the mouse will appear as a rectangle on the screen. If you have a graphics screen, you have the option of having the screen in graphics or text mode. When the screen is in graphics mode the mouse will appear as an arrow; when the screen is in text mode the mouse is represented as a rectangle. The modes can be changed by accessing the **Options Menu** and selecting **Work Settings**.

The mouse has two buttons. When using the mouse with Works, the left button can be used for Clicking or Dragging. Clicking is the process of simply pressing and then releasing the button once. Dragging is the process of holding down the button while repositioning the mouse.

To select a menu or option, simply position the mouse on the option name of your choice and click. If you want to leave a menu, you can close the menu by positioning the mouse on the screen anywhere other than on the menu and clicking.

There are some functions in Works that require special handling of the mouse to achieve the desired results. There is a section later in this chapter instructing you on how to utilize the mouse in these cases.

The Printer

The printer is the main output device used to obtain a printed copy of your work. To use a printer with Works, you must give the program information about the printer you are using and how that printer is connected to your computer. Instructions will be given in the Installation section of this chapter on how to set up your printer.

The Disk Drive(s)

Disk drives are the auxiliary storage units that your computer is most likely to use. The computer can only carry out instructions or manipulate data that are in its main memory. Since this memory is limited and the information in memory is lost when the computer is turned off, disks are used to store both the programs that tell the computer what to do as well as the output of the programs. Anything stored on a disk is stored in a file.

There are two types of disk drives: floppy drives and fixed (or hard) drives. Floppy disk drives have openings into which you insert a diskette (which we will refer to as a disk). Disks are currently either 5.25 inches or 3.5 inches in size, and are transportable. This portability makes floppy disks excellent storage facilities for data. The names **Drive A** and **Drive B** are usually applied to floppy disk drives. **Drive A** is also referred to as **A:** or **a:** and **Drive B** is referred to as **B:** or **b:**.

Many computers also have at least one fixed disk drive. Fixed disk drives are usually not easily portable, but they hold much more information than floppy disks and are accessed at faster speeds. If a computer has one fixed disk drive, that drive typically is referred to as **Drive C** or **C:**.

You must use disk drive names whenever you want the computer to read information from a disk or to store information to a disk.

Care and Handling of Disks

You already have a floppy disk containing the Works program, and will be creating and saving files of your own. Floppy disks are data storage facilities that may be used again and again. They must be handled carefully, however, because when a disk gets damaged there is a good chance that the files on it will be partially or totally destroyed. You will learn how to make backup copies of both individual files and entire disks later in this chapter; for now here are some ways to avoid damaging disks and losing files as a result.

Floppy disks are sensitive to heat, cold, dust, moisture, and magnetic devices, so keep the following guidelines in mind:

- Never store your disks in a location where the temperature will be above 125°F or below 50°F
- Always store 5.25 inch disks in their disk jackets
- Avoid eating and drinking at your computer work area or disk storage area
- Never write on a label on a 5.25 inch disk with a ball point pen; use a felt tip instead
- Never expose your disk to a magnet or leave a disk on top of a computer, television, stereo, or other electrical device, as these generate an electromagnetic field
- Avoid passing your disks through magnetic sensors such as those in libraries, stores, and airports
- Never touch any exposed area of a disk
- Never paper clip a disk to another disk or to papers, as the paper clip may put a crease in the disk
- Never bend a disk

Note

People often bend disks inadvertently while trying to insert them into disk drives. NEVER try to force a disk into a drive. If the disk does not slip into the drive smoothly, pull it back out and make sure you are holding it correctly. Then gently try to insert it again; you may find that you need to adjust the angle of insertion.

To insert a 5.25 inch disk into a disk drive:

1. Remove the disk from its jacket.
2. Hold the disk so that the label faces up and the small notch in the side is on the right. (This is called the write protect notch; when it is covered with a piece of tape, called the write protect tab, no new information can be stored on the disk and existing files cannot be erased or changed.)
3. Carefully insert the disk into the disk drive and close the door.

To insert a 3.5 inch disk into a disk drive:

1. Hold the disk so that the label faces up and the end with the sliding metal cover enters the drive first.
2. Carefully insert the disk into the drive until it clicks into place.
3. To write protect a 3.5 inch disk, push the black plastic tab on the left-hand side of the disk so that the square notch is open.

DOS (The Disk Operating System)

There is really very little you need to know about DOS to work with Microsoft Works. However, understanding a few concepts and basic commands is essential for your ability to work with Works or any other package. There are many commands which DOS provides that help organize and manipulate your diskettes and run your computer system effectively and efficiently. Many file manipulation commands such as those erasing unwanted files and copying and formatting disks are now provided in Microsoft Works. However, most software companies will recommend that you copy all software disks before trying to use or install their package, so you will have a backup copy should anything happen to the original. Because of this you should use DOS to make the disk copies rather than attempting to run Microsoft Works and use its file manipulation options.

PC-DOS or **MS-DOS** is the Disk Operating System typically used with IBM or IBM-compatible personal computers. DOS is the collection of programs that lets you begin to use your personal computer. It serves as the intermediary between your software program and the CPU. Without first "loading" DOS, you would be unable to proceed to the next step, which is loading the actual software you wish to use. To *load* a program means to copy at least part of it from the disk into the computer's memory. Loading DOS is sometimes referred to as *booting* the disk or booting the system, because DOS "pulls itself up by its own bootstraps" without the help of other programs.

Thus far, we've provided general information about Works or about computers. Hereafter, you'll be trying activities as they are discussed. Turn the computer on and try some **DOS** commands. Instructions for starting your computer are given separately for computers with and without hard drives.

If your computer has only floppy disk drives:

1. Put your **DOS** disk in Drive A and close the door.

Note If your computer has more than one floppy disk drive, drive A is usually the left or top drive.

2. Turn on the system unit, monitor, and printer. Don't worry if nothing happens for a while. The computer is checking that its components are working.

The following message will appear:

Current Date is Tues 1-01-1980
Enter new date (mm-dd-yy):

Some versions of DOS have slightly different default dates.

3. Type the date in the form: **mm-dd-yy**

For example, if the date is September 11, 1989, type: 9-11-89

4. Press **ENTER**. In most cases, when you have completed giving DOS a command or the information it requests, you must press **ENTER** to tell DOS that you are done.

A new message will appear on the screen:

Current time is 0:00:23:23
Enter new time:

5. Enter the current time in the form: **hh:mm**

DOS uses a 24-hour clock. Therefore, to enter P.M. times, add 12 to the current time. For example, if it is 1:30 P.M., type: 13:30

6. Press **ENTER.**

The system prompt, *A>*, should appear on your screen.

If your computer has a hard disk:

1. Be sure that there are no disks in the floppy disk drives.
2. Turn on the system unit, monitor, and printer.

As with the computers that only have floppy drives, the computer will check that the necessary components are functioning. What appears on your screen next will vary depending on how the hard disk was set up. If you are prompted to enter a date and time, proceed with steps 3–6 above.

3. Your screen should contain the system prompt, *C:\>*, or instructions on how to get to the C prompt or how to enter DOS commands.

The Current Drive

The *current drive*, which is sometimes called the *active* or *default drive*, indicates where the computer will search when it needs to find a file or to save a file. When you first turn the computer on, the active drive is the one that contains the DOS files. The name of the active drive is included in the prompt that appears on the screen. Unless you give the computer other instructions, it will look on the disk in the active drive for any files it needs and will assume that any commands you give it apply to the disk in the active drive.

*The **FORMAT** Command*

The **FORMAT** command is important because it gets your data disks ready for use. It erases the disks and puts tracks, sectors, and space for a directory on the disk so that files may be kept in order and may be accessed readily.

It is necessary to format a disk in order to store Works data files once they are created. Be sure to follow the directions carefully. Since the **FORMAT** command erases the disk, if you accidentally format a disk that contains information, the information will be lost.

Note Some of the DOS responses and the exact format of the commands may be different in your system than those described here. These discrepancies are caused by the many revisions that have been made to DOS. The commands and prompts given in this book are from DOS version 3.2. Versions of DOS that differ only by the decimal (e.g., DOS 3.0 and DOS 3.1) contain minor variations. A change in the integer portion (whole number) indicates a greater revision. None of the differences between versions has a major effect on the commands shown here. Any significant variations will be noted.

If you are using a system with only floppy drives:

1. Be sure the DOS disk is still in Drive **A**.
2. Place a blank disk in Drive **B**.
3. Type: **format b:**

Note You may use any combination of uppercase and lowercase letters when you type a DOS command.

Your screen display should be: *A>Format B:*

Note If you omit the **B**:, DOS will assume that you want to format the disk in the A drive, since that is the current drive.

4. Press **ENTER**.
5. You will be prompted to enter a new diskette for Drive B. Since you have already done that, press **ENTER**.
6. When the formatting is complete, DOS will give a message telling how much space is available on the disk and if any part of the disk is bad. It will then ask if you want to format another.
7. The next response is up to you. Many people like to format an entire box of disks at one time. If you want to format another disk, type: **y**. If you do not want to format additional disks, type: **n**. Press **ENTER**. (**Note:** It is not necessary to press **ENTER** if you are using early versions of DOS.)
8. Remove the last formatted disk from the disk drive. Put on a label with some identification of the type of data you will saving on the disk.

If you are using a system with a hard drive:

1. Put a blank disk in Drive A.
2. Type: **format a:**

Note You may use any combination of uppercase and lowercase letters when you type a DOS command.

The screen display should be: C >*Format A:*

Note If you omit the **A:**, DOS will assume that you want to format the disk in the C drive, since that is the current drive.

3. Follow steps 4–8 above to finish the command.

DISKCOPY

The **DISKCOPY** command is important because it makes an exact duplicate of any floppy disk. **DISKCOPY** is a very powerful command; it also can be dangerous. In the process of copying all of the files from one disk (the *source* disk) to another (the *target* disk), **DISKCOPY** also formats, and therefore erases, the target disk. For this reason, **DISKCOPY** should only be used when the disk that you are copying to is blank, or contains information that you are sure you will not want to use again.

Use the **DISKCOPY** command to make a *backup* copy of software or data disks. You should use the backup copy as the working copy and store the original disks in a safe place. That way if your backup disk is accidentally ruined, you can get the original disk, make another copy and continue working.

Once you start saving your own data on disks, you will probably want to use **DISKCOPY** frequently to make backup copies of your work disks.

The general format of the **DISKCOPY** command is:

DISKCOPY <source> <target>

where **<source>** is the letter, followed by a colon, of the drive containing the disk you want to copy, and **<target>** is the letter, followed by a colon, of the drive containing the disk onto which the copy will be made. **If your computer has only floppy disk drives:**

1. Insert the DOS disk in Drive A.
2. Type: **diskcopy a: b:**

You will see the following prompts to insert the source and target diskettes in the drives you designated in the command.

Insert source diskette in drive A:
Insert target diskette in drive B:
Strike any key when ready

3. Remove DOS from Drive A and replace it with the disk you want to copy.
4. Put a blank disk in Drive B and press any key.

Screen prompts relating to the copy process will appear. When DOS is finished, you will be prompted:

Copy another (Y/N)?_

5. If this is the only disk that you want to copy, type: **n**
6. Remove and label the disk. Now put the original away in a safe place.

If you are using a computer with DOS on the hard disk and one floppy drive, the process is somewhat more complicated because the same disk drive is used for the source and the target. DOS will prompt you to change drives.

1. Be sure you are at the **C>** prompt.
2. Type: **diskcopy a: a:**

You will see the following prompts:

Insert source diskette in drive A:
Strike any key when ready

3. Insert the disk you want to copy into Drive A. Press any key.

When the contents of the disk are copied into the computer's memory, you will be prompted to:

Insert target diskette in drive A:
Strike any key when ready

4. Remove the original disk and insert the blank disk in Drive A. Press any key.
5. Depending on the amount of computer memory available, you may have to swap the Source and Target disks a few more times. If this is necessary, you will be prompted. Follow the screen prompts.
6. When the diskcopy is completed, you will be prompted:

Copy another (Y/N)?_

7. If this is the only disk that you want to copy, type: **n**. Otherwise type: **y**
8. Remove and label the backup copies.

COPY

The **COPY** command is used to make copies of one or more files. Just as **DISKCOPY** is used to backup an entire disk, **COPY** is used to backup individual files. Even if you want to copy all of the files from one disk to another, you must use the **COPY** command rather than **DISKCOPY** if the disk you are copying to already contains files you wish to keep.

The **COPY** command can be used to copy a file from a disk to another disk, or if the name is changed, to another location on the same disk. For example, if you have a filename **LABEL.WPS** on a disk in drive **A** and you want to make a copy of it on the disk in drive **B**, you would type: **Copy A:LABEL.WPS B:**.

The rules and procedures for copying files are beyond the scope of this short DOS introduction. Works also allows you to make copies of disks by using the **File/File Management/Copy** command. For most file copying activities, this is easier than using DOS because it provides menus to help guide you through the command. However, there is one time when you will want to use the DOS **COPY** command. Before using the setup program to get Works ready to run on your computer system, you should make backup copies of all your disks. This may be done using the DOS **COPY** command.

To copy all files on one disk to another, you can use the **COPY** command with a special syntax. If you are using a system with two floppy disk drives:

1. Insert the disk with the files to be copied in drive A:.
2. Insert a blank formatted disk in drive B:.
3. Type: **copy a:*.* b:**

The *.* tells DOS to copy all files with any filename and any extension.

4. Press **ENTER**. DOS will list the name of each file as it is copied from one disk to the other.

This same procedure can be used if you have only one disk drive. However, this procedure requires you to frequently change the disk in your disk drive and it is not a good procedure to use when copying multiple files. If you have only one disk drive, make sure that the disk to which you are copying the files is blank, and use the **DISKCOPY** command described in the previous section.

1. Format a blank disk.
2. Copy all the files from one of your Microsoft Works disk to the blank disk.

---

1. *Put a blank disk in Drive A: and type:* ***Format A:*** *and then press* ***ENTER.***
2. *Use either the* ***DISKCOPY*** *command or the* ***COPY *.**** *command. See the* ***DISKCOPY*** *or the* ***COPY*** *section in this chapter for the exact syntax.*

Installing Works

It does not take long to install Works on your computer system, and it has to be installed only once. The Setup Program copies Works to your hard disk or floppy disks, and tells Works about the equipment you have.

Setting up and using Works on a hard disk: You must use the Setup Program before you use Works for the first time. Before running the Setup Program, you need the following:

- The Works disks you have purchased
- The type of Video card you have
- The name of your printer (if you have one)
- The name of your mouse (if you have one)

To set up Works:

1. Turn on your computer.
2. Insert the Setup Disk in Drive A.
3. At the DOS prompt, type: **a:setup**
4. Press **ENTER.**
5. Follow the directions on the screen:
   a. The first screen pauses to determine if you want to continue to use the Works Setup. Press **ENTER** to continue.
   b. Next, you are asked whether you want to create a new copy of

Works, or change a previous installation. If this is the first installation, press **ENTER**.

c. The next screen asks where you want Works installed. If you have a hard disk, you most likely want it on the *Hard Disk C*.
d. Works then will be created in a subdirectory called *Works*. To accept this, press **ENTER**.
e. To continue you need to enter the type of video card you have. The Setup program has already marked the type of video card it thinks you have. If you are not sure, press **ENTER**. The marked video card is likely to be correct.
f. You can run Works in either Text or Graphics mode. Graphics mode allows you to have nicer looking screens, but it is very slow. It is suggested you run Works in Text mode. (*Note*: Depending on the monitor you have, you will sometimes have additional messages appearing on the screen.)
g. The next screen asks about the colors seen on the screen. Pick the appropriate response.
h. You must then choose a printer. Use your arrow keys to find your printer. They are arranged alphabetically. Depending on the type of printer you have, you might also be asked for the appropriate cartridge.
i. The next screen asks for the printer port. Your choice most likely should be **LPT1**.
j. You have the option to copy the tutorial to your hard disk. If you are completely unfamiliar with Works, it is suggested.
k. Setup will then copy the disks and prompt you to change the disks when necessary. **REMEMBER**, NEVER REMOVE A DISK FROM THE DRIVE WHEN THE DISK LIGHT IS ON!!!!
l. You need to tell Setup you country so it uses the right conventions.
m. Finally, if you have a mouse, you can use it in Works. This question is only if you have a mouse.
n. If you are not sure if you have the right number of files open in your **CONFIG.SYS** file, answer YES, and have the Setup program create the space it needs.

Setting up and using Works on floppy systems: Before you can set up Works to run on Floppy systems, you must first make backup copies of your disks. If you need help copying the disks, see the previous segment of this chapter. Also, be sure you have a box of blank formatted disks and the DOS program that came with your computer prior to starting this procedure.

To set up Works:

1. Insert your DOS disk in the A drive and turn on your computer.
2. When the DOS prompt appears on the screen, remove the DOS disk and insert the Works Setup disk in the A drive.
3. At the DOS prompt, type: **A:setup**
4. Press **ENTER**.
5. Follow the same directions above for a Hard Disk system beginning with instruction 5.

Starting

In order to use the Works program, or any program, it must be copied into computer memory. This is called *loading the program*. The procedure is easy, but operates a little differently depending on whether Works is installed onto your fixed disk or you are using the floppy disk.

Loading Works from a floppy disk system:

1. To start your computer:
   a. Put your DOS diskette in Drive A.
   b. Turn on the computer system.
   c. Enter the correct date and time.
   d. Remove the DOS diskette from Drive A.
2. Once the A> prompt appears on the screen, Works is ready to be loaded.
   a. Place the Works disk in Drive A.
   b. Type: **Works**
   c. Press **ENTER**.

Loading Works from a fixed disk system:

1. To start your computer:
   a. Be sure that there are no disks in the floppy disk drives.
   b. Turn on your computer system.
   c. Enter the correct date and time, if necessary.
2. When the C> prompt appears on the screen, you are ready to load Works.
   a. Type: **cd\directory** (Where directory is the name of the subdirectory. This will change the current directory to the Works subdirectory you created when you installed Works on your hard drive.) If you installed Works using the defaults, type: **cd\Works**

b. Type: **works**
c. Press **ENTER.**

Now that you have examined the hardware and DOS, and you have installed Works, you are ready to begin to use it.

At the Beginning—Creating a New File

When you start Works, a screen containing copyright information and a few command options appears (Figure 1.2). This exact screen only appears when Works is first loaded. The same screen also appears without the copyright information when all files have been closed, as you'll see at the end of this chapter.

In order to use Works, you must be working on a file using one of the four tools—the Word Processor, Spreadsheet, Database, or Communications. That's why the File Menu is opened when you first load Works. The File Menu and general procedures for using all menus will be fully discussed later in this chapter. For now, just use the following directions to open a word processing file so that you can begin exploring Works.

1. To choose the **Create new file** command:

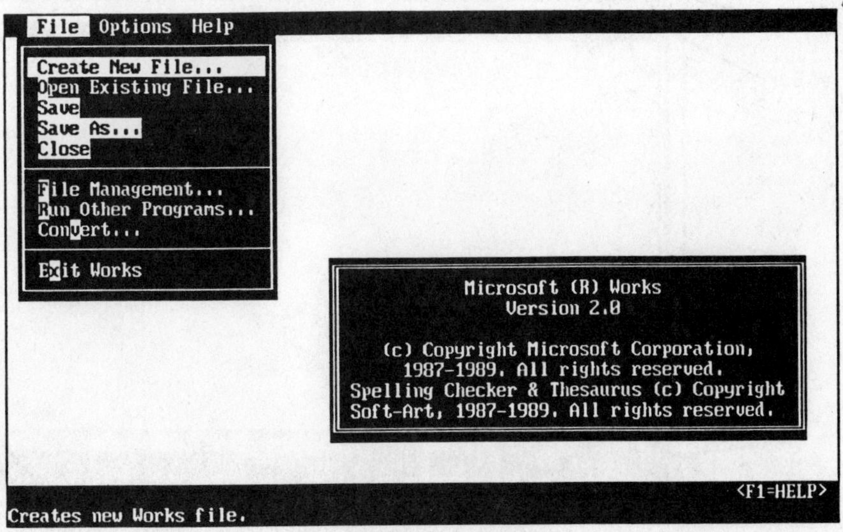

Figure 1.2. Opening screen

- Either move the highlight to *Create New File* and press **ENTER** or
- Type the highlighted letter in *Create New File*: **N**

A box naming the four tools appears on the screen. Each of the tool names and the word *Cancel* are enclosed in brackets.

2. *New Word Processor* should be enclosed in highlighted brackets. If it is not, press the **UP** or **DOWN** arrows until it is.
3. Press **ENTER** to open a new word processor file. The word processor screen appears (Figure 1.3).

The Works Screen

The screen for each Works tool is slightly different. However, there are many similarities. One of the changes made in Version 2 of Works was increasing the similarities among screens, to make learning your way around Works even easier. Here, the word processor screen is used to see the common elements.

The first line on the screen is the *Menu Bar*. It lists the names of the command menus. Most tasks in Works except for entering text or data, involve the use of the menus. The Menu Bar on the copyright screen contains fewer

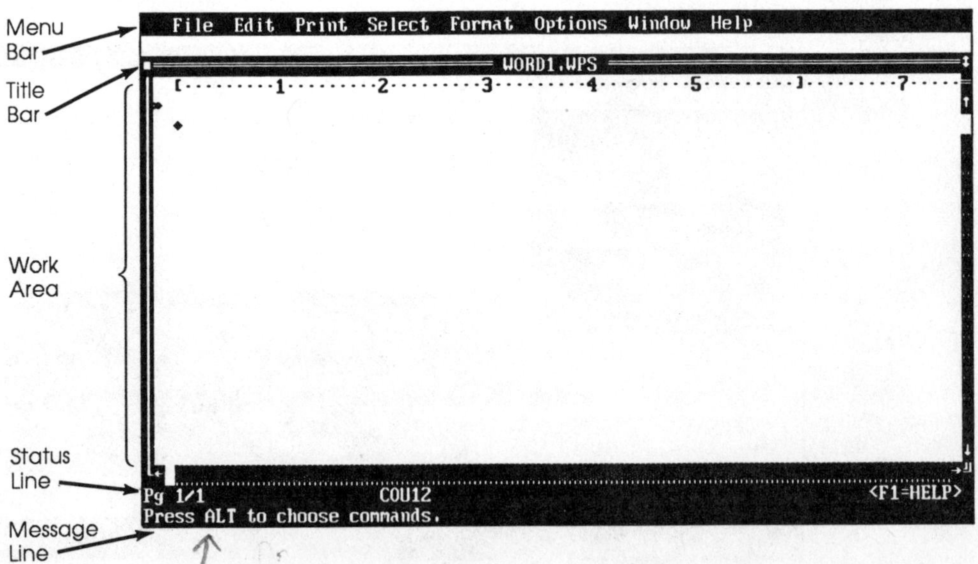

Figure 1.3. Word processing screen

items than the one on the word processor screen because there are only a few things that you can do when you start. All of the word processor menus also appear on the Menu Bar in the spreadsheet and database, although some of the options on the individual menus are different in the other tools. More important, once you learn how to select from the menus, the same procedures can be used in each of the tools.

Immediately under the Menu Bar is the *Title Bar,* which lists the name of the file. It currently displays **WORD1.WPS**, the default name Works assigns to the first new word processing file opened in a session. Subsequent new word processing files are named **WORD2.WPS**, **WORD3.WPS**, and so on. Database files are similarly named beginning with **DATA1.WDB**, spreadsheet files **SHEET1.WKS**, and communications files **COMM1.WCM**.

The *Work Area*, which takes up most of the screen, is used to enter and edit information.

The *Status Line* helps you keep track of your work. It contained minimal information on the copyright screen because there was no work to track. In each of the tools, however, it tells which part of the file is displayed on the screen. For example, the word processor indicates which page of the document is displayed on the screen. Information on tasks in progress is also displayed on this line. When a tool is selected, the font type will also appear on the Status Line. For example, if your font is Courier 10 pitch, *COU10* will appear on the Status Line. The information on your screen will probably be different than the illustrations since you are probably using a different font.

The *Message Line* displays prompts, instructions, or descriptions that primarily are designed to help you to use the menus.

Special Mouse Symbols on the Works Screen

The Works screen includes a set of symbols that can be used to scroll the screen or can be used as shortcuts to some of the commands (see Figure 1.4). When you are using a mouse, a separate mouse cursor will appear on the screen. This cursor is either in the form of a rectangle or an arrow. To use the symbols, move the mouse cursor to the symbol and either *click* on it or *drag* it. To click on a symbol, press the left mouse button once. To drag a symbol, depress the left mouse button and keep it depressed while moving the cursor.

The mouse symbols are described below. Directions in this book will use keyboard strokes, but the use of the mouse will be mentioned when new tasks are introduced.

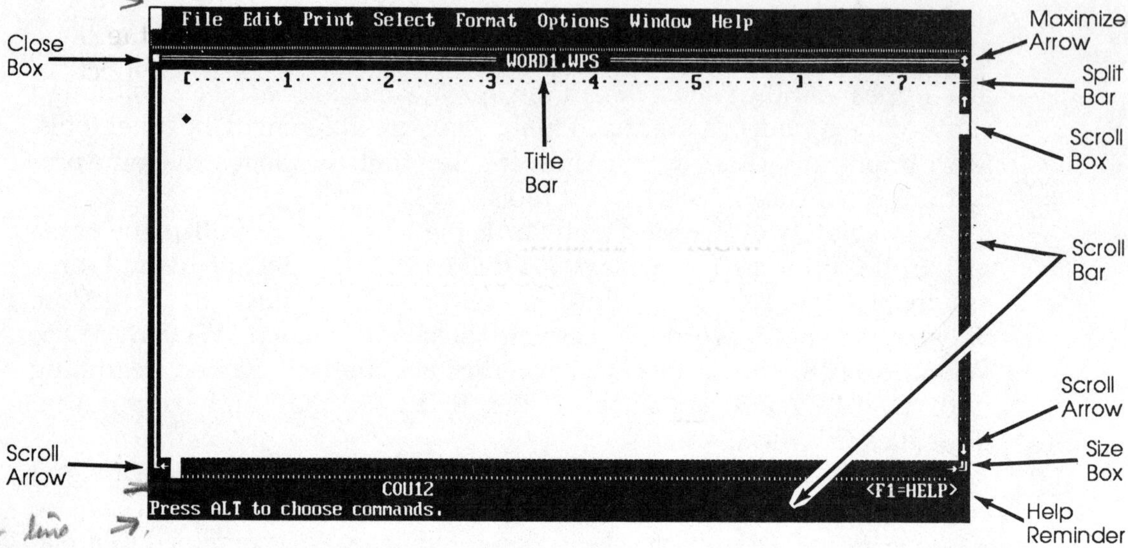

Figure 1.4. Mouse symbols

Three symbols are used to scroll the screen. These symbols are used frequently in all of the tools.

1. **Scroll Bar**: Clicking within the shaded bar on the right and bottom of the screen scrolls one screen per click.
2. **Scroll Arrows**: Located at each end of the scroll bars, the scroll arrows are used to scroll the screen one line, character, row, or column at a time.
3. **Scroll Box**: The black boxes located in the scroll bars can be dragged to scroll quickly by large amounts. The box indicates the approximate position of the current screen in the file.

Two of the mouse symbols replace general commands. Their use will be demonstrated later in this chapter.

1. **Close Box**: The small box located at the top left of the Works screen is used to close a file.
2. **Help reminder**: The Help reminder on the Status Line tells you which key to use to access help. Help can also be accessed by clicking on the reminder.

Four of the mouse symbols can be used in place of the Window Menu commands. Their use will be described in Chapter 8.

1. **Title Bar**: Clicking on the line containing the file name has the same effect as **Window/filename**; dragging it has the same effect as **Window/Move**.
2. **Maximize Arrow**: The double arrow at the right of the title bar is used instead of the **Window/Maximize** command.
3. **Split Bar**: The two lines under the maximize arrows are used in place of the **Window/Split** command.
4. **Size Box**: The small right angle symbol in the bottom right corner of the screen has the same use as the **Window/Size** command.

Using the Work Area

When you create a new file, you may begin by either entering information on the Work Area, or by using the menus to issue a command. The type of information entered on the Work Area varies with each tool. The rest of this chapter will be devoted to looking at the command menus, however, start by entering some text on the screen so that you can have a usable file.

1. Type your name or a sentence.
2. It will appear in the Work Area.

A First Look at Menus

Opening a Menu

The Message Line contains instructions on how to begin choosing commands. Follow the instructions to get a closer look at the Works Command Menus.

1. Press **ALT**.

Pressing **ALT** *activates* the Menu Bar. Three changes occur on the screen (Figure 1.5.):

- The cursor no longer appears in the Work Area
- One letter in each of the menu names is **bold** (or underlined on some monitors) and the first menu name **File** is in an inverse highlight box (we will refer to this inverse highlight box as the highlight)
- A new instruction appears in the Message Line

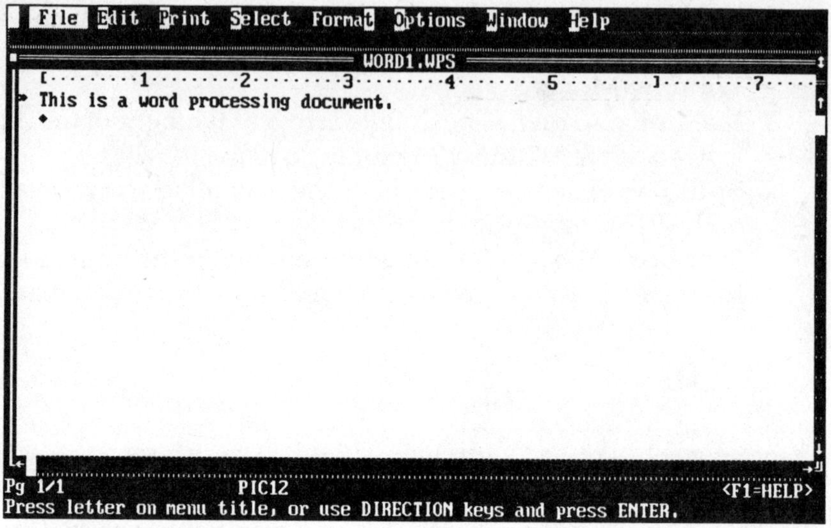

Figure 1.5. Screen after activating the Menu Bar

As the new prompt on the Message Line indicates, there are two ways to open a menu—either type the **bold letter** in the menu name, or use the **RIGHT** or **LEFT ARROW** to move the highlight bar to the menu name you want and then press **ENTER**. To use the bold letter method to open the Help Menu:

2. Type: **H**

The Help Menu opens, displaying a list of commands (Figure 1.6). Each of the commands in the Help Menu now has a letter in bold, but none of the letters on the top Menu Bar remains bold. Therefore, you cannot use the bold letter method to open another menu until you close the Help Menu.

Closing a Menu

What happens if you open the wrong menu? To **Close** the menu:

1. Press **ALT** again.

This will close the Help Menu, but keep the Menu Bar activated; one letter in each menu name is once again highlighted.

2. Type: **t** to open the Format Menu.
3. Now press **ESC**.

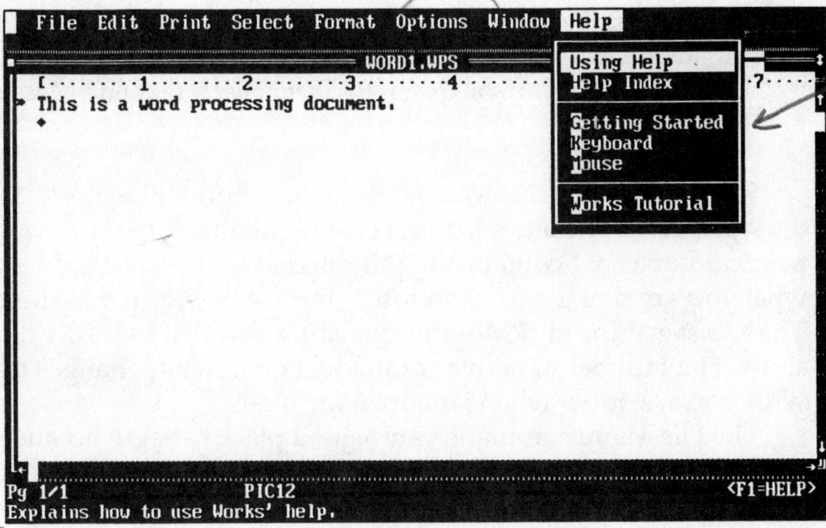

Figure 1.6. Screen with the Help Menu opened

ESC closes the menu and deactivates the Menu Bar. Therefore, no letters on the Menu Bar are highlighted, and the cursor returns to the Work Area. To open another menu, start from the beginning and press ALT.

To select the Help Menu again, this time using the **ARROW** key method:

1. First press **ALT** to activate the Menu Bar.
2. Then use the **RIGHT** or **LEFT ARROW** to move the highlight to Help.
3. Press **ENTER**.

Once one menu is opened, the **ARROW** keys can be used to open other menus without pressing **ENTER**.

4. Use the **RIGHT** or **LEFT ARROW** keys to open the Options Menu.

Browsing Menus

Once a menu is open, the highlighted command is described on the Message Line. Therefore, the tasks performed by each command can be viewed by highlighting each of the menu options and reading the Message Line.

The first Options Menu command *Works Settings* is described on the Message Line when the menu is first opened. To look at the other Options Menu commands:

1. Press the **DOWN ARROW**. The next command is highlighted on the Menu and described on the Message Line.
2. Now move the cursor down to *Show Footnotes*. The Message line says *No footnotes*.

Review the Options Menu commands. Some like *Works Settings* are in dark print and one letter is in reverse highlight. *Show Footnotes* is in lighter print and does not contain a highlighted letter because it does not apply to what you are doing and, therefore, may not be selected at the current time. The Message Line indicates this by telling you that there are no footnotes to show. The number of active commands on a menu changes depending on what you are doing when you open the menu.

The File Menu commands are a good place to begin because they are the same in each of the tools and at least some of them must be used each time that you use Works. Most of the File Menu commands also require additional information before they are executed. Therefore, you'll learn how to provide all of the types of information Works ever needs to execute commands.

Selecting a Command—The File/File Management Command

Now that you've created a file, you should save it. Since all files must be saved to a formatted disk, the first step is to format a disk. You may have already formatted a disk using the DOS commands presented earlier. However, the Works File Management command lets you perform some of the basic DOS file management tasks without exiting to DOS and it provides more help in performing the task than most versions of DOS do. Therefore, we'll begin by using the **File Management** command to format a disk.

1. Use the **ARROW** keys to pull down the File Menu (Figure 1.7).

Just as there are two ways of opening a menu, once a menu is opened, a command can be executed by either:

- Highlighting the command and pressing **ENTER** or
- Typing the highlighted letter

Therefore,

2. To select **File Management**:

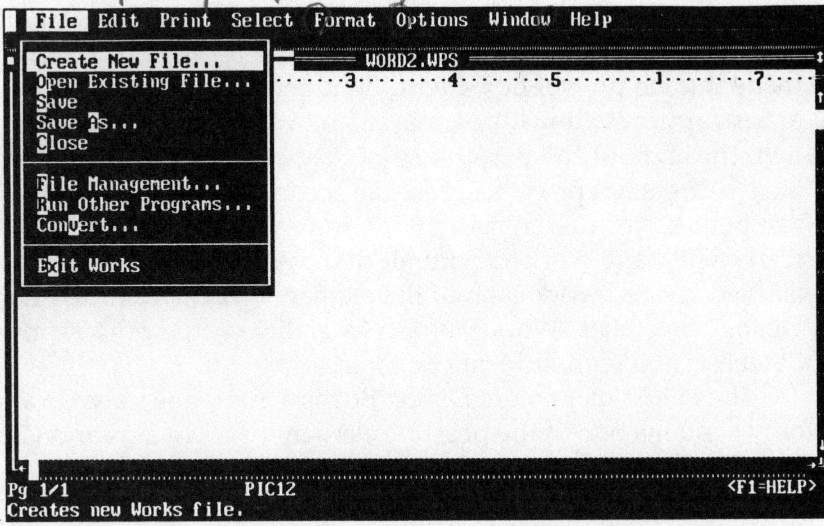

Figure 1.7. File Menu

- Move the cursor to **File Management** and press **ENTER** or
- Type: **F**

Note

Typing the bold letter in the command name you want to use is faster, but may not be the best approach when you are learning Works. As you've just seen, using the **ARROW** keys to move the cursor causes a description of the highlighted command to appear on the Message Line. This is not only a good way to learn about Works, but you can check that the highlighted command is the one that you actually want to choose.

Works responds in several different ways when you select a command. Sometimes, it immediately carries out the command. At other times, instructions appear on the Message Line and the command is executed as soon as you carry out the instructions. Some commands, such as **File Management...** are followed by an ellipsis (. . .). The ellipsis indicates that more information is necessary before the command can be carried out. Whenever Works requires more information it displays a *Dialog Box* on the screen.

Works Dialog Boxes

Dialog Boxes, used throughout Works, are a means of allowing you to specify the information needed to carry out a task. Every Dialog Box contains one or more of five elements: *Text Boxes, Check Boxes, Option Boxes, List Boxes,* and *Command Buttons*. There are some differences in the way selections are made in each type of box. Learning to move around the Dialog Boxes may, at first, appear to be a little tricky. Don't worry, you'll get lots of practice and help throughout the book. A summary of the selection procedures associated with each type is included in a section near the end of this chapter and can be used as a reference. By the time you conclude this chapter you already will have worked with all five elements. What's more, once you've learned how to work each of the elements, you've learned how to use any Dialog Box that Works opens—in the word processor, spreadsheet, database, and communications tools.

The File Management Dialog Box is a good one to begin with because it only contains two of the possible elements—a List Box and Command Buttons (Figure 1.8).

Changing an Option in a List Box

A List Box is a list of options, only one of which may be selected at a time. The List Box in the File Management Dialog Box shows the different file management tasks that can be performed. The first option, *Copy File,* is highlighted. That means that *Copy File* is the currently selected option and would be executed if you pressed **ENTER** now.

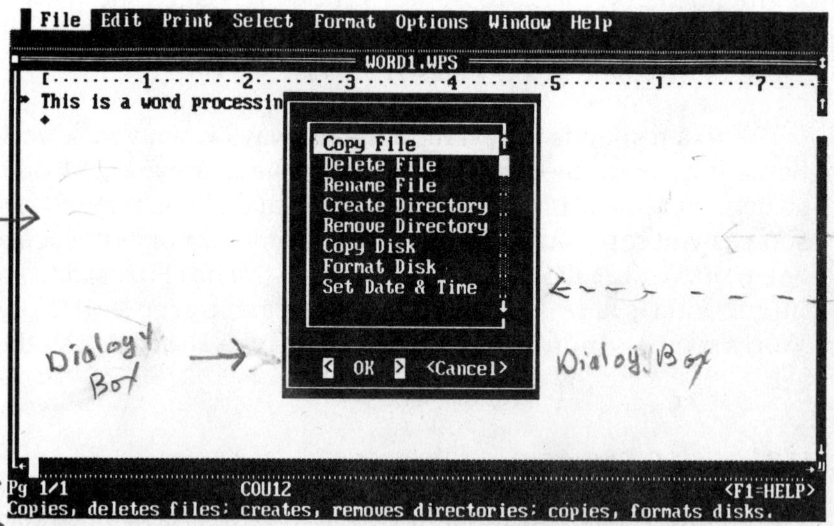

Figure 1.8. File Management Dialog Box

To change the selected option in a List Box, use the **UP** or **DOWN ARROWS** to move the highlight to the desired option.

3. Use the **DOWN ARROW** to highlight **Format Disk.**

The Command Buttons

Now that you've selected the option that you want, you need to choose a **Command Button** to carry out the command. Every Dialog Box contains buttons that ask you whether you want to carry out or cancel the task. Most Dialog Boxes contain only two buttons—one such as **<OK>** or **<Print>** (if we're using the Print command), which tells Works to carry out the command using the current settings in the Dialog Box, and one that says **<Cancel>**. A few boxes contain additional Command Buttons. As you might remember, all of the items in the Create New File Dialog Box were enclosed in brackets (<New Word Processor>, <New Spreadsheet>, etc.). Each one of these was a button.

The brackets around **<OK>** in the File Management Dialog Box should be highlighted. In every Dialog Box, one button is enclosed in highlighted brackets. This is referred to as the *preset* button because it is automatically highlighted when the Dialog Box appears. The button in the highlighted bracket will be selected if you press **ENTER**.

4. Press **ENTER** to tell Works that it's **<OK>** to proceed with the Format command.

Usually when a Dialog Box is completed, the command is executed and the cursor returns to the Work Area. In this case, however, what happens next depends on your computer configuration. If your computer contains more than one floppy disk drive, Works needs to know which drive will contain the disk to be formatted. Therefore, it will display a new Dialog Box (Figure 1.9). The directions in the next section tell you how to make a selection in this box. If your computer only contains one floppy disk drive, no Dialog Box will appear because Works will only Format floppy disks. Read the next section, even if a Dialog Box is not displayed so that you will be introduced to the use of the Options Boxes. The information displayed on your screen should be the DOS Format prompt, so begin following the instructions again with step 5 in next section.

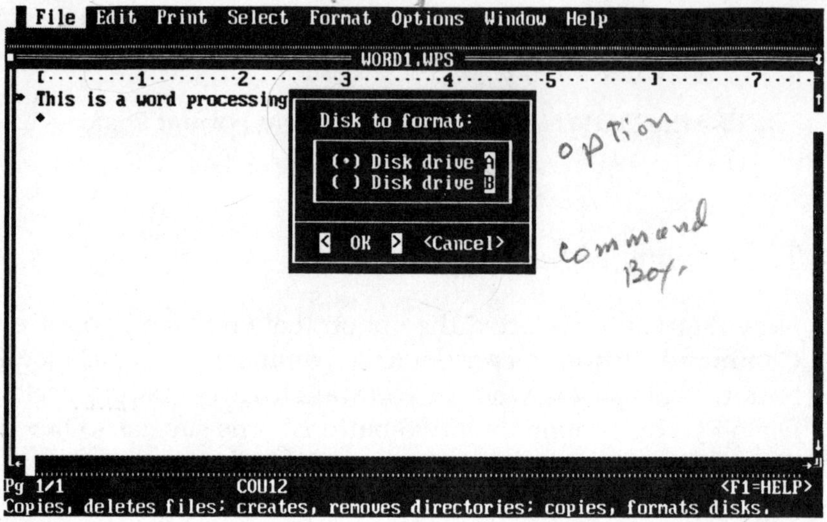

Figure 1.9. Format command Dialog Box

Changing an Option in an Option Box

The new Dialog Box is also simple in that it only contains two elements: an Option Box and Command Buttons. An Option Box, like a List Box, contains several choices only one of which can be selected at a time. Option Boxes are used instead of List Boxes when there are only a few choices, and when those choices are the same each time the Dialog Box appears. Each choice is preceded by a set of parentheses ( ), one of which contains a dot. The option preceded by the parentheses containing the dot is the selected option. In the Disk to format Option Box, *Disk drive A* is currently selected.

1. To change the selected option, use the **ARROW** keys to move the dot to the correct option.

As discussed earlier in this chapter, A and B are the names given to the floppy disk drives. If you have two floppy disk drives, drive A is usually the one on the top or the left.

2. Decide which drive you are going to use to format a disk, and move the dot to that option.
3. If there is any information on a disk when it is formatted, that information is destroyed. Therefore, be sure that the disk that you are formatting is blank.

4. The **OK** Command Button should have been preselected; press **ENTER** to begin formatting a disk.
5. The DOS Format command instructions will now appear on the screen. If you have any questions about how to respond to these prompts, refer to the earlier section of this chapter that discusses the use of the DOS Format command.

If the message, *Not ready error reading drive B (or drive A) Abort, Retry, Fail?* appears, put an already formatted disk in the drive named in the error message and type: **R** (for retry). If that drive is also the drive that you are using to format a disk, be sure to replace the formatted disk with an unformatted disk before continuing with the format command.

6. When asked if you want to format another disk, type: **N** and press **ENTER**.

The File Management Dialog Box is displayed again because people often want to perform several file management tasks in a row. When all file management tasks are completed, the Dialog Box must be canceled.

Canceling a Dialog Box

There are two ways to cancel a Dialog Box.

1. To cancel the File Management Dialog Box, either:
   - Use **TAB** to move the cursor to the Cancel Button and press **ENTER** or
   - Press **ESC**

Now that you have a formatted disk, you can save your word processing document. In later chapters, we discuss several ways to do this. The instructions below use the **Save As** command.

1. Press **ALT** to activate the Menu Bar.
2. Press **ENTER** to open the File Menu.
3. Select **Save As**.

Note In future directions, the steps involved in selecting a command will be abbreviated; steps 1, 2, and 3 will be abbreviated as: select **File/Save As**.

The Save As Dialog Box

The Save As Dialog Box is more complex than those that you have used so far. Some of the specific information on your screen may be different than that shown in Figure 1.10 because your computer setup may be different than the one used to take these screen shots. It contains all five of the possible Dialog Box elements.

You've already used three—List Boxes, Option Boxes, and Command Buttons. The following list describes all five of the elements, and the way that they are used in the Save As Dialog Box.

1. **Text Boxes**: allow you to type in new information or to change information that is in the box. The Save file as Text Box contains the current name for the file, **WORD1.WPS.**
2. **List Boxes**: contain a list of options, only one of which can be selected at a time. List Boxes are used when the options may be different each time the Dialog Box is used or for long lists of choices. The Directories List Box contains the name of the drives or subdirectories to which you may save a file on your computer. Therefore, the list on your screen may be different than the list in Figure 1.10.
3. **Option Boxes**: also contain a list of options, only one of which can be selected at a time. Option Boxes are used instead of List Boxes when the

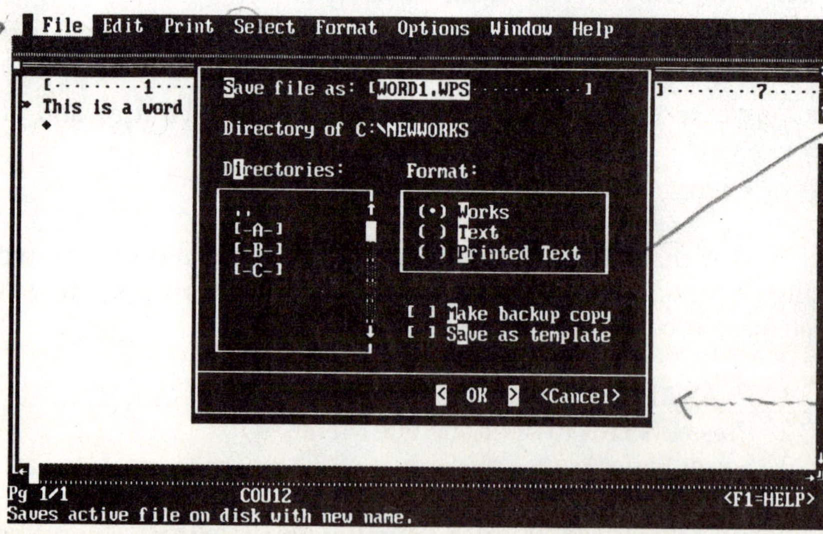

Figure 1.10. Save As Dialog Box

possible choices are few and are the same each time the Dialog Box appears. Each choice is preceded by a set of parentheses ( ), one of which contains a dot. The option preceded by the parentheses containing the dot is the selected option. In the Save As Dialog Box the Format Option Box gives you a choice of three formats in which to save the document. The selected choice is *Works*.

4. **Check Boxes**: function like on/off switches. There may be one or several in the same Dialog Box and they may be separated or enclosed in a box. They are similar to Option Boxes, but are preceded by brackets [ ] instead of parentheses and more than one may be selected at a time. A selected box is preceded by an X or a dash [-]. The two Check Boxes in the Save As Dialog Box allow you to save the file as a template or make backup copies each time you save a file. Neither one is currently selected.
5. **Command Buttons**: appear on the bottom of the screen and ask you if, or how, you want to carry out the command with the settings that you have chosen in the boxes previously described. The Command Buttons in the Save As Dialog Box, *<OK>* and *<Cancel>*, are the ones typically used to tell Works to carry out or cancel the command. The selected Command Button *<OK>* is indicated by the highlighted brackets surrounding it.

Moving Between Elements in a Dialog Box

When a Dialog Box appears the cursor is in the top-most or left-most box. Therefore, in the Save As Dialog Box, the cursor is in the Save file as Text Box. Unfortunately, the first task that should be done is using the Directories List Box to change the Current Directory. There are two ways of moving from box to box—the **TAB** key method and the **ALT** key method. Try the **TAB** key method first:

1. Press **TAB** once.

The highlight disappears from the Save file as Text Box and the cursor moves under the first entry in the Directories List Box.

2. Continue pressing **TAB** until the cursor moves back to the Save file as Text Box.

The cursor will move to each of the boxes going from top to bottom and left to right. If you continue to TAB, the cursor will move to the OK and Cancel buttons.

Note Since the **TAB** key, like most computer keys, repeats when it is held down, the cursor may jump rapidly from box to box if the key is held down too long.

Now try the **ALT** key method.

In Text and List Boxes, only a letter in the **name of the Box** is bold. In Option Boxes, a letter in **each option** is bold. This difference affects what happens when the **ALT** key method is used with the different types of boxes.

1. While holding the **ALT** key down, press the letter **I**. Then press the **ALT** and **S** keys. The cursor or highlight box moves first to the Directories List Box and then back to the Save file as Text Box, but does not change the option in the box that is selected.

Note If the cursor is in a Text Box and you accidentally type a letter without simultaneously pressing **ALT**, the letter you typed will replace the text box entry. If this happens, press **ESC** to cancel the Dialog Box and select **File/Save As** again.

2. Now press **ALT-T**.

When you use the **ALT** key method to move to an Option Box, Works simultaneously moves to the box **and** moves the mark to the option whose key letter you typed, if that was not already the selected option.

Note The notation **ALT-LETTER** will be used to indicate that you should press the first key and then hold it while pressing a second key simultaneously. Therefore, press **ALT-T** means press the **ALT** key and then hold it while pressing **T**.

3. Press **ALT-W** or just press the letter **W** to change the selected option back to *Works*.

Note Once the cursor is in a box, you may move it to a **different option in that box**, or options in some, but not all, other boxes by typing the bold letter **without** the **ALT** key. Since it is always permissible to use the **ALT-LETTER** combination, many people find it easier to always use the key combination than to remember when the **ALT** key is needed and when it is not!

4. Use either the **TAB** or the **ALT** key method to move the cursor to the **Directories** List Box.

Changing the Current Directory

When disk drives and DOS commands were discussed at the beginning of this chapter, the drive names used to tell the computer where to find or save files were described. The first time you try to open or save a file after loading Works, it assumes that you will search for the file on the drive and directory that contains the Works system files. The computer used for Figure 1.10 loaded Works from the Newworks subdirectory on Drive C. This is indicated by the second line in the Dialog Box: *Directory of C:\NEWWORKS*. If you are using Works from a subdirectory named C:\WORKS, your screen will display *Directory of C:\WORKS*. If you loaded Works from a disk in Drive A, the line would say *Directory of A:*.

If you save your word processor file now, it will be saved on the drive and subdirectory indicated in the Dialog Box. Since you do not want to clutter this subdirectory with the exercises from this book, it's better to save these exercises on a separate floppy disk which contains nothing but these activities. Therefore, you should use the Directories List Box to change the current drive to the drive containing the disk you previously formatted. Once you change the current drive, Works will continue to save files to that disk drive until you change it again or exit from Works.

1. In the File Management Dialog Box one of the items in the List Box was preselected by Works. In other cases, such as the Directories List Box, the cursor appears under the top item in the list, but none of the options are selected. In these situations, even if you want to select the first item in the box, you must press the **DOWN ARROW** once.

   Press **DOWN ARROW** once.

   The first entry in the list is now selected (Figure 1.11).

Note Since the active directory in Figure 1.11 is a subdirectory, the first entry is a double period (..). Selecting the double period will take you up one directory in the directory tree. This option is not appropriate in the current example, since you will be saving to a floppy disk.

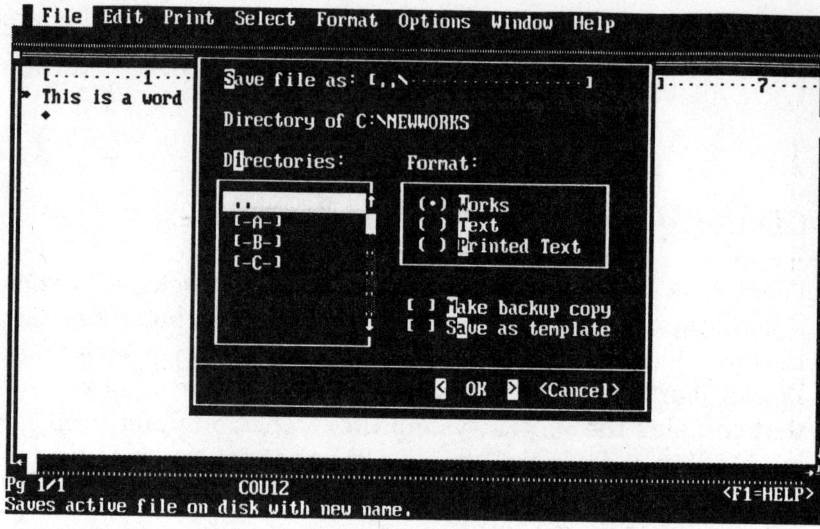

Figure 1.11. Selecting entries in a List Box

2. If the first drive is **not** the drive that contains your exercise disk, continue pressing the **DOWN ARROW** until the correct drive is highlighted. If you are using a system with two floppy drives, the exercise disk should be in Drive B. If Works is on the hard drive, the exercise disk is probably in Drive A.
3. The selected drive should appear in the Save file as Text Box. However, as shown in Figure 1.12, the second line of the Dialog Box contains the original directory listing. In order to change the current directory listing to the one selected in the Directories List Box, Press **ENTER**.

Note When you change the current directory, Works checks to make sure that there is a formatted disk in the new drive. If there is not, Works displays the message *Cannot find directory*. Press **ENTER** to acknowledge the error message, and put a formatted disk in the drive. If you have selected the wrong drive, select another one. Press **ENTER** again.

Using a Check Box

The *Make backup copy* Check Box can be used to make a backup file that is updated every time that you save a file. It is not necessary to select this feature, but it can be useful if your real file is accidentally destroyed. A Check Box can be selected by:

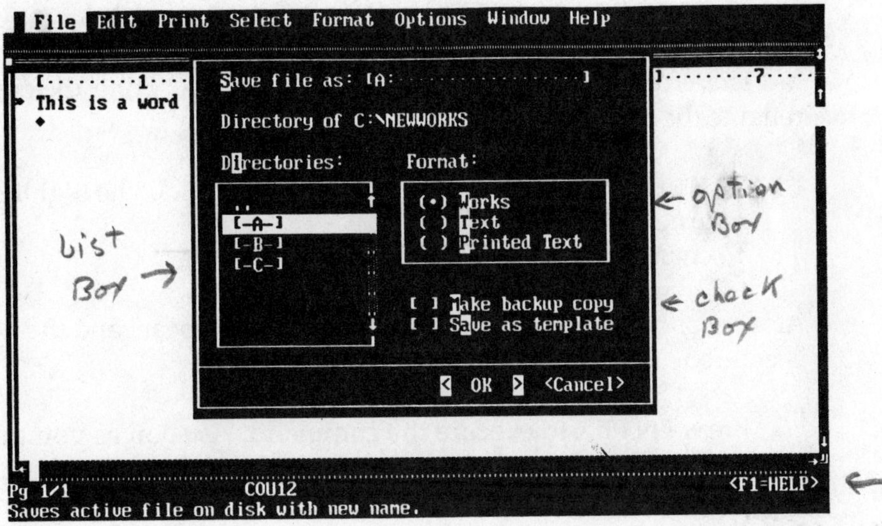

Figure 1.12. Effects of highlighting a new directory

- Using the **TAB** key to move to the Check Box and pressing **ENTER**, or
- Holding down **ALT** and pressing the bold letter of the option that you want

In Check Boxes either method works as a *toggle key*. This means that if the check box is turned off, selecting it will turn it on, but if it is already turned on, selecting it will turn it off. To try this:

1. Press **ALT-M** or **TAB** to the Make backup copy Check Box and press the **SPACE BAR**. An **X** should appear in the brackets preceding *Make backup copy*.
2. To turn the backup feature off, press **ALT-M** or the **SPACE BAR** again.
3. Repeat the last step one more time so that the Check Box is once again selected.

Using a Text Box

So far you've changed two of the settings in the Dialog Box. There are two more boxes that could be changed: the Format Option Box and the Save file as Text Box. The *Works* option has been preselected in the Format Option Box. The only time the other options are used is if you want to save a file in a text or ASCII (American Standard Code for Information Interchange) format. These formats will not be used in this book.

Therefore, the one remaining step before executing the command is to rename the file.

1. **TAB** to the Save file as Text Box or press **ALT-S**. The highlight should be returned to the Text Box.
2. To change the filename to 1stfile, type: **1stfile**

As soon as you begin typing, the old entry disappears and the new file name is entered.

3. Press **ENTER** to execute the command. As soon as you press **ENTER**, Works adds the extension *.WPS* to the filename. The light on the disk drive to which the file is being saved will also be turned on.

If you didn't see the extension added in the Save file as Text Box, you can see it in the Title Bar on the Word Processing screen.

Rules for Naming a File

DOS, the disk operating system described earlier in this chapter, has a set of rules that all programs, including Works, must follow in naming files. According to DOS, each file must have a *filename* of from one to eight characters. At the end of the filename, it is possible, but not necessary, to add an extension by typing a period (.) and one to three additional letters. The extension is typically used to group files.

When using Works, it is recommended that you just *type the filename without the period or extension* and allow Works to add one of its extensions:

.WPS word processing file
.WKS spreadsheet file
.WDB database file
.WCM communications file

As you'll see when you retrieve the file that you just saved, Works uses its extensions to organize and display a listing of the files on the disk. Therefore, even though you can use a file with a non-Works extension, Works will list the file under "Other Files" instead of under "Word Processor."

DOS also limits the acceptable characters in file names to letters, digits, and the following special characters:

@ ! # $ % ^ & () _ - { } " ~ '

Filenames may **not** include a blank space. Some acceptable file names are:

ACCTS-NY   NEW _EMP   BUDGET1   88BUDGET

Can you explain what's wrong with the following filenames?

INVENTORY   *SALES*   NEW EMP

The only other trick to naming files is remembering that you may need to retrieve the file in a week or a month. Selecting meaningful filenames is difficult because of the eight-letter limit on filename length, but your skill will improve with practice.

Now you've chosen several commands and used each of the types of boxes Works uses to obtain information about how you want a command executed. Your introduction to Works is almost over—only a few more of the important File Menu commands remain. Before trying them, take a look at Tables 1.1 and 1.2 for a summary of the methods of selecting commands and using the different elements in the Dialog Box. If you are using a mouse, look at the instructions for performing these same tasks with a mouse. Then use these references to help yourself become more independent with the tasks that follow.

Table 1.1 Selecting commands

Task	**ALT Key Method**	**ARROW Key Method**
Activate the Menu Bar	Press **ALT**	Press **ALT**
Open a Menu	Type the bold letter in the Menu name	Use the **RIGHT ARROW** to move the highlight to the Menu name and press **ENTER**
Select a Command	Type the bold letter in the Command name	Use **ARROW** keys to highlight the Command name and press **ENTER**
Close a Menu	Press **ESC**	Press **ESC**

Table 1.2 Selecting Options

Box	Either	Or
Option Boxes	**TAB** to box; use an **ARROW** key to move the mark to the option you want	Press **ALT** plus the bold letter in the option you want
List Boxes	**TAB** to box; use the **UP** or **DOWN** **ARROW** to highlight the option you want	Press **ALT** plus the bold letter in the box name; use the **ARROW** keys to highlight the option you want
Text Boxes	**TAB** to box; type the information in the box	Select the information from a List Box (only possible in some Dialog Boxes)
Check Boxes	**TAB** to the Check Box and press the Space Bar (you may toggle an option both on and off this way)	Press **ALT** plus the bold letter in the option (you may toggle the option both on and off this way)
Command Buttons	**TAB** to the button you want and press **ENTER**	Press **ALT** plus the bold letter in the button you want (this will not work with the **<Cancel>** button, but you may press **ESC** to cancel a command)

Using a Mouse with Command Menus and Dialog Boxes

The mouse can be used to issue all of the menu commands. Specific instructions for using the mouse are included in Table 1.3. However, in general, menus are opened, commands are selected, and choices are made within dialog boxes by clicking once on the desired option with the left mouse button. Some actions are easier with a mouse than using the keyboard. For example, when using a mouse, the menu bar is activated and the menu opened in one step instead of two.

Table 1.3. Using the Mouse

Task	Action
Open a Menu	Click on the Menu name
Select a Command	Click on the Command name
Close a Menu	Click anywhere outside the menu before choosing a command
Change Information in:	
Text Box	Click on the Text Box and type the new information
Option Box	Click on the option or in the parentheses preceding the option that you want to select
Check Box	Click on the option or in the brackets preceding the option to toggle the option on or off
List Box	Click on the option. If the option you wish to choose is not visible in the box, click on the arrows on the side of the box to move the list up/down one item at a time, or click within the scroll bar to move the list up/down one screen at a time
Command Button	To execute or cancel the command, click on the appropriate command button

Getting Help

Works has on-screen context-sensitive help available. What this means is that when you access Help, Works considers what you are currently doing and presents information on a related topic. The Help screen that is displayed includes Command Buttons that let you move to other Help screens or to the Help Index. To explore Help:

1. Open a menu and highlight one of the commands. The Help key is **F1** except when you are involved in certain tasks in the Communications tool. The current Help key is always indicated on the right corner of the Status Line. The Help key can be used to access help from any activity in Works—when the cursor is on the Menu Bar, on an open menu, in a Dialog Box, or on the Work Area.

2. Press **F1**.

A Help Screen will be displayed. Figure 1.13 shows the Help Screen displayed when the **File/File Save As** command is highlighted.

3. To explore Help further you may use the following Command Buttons:

Page Up and **Page Down**: Move to the following/preceding Help Screen. These are continuations of the current screen or related topics. Select this by tabbing to the button and pressing **ENTER** or the **PGUP** or **PGDN** keys.

Basic Skills: Moves to an index of help topics on basic skills.

Index: Moves to the Help Index related to the current topic. The screen includes instructions on how to select help topics.

Lesson: If the tutorial includes a lesson on the current topic, this gives you access to the lesson.

Cancel: Exits from Help. This can be selected by tabbing to the button and pressing **ENTER**or **ESC**.

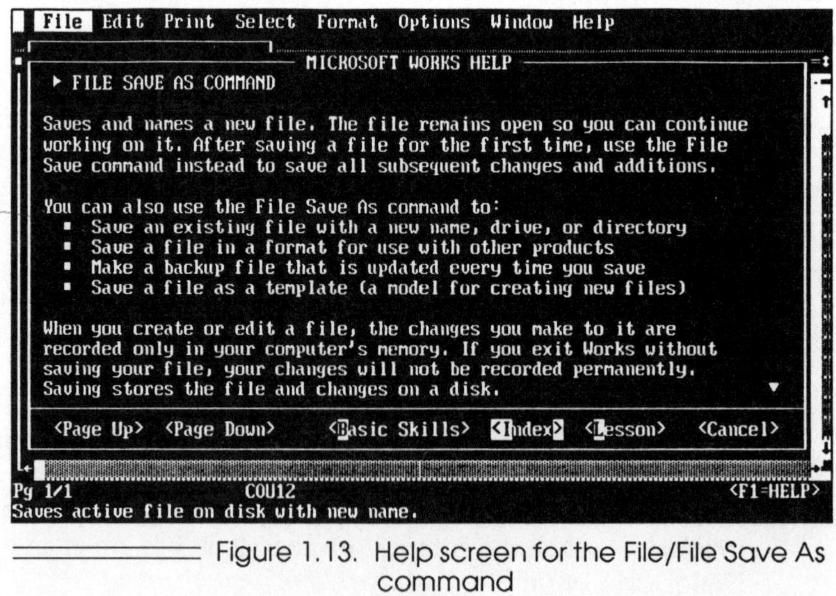

Figure 1.13. Help screen for the File/File Save As command

General instructions on using Help and the Help Index can also be accessed by using the **Help/Using Help** and the **Help/Help Index** commands. **F1** must be used instead of the Help Menu commands when another menu is open.

Using Help with a Mouse

To use a mouse to access Help, click on the Help Reminder on the right side of the Status Line.

A Second Look at the File Menu

So far in this chapter we have dicussed three of the main File Menu commands—**Create New File**, **Save As**, and **File Management**. There are three more that should be explored:

1. **Open Existing File** is used to retrieve a file that you have already created and saved on a disk; once opened you can add to or edit the file.
2. **Close** is used to remove a file from the computer's memory. If you have already saved the file it remains on your disk, but must be opened again before you can work on it.
3. **Exit Works** is used to exit from Works.

Closing a File

Works allows eight files to be opened at one time. Methods of working with more than one file simultaneously will be discussed in Chapter 8. However, consider the common situation when you have finished using one file and wish to start another. In that case, it is neater if you close the current file before creating or opening another file. It is also necessary to use the close command if you already have eight open files and wish to open a ninth.

Use the **File/Close** command to close **1STFILE.WPS**.

1. *Press **ALT** to activate the Menu Bar and then press **ENTER** to pull down the **File** menu.*
2. *Type **C** or highlight **Close** and press **ENTER**.*

*The **Close** command is not followed by an ellipsis. Therefore, no further information is ordinarily needed before it is executed. If you have not made any changes to the file since you last saved it, the file will be closed and the opening screen without the copyright information will be displayed (Figure 1.14).*

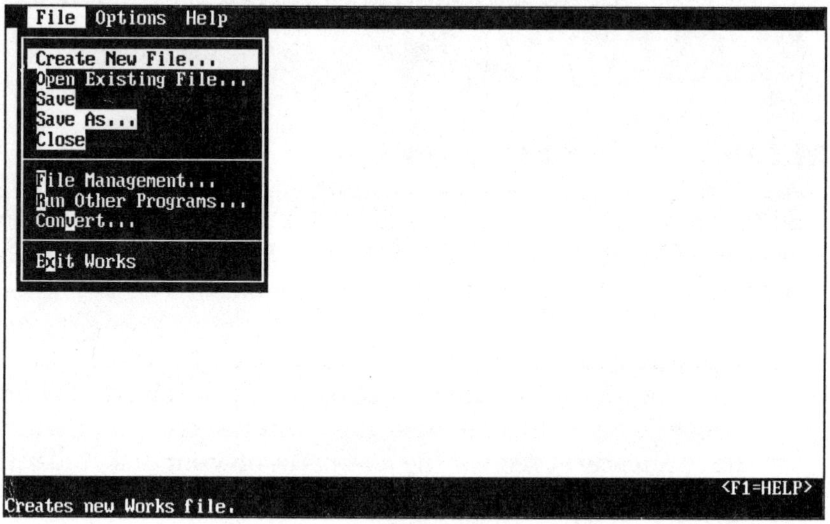

Figure 1.14. Works screen with no open files

A Works Warning

If, however, you have changed the document since it was last saved, Works displays a Dialog Box with the warning *Save changes to:1STFILE.WPS?* (Figure 1.15.). This screen contains three Command Buttons. If you press **ENTER**, Works will save the file again, replacing the previous version with one containing the revisions. If you type an **N**, the file will be closed and any changes made since last saving the file will be lost. Works is usually good about including similar warnings in other situations where executing a command may cause unexpected results. You must always choose one of the Command Buttons on the warning message before Works will continue with the command.

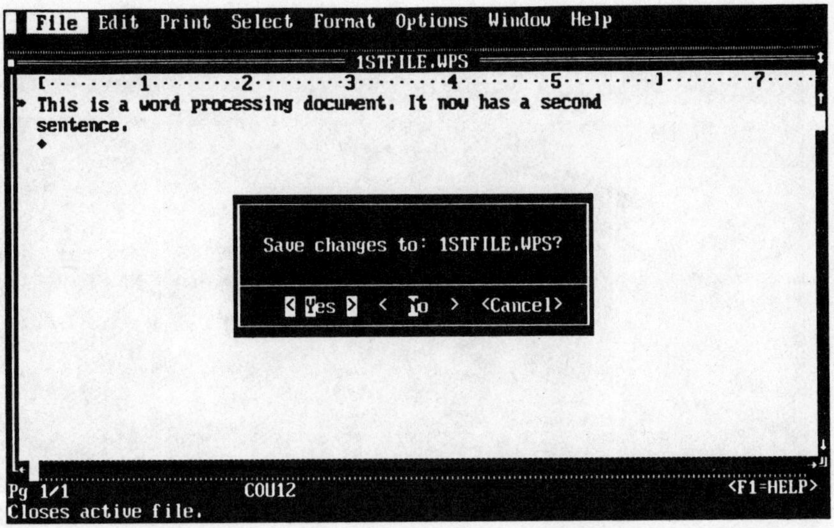

Figure 1.15. Works Warning Box

Using the Mouse to Close a File

Click on the small rectangular box on the left-side of the Title Bar. This has the same effect as the **File/Close** command and will display the same warning messages if they are appropriate.

Opening an Existing File

Often you want to edit or continue working on an already existing file. Open the file **1STFILE.WPS** to see how this is done.

1. The File Menu should already be opened. If it is not, open it.
2. Select **Open Existing File**. A Dialog Box will be displayed (Figure 1.16).

The Open Dialog Box looks a lot like the Save As Dialog Box. It contains a Text Box in which to enter the name of the file to be opened, a line that tells what the current directory is, and a Directories List Box that lets you select a different directory if the file you want is not saved in the current directory. These are all also present in the Save As Dialog Box.

The new parts of the Open Dialog Box are the Files List Box that lists all of the files in the current directory and a Check Box that asks if you want to

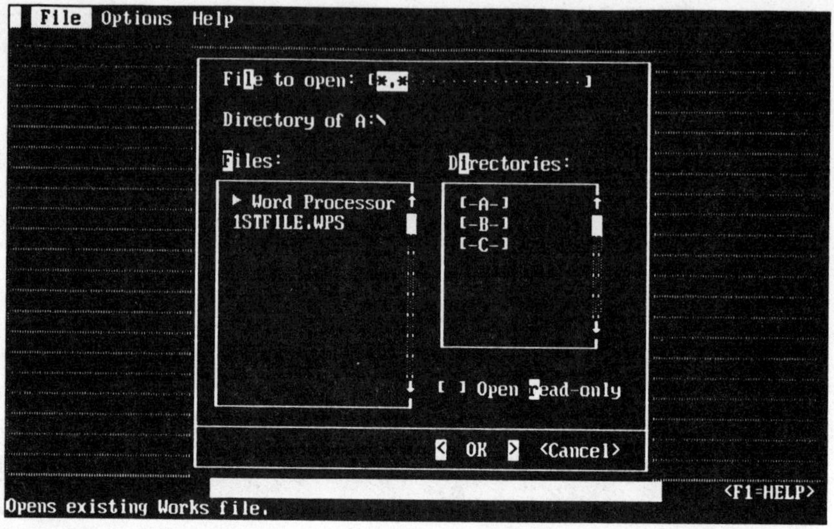

Figure 1.16. Opening Existing File Dialog Box

open a file on a *read-only* basis (i.e., to open the file so that you can view it without being able to make changes).

It's possible to open a file by typing the filename directly into the File to open Text Box. However, most typically you will want to select the filename from the Files List Box.

1. Move the cursor to the Files List Box.

In Figure 1.16 there is only one file on the disk in drive A, **1STFILE.WPS**. Works has added the heading *Word Processor* to help make the file listing easier to read. It also uses the headings Database, Spreadsheet, Communications, and Other Files if you have files fitting these categories in the current drive/directory.

2. Highlight **1STFILE.WPS.** As each filename is listed, it should also appear in the File to open Text Box.
3. Press **ENTER** to select the OK button. **1STFILE.WPS** should be displayed on the screen.

Exiting Works

The command to exit Works is also included on the File Menu. Therefore, to exit Works:

1. Select **File/Exit Works**. If you have not changed the open file, Works should be closed and your screen should appear as it did before you entered Works.
2. Just as with the **Close** command, if you have made changes to Works since opening or last saving the file a warning will appear asking if you want to save the file again.

Here we've briefly discussed the physical components of your computer system and some of the related terminology. You've also had an opportunity to practice three basic DOS commands—**FORMAT**, **DISKCOPY**, and **COPY**. This information was preparatory to the main goal of learning Works.

You've also taken a first look at the Works interface—a Works screen, some of the commands that you'll be using, and how to work with the frequently displayed Dialog Boxes. Don't worry if you haven't mastered all of these tasks. The commands and procedures will be reviewed as they are used in the various tools. Each time you repeat a process, it should feel a little more comfortable.

Use this chapter as a reference for filename limitations and the basic procedures required in using the menus and Dialog Boxes.

Exercise

1. Start Works.
2. If you are using Works from a fixed disk:
   a. Select the **File/Open Existing File** command.
   b. Look at the list of files. If you have copied all of the Works files onto the disk, several Word Processing, Database, and Spreadsheet files should be listed.
   c. Select one of these files.
   d. Use the **File/Save as** command to save the file to your exercise disk. Use the same name or enter a new filename.
   e. Close the file.
3. Create a new word processing file.
4. Type a couple of words into the file.
5. Save the file on your exercise disk using a name of your choice.
6. Close the word processing file.
7. Exit Works.

2

Introducing the Word Processor

Our investigation of Microsoft Works begins with the Word Processor, a tool that allows you to create letters, memos, reports, or any documents consisting mainly of text. In this chapter you will learn how to:

- Create a word processor file
- Enter text
- Use simple editing commands to delete, insert and replace text
- Copy and move text
- Save and retrieve files
- Print a document

What Is a Word Processor?

The advantage of the word processor over the typewriter or pen and paper is the ease with which documents can be edited, reformatted, and enhanced. Paragraphs can be copied, moved, deleted, or inserted with only a few keystrokes. The current date can be entered and changed automatically to reflect the date the document is printed. Pages can be numbered and renumbered automatically. Page lengths, margins, and paragraph indentations can be changed quickly.

Many word processors may be used with other types of programs to create personalized form letters or to insert graphs or sections of spreadsheets in the middle of documents. Since Works combines word processing, database, and spreadsheet functions in one program, this integration of materials between tasks is facilitated.

Creating a New Word Processor Document

After starting Works, the Main Menu will be on the screen.

1. If the File Menu is not displayed, press **ALT**. **Create New File** should be highlighted.
2. Press **ENTER** to select **Create New File**.
3. **New Word Processor**, the first option, will be marked. Press **ENTER** to create a new word processor file.

Note || The instructions for starting Works are in Chapter 1.

The Word Processor Screen

The Word Processor Screen (Figure 2.1) is comprised of several components: the Menu Bar (the very top line of the screen), the File Name Bar (the second line of the screen), the Work Area (the portion of the screen where you enter text), and the Status and Message Lines (on the bottom of the screen).

The Menu Bar

The top line on the screen is the Menu Bar. In order to examine the word processor menu choices, follow these steps:

1. Select **File** by pressing **ALT-F**.
2. Use the **RIGHT ARROW** to pull down the **Edit** menu. Press the **DOWN ARROW**. The Message Line on the bottom of the screen will have a description of the highlighted command.

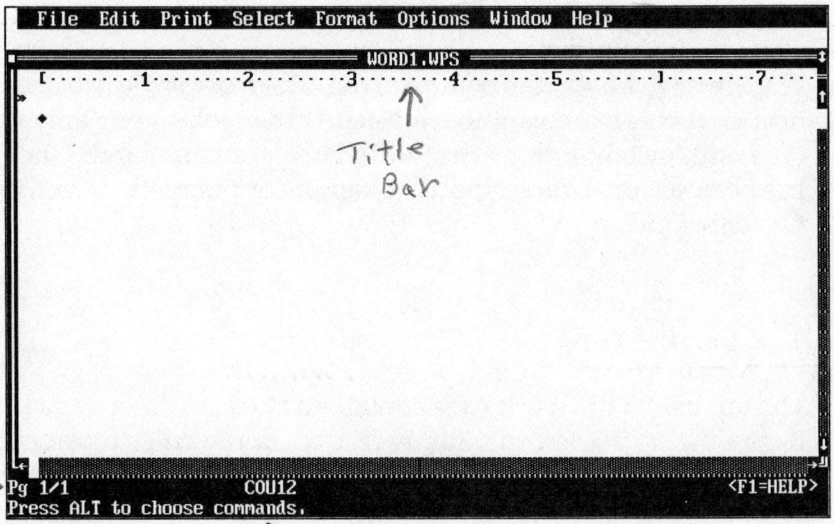

Figure 2.1. Word processor screen

3. Pull down the other menus and look at the Message Line as you highlight each command to see what the Works word processor can do with a document.
4. Press **ESC** when you have finished examining the menus.

The Title Bar

The name of the current document is shown on the second line of the screen. Works automatically names the first word processor document **WORD1.WPS**, the second one **WORD2.WPS**, and so on. The document's name can be changed to a more meaningful one when it is saved.

The Status Line

The Status Line, the second to last line on the screen, provides information about your document. In the word processor, the first piece of information tells both the current page location of the cursor and the total number of pages in the document. The current font is displayed in the middle of the line and the right-hand side of the Status Line specifies the key associated with the Help facility.

The Message Line

The Message Line at the bottom of the screen displays instructions about the next step you may want to execute. At this point your only options are to type and/or edit a document or to choose a command. Once a command has been selected, more specific prompts or instructions will appear on the Message Line.

The Work Area

The top line of the Work Area contains a ruler that keeps track of the cursor. Beginning at the left margin, each dot on the ruler represents a column; every tenth column is indicated by a number. Works, like most programs, comes with predetermined settings called *default settings*. Most of the defaults can be changed from within the program. Among the word processor defaults are left and right margins of 1.3 and 1.2 inches, respectively, and tabular settings at 0.5-inch intervals. The space between the left and right brackets represents the left and right margins (**[** and **]**) which indicates the current line length. The default line length is 60 characters. The cursor, represented by the flashing dash below the ruler, indicates where text appears as it is typed.

The **>>** symbol at the beginning of the top line indicates the beginning of the document. The same symbol appears at the beginning of each page of a multipage document. The diamond on the following line is the symbol for the end of a document. The cursor is the only symbol between the beginning and end of the document symbol at this time, because text has not been entered yet.

Creating a Letter

In order to practice entering text, try typing a letter. Figure 2.2 is a copy of the first draft of a letter. Instructions for entering it follow. If you notice errors as you type a word, press **BACKSPACE** until you erase the incorrect characters. Then retype the word. Don't be worried about errors that you don't notice until you have passed them. You will learn how to correct them shortly.

Remember to read the instructions before you enter each segment of the letter.

==

Today's Date

Dr. Daniel Farkas
1 Springhurst Road
Bedford, NY 10605

Dear Dr. Farkas,

Thank you for calling and inquiring about our computer courses. We have classes on Works quite often. Enclosed is a listing of the courses scheduled for November and December.

We feel certain you will grasp the concepts quickly. All of the students who have taken our courses have been very satisfied.

If you have any questions, please feel free to telephone us at 555-4328. Our office hours are Monday through Friday, 9:00 to 5:00.

Karen Johnson

==

Figure 2.2. Document to be entered

Uppercase Letters

To type an uppercase letter, hold down the **SHIFT** key and type the letter. Do not press **CAPS LOCK** to type a single capital letter. Once **CAPS LOCK** is turned on, all letters are capitalized until **CAPS LOCK** is turned off. If the letters **CL** appear on the Status Line, **CAPS LOCK** has been turned on. Press **CAPS LOCK** again to turn **CAPS LOCK** off.

1. Type today's date. Capitalize the first letter of the month.
2. Since the date is the only information on the first line, press **ENTER**. The cursor will move down to the left margin of the next line.

Including Blank Lines

Try pressing **DOWN ARROW**. Works will beep, indicating that you are attempting to do something that is not allowed. In order to insert a blank line, you must press **ENTER**.

3. Press **ENTER** three times to introduce three blank lines.
4. Type the following address and press **ENTER** at the end of each line:

   Dr. Daniel Farkas
   1 Springhurst Road
   Bedford, NY 10605

5. Leave a blank line between the address and the salutation by pressing **ENTER**.
6. Type: **Dear Dr. Farkas,** and then press **ENTER**.
7. Leave a blank line after the salutation.

The Tab Key

The **TAB** key can be used to indent paragraphs or to type text in columns. Press **TAB** once at the beginning of each paragraph to indent the text to the first tab stop.

8. Press **TAB** to indent the first line of the paragraph.

Word Wrap

One of the major changes from old-fashioned typewriters, is that you do NOT press **ENTER** at the end of the line in the middle of a paragraph. The word wrap feature automatically brings the cursor to the start of the next line when you reach the right margin. If you reach the right margin in the middle of typing a word, the part of the word that you have typed will be brought to the beginning of the next line as you complete it.

At the end of a paragraph press **ENTER** to move the cursor to the next line. Similarly, when you type an inside address, salutation, or any other text that does not take up the whole line, press **ENTER**.

9. Type the first paragraph in Figure 2.2 **without** pressing **ENTER** at the end of each line. Press **ENTER** twice at the end of the paragraph.

10. Type the remaining paragraphs being sure to indent the first line and leaving a blank line between each paragraph.
11. Leave a blank line after the last paragraph.
12. Press **TAB** six times to indent the closing. Type: **Karen Johnson**
13. Press **ENTER**.

How Works Scrolls the Screen

As you begin typing on the last line of the work area, the text is automatically scrolled so the last line is moved from the bottom of the screen to the middle of the screen. This adjustment will occur whenever you edit or enter text on the last line of the screen. When you move the cursor through previously entered text to the borders of the screen, only one line at a time scrolls off.

Moving Around the Screen

In order to read or edit parts of the document that have scrolled off the screen, you must move the cursor. The four **ARROW** keys can be used to move the cursor one character or row at a time. However, there are a number of ways to move the cursor around the screen more quickly. Try moving around the screen.

1. Press the **UP ARROW** once or twice.
2. Hold down the **UP ARROW** until the cursor reaches the beginning of the document. Since the cursor can be moved only to parts of the screen containing text (or the hidden characters indicating such things as blank lines), the **UP** and **DOWN ARROWS** may move the cursor through the text in ways you don't expect.
3. Use the **ARROW** keys to move the cursor under the *D* in *Dear*.
4. Press **PGDN** (Page Down) until the cursor moves to the end of the document.
5. Press **PGUP** to return to the beginning.
6. There is a faster way to move to the end of the document: press **CTRL-END.** What effect does **CTRL-HOME** have?
7. There are faster ways to move to the end and beginning of a line. Press **END**. Then press **HOME**.

8. Now use **CTRL-RIGHT ARROW** to move across the line one word at a time. What does **CTRL-LEFT ARROW** do?

Table 2.1 reviews and summarizes the key movements you've been using.

Scrolling the Screen with a Mouse

Scrolling with a mouse is different than with the cursor. On the right-most side of the screen is a vertical bar called the *scroll bar*. On the bar there are several symbols. One symbol is a black box called the *elevator*; the others are an up arrow on the top of the bar and a down arrow on the bottom of the bar. All these symbols are used for scrolling purposes. Here are some methods of scrolling the screen with the mouse:

- To move the screen up one line at a time, position the mouse on the up arrow on the scroll bar and click the left button (if the screen is already at the top, no change occurs)
- To move the screen down one line at a time, position the mouse on the down arrow on the scroll bar and click the left button
- To move one screen up, position the mouse on the bar anywhere above the elevator and click the left button
- To move one screen down, position the mouse on the bar anywhere below the elevator and click the left button

Table 2.1. Summary of Key Movements Used

Key	Movement
ARROW Keys	One space or row in the direction of the arrow
CTRL-RIGHT ARROW	Beginning of next word
CTRL-LEFT ARROW	Beginning of previous word
HOME	Beginning of line
END	End of line
PGUP	Up one screen
PGDN	Down one screen
CTRL-HOME	Beginning of document
CTRL-END	End of document

- The scroll bar can be thought of as representing the length of your document. The top of the bar is the beginning of your document and the bottom of the bar is the end of your document. The elevator can be repositioned on the scroll bar and the document will be adjusted on the screen accordingly. For example, if you have a multipage document and currently page one is displayed on the screen, when you drag the elevator to the bottom of the bar, the end of the document will be displayed.

To move more than one page at a time, you can change the relative position of the elevator which is called dragging the elevator. Position the mouse on the elevator; since the elevator is a solid black rectangle the exact size of the mouse, the mouse seemingly disappears. Click the left button and hold it down while moving the mouse up or down. The document will be relatively adjusted.

---

1. Using one keystroke, move to the end of the document.
2. Using one keystroke, move to the beginning of the document.
3. Move the cursor to *T* of *Thank* in the first paragraph.
4. Using one keystroke, move the cursor to the *y* of *you*.
5. Using one keystroke, move the cursor to the end of the current line.

---

1. *Press* **CTRL-END**.
2. *Press* **CTRL-HOME**.
3. *Press* **DOWN ARROW** *until you reach the first paragraph. Press* **RIGHT ARROW** *once.*
4. *Press* **CTRL-RIGHT ARROW**.
5. *Press* **END**.

Editing a Document

Deleting Text

The **BACKSPACE** key typically is used to delete text immediately after you enter it, since it deletes text to the left of the cursor.

The **DEL** (delete) key can be used to delete text at the cursor position. Use the following directions to delete the words *calling and* from the first paragraph of the letter (Figure 2.3).

==
Thank you for calling and inquiring about our computer courses. We have classes on Works quite often. Enclosed is a listing of the courses scheduled for November and December.
==

Figure 2.3. Text to be deleted

1. Put the cursor under the *c* in *calling*.
2. Press **DEL** until *calling and* and the space that follows it are deleted. In order to maintain full lines of text, Works will adjust the entire document when text is deleted or added.

Did You Let Word Wrap Work?

Did your paragraph word wrap to fill in the space left when you deleted *calling and*? Often, when people first use word processors, they press **ENTER** at the end of lines within a paragraph. Each time you press **ENTER**, Works enters a paragraph code. If there are paragraph codes at the end of lines in the middle of paragraphs, word wrap will not work correctly when you revise the letter.

Check to see that your letter does not contain any extra paragraph endings.

1. Compare the three paragraphs of your letter with Figure 2.4. Spaces are indicated by dots and tabs by arrows. Each time you pressed **ENTER**, a paragraph sign was inserted.
2. If the special symbols do not appear on your screen then select **Options/Show All Characters**.
3. Be sure that there are no paragraph signs in the middle of paragraphs. If there are, move the cursor under any extra paragraph symbols, and press **DEL** to remove them.
4. Select **Options** again. The mark preceding **Show All Characters** indicates that this command has previously been activated. Select this command again in order to deactivate it.

Now that you know how to toggle **Show All Characters** on and off, use this option as you wish when entering and editing text.

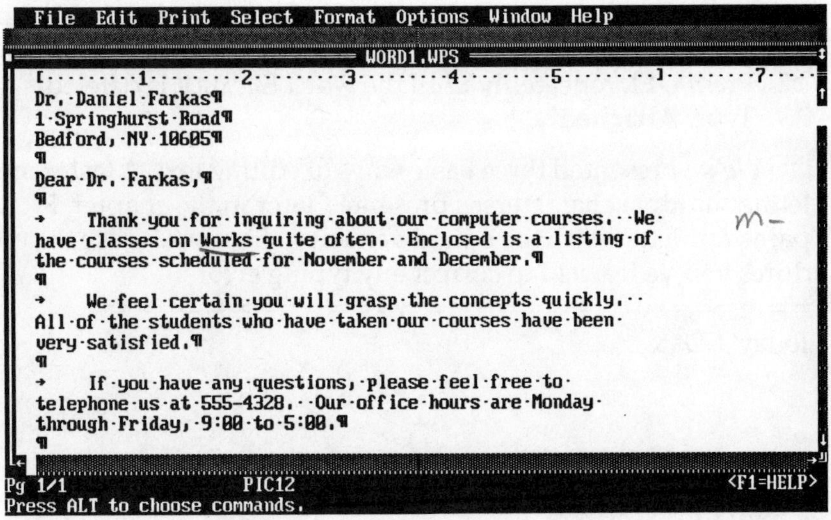

Figure 2.4. Document with all characters showing

Inserting Text

Anything you type in the middle of existing text is automatically inserted into the text. The only trick to inserting text is to be sure that the cursor is immediately after the point at which you want to insert text. For example, to insert the word **Microsoft** before *Works* in the first sentence of the first paragraph, do the following:

1. Move the cursor to the *W* in *Works*.
2. Type: **Microsoft**

Press the **SPACE BAR** once. *Microsoft* is inserted into the text and the rest of the lines in the paragraph are adjusted.

Replacing Text

Sometimes, instead of adding or deleting text, you want to correct a typographical error or replace one word with another. Some word processors include an overwrite or replace mode that allows you to substitute newly entered characters for existing ones. In Works, to replace text, you must first delete the unwanted characters and then insert the correct ones. To change the word *Enclosed* in the first paragraph to **Attached**:

1. Move the cursor to the *E* in *Enclosed* in the second line of the first paragraph.
2. Press **DEL** repeatedly until the word *Enclosed* is deleted.
3. Type: **Attached**

We've presented three basic ways of editing text. A faster method for deleting multiple characters is presented later in the chapter. Right now, compare your letter with the edited version in Figure 2.5. Use the editing procedures you've learned to correct any typing errors.

==============================

Today's Date

Dr. Daniel Farkas
1 Springhurst Road
Bedford, NY 10605

Dear Dr. Farkas,

Thank you for inquiring about our computer courses. We have classes on Microsoft Works quite often. Attached is a listing of the courses scheduled for November and December.

We feel certain you will grasp the concepts quickly. All of the students who have taken our courses have been very satisfied.

If you have any questions, please feel free to telephone us at 555-4328. Our office hours are Monday through Friday, 9:00 to 5:00.

Karen Johnson

==

Figure 2.5. Edited document

1. Delete *November and* from the first paragraph of the letter.
2. Insert area code (914) before the telephone number in the last paragraph.

3. Replace the office hours of 9:00 to 5:00 with 8:30 to 4:30.

---

1. *Move the cursor to the* N *of* November *and press the* **DEL** *key until the phrase* November and *has been deleted.*
2. *Move the cursor to the first* 5 *in* 555-4328 *and type* **(914)** *and then press the* **SPACE BAR** *once.*
3. *Move the cursor to the* 9 *of* 9:00 *and press* **DEL** *until* 9:00 to 5:00 *has been deleted and then type:* **8:30 to 4:30.**

Spell Checking

Before you print the final copy of your letter, you should use the spell checker. The spell checker will locate misspelled words, duplicate words (such as *and and*), incorrect hyphenation, and incorrect capitalization. Works has a built-in dictionary which does not have proper names or colloquialisms. However, you can update a personal dictionary to contain often-used words.

When the spell checker finds a misspelling, you can type in the correct spelling or ask Works to suggest possible spellings from which you can choose. The selected correction then replaces the misspelled word and the spell checker continues onto the next error.

It is important to have your cursor at the point in the document where you want to begin spell checking. If your cursor is on line 2 of the document, none of the words on line 1 will be checked for errors. The options on the Spell Checker menu (Figure 2.6) are:

Change All replaces all occurrences of a misspelling in a document with the text entered in the **Replace with** text box.

Change replaces only the current occurrence of a misspelling with the text entered in the **Replace with** text box.

Ignore All considers all occurrences of the flagged word in the document correctly spelled.

Ignore considers only the current occurrence of the flagged word as correctly spelled.

Suggest lists possible spellings for the misspelled word.

Add inserts the flagged word to a personal dictionary and will always consider this word spelled correctly.

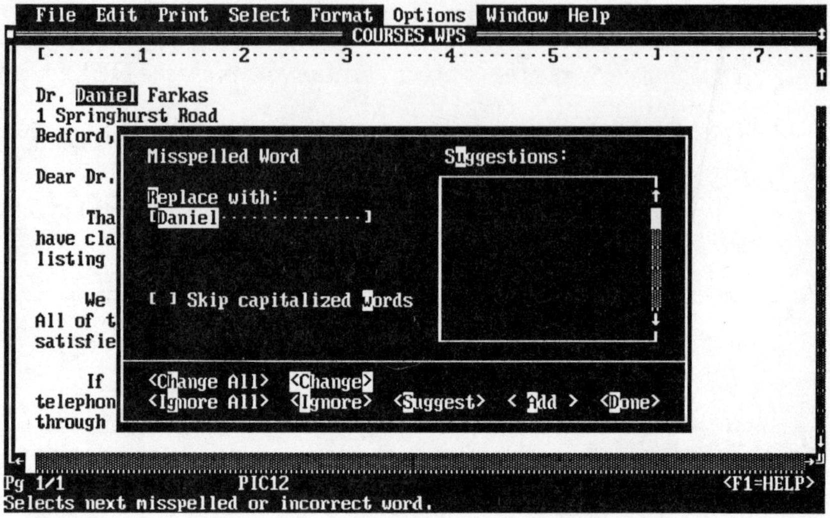

Figure 2.6. Spell Checker Menu

Done terminates the spell checker.

Skip capitalized words skips over capitalized words. This can be helpful in skipping proper names. However, this also passes misspellings that are the first words in a sentence.

1. To be sure that you have some errors in your document:
   a. Change the word *Thank* in the first paragraph to **Thaank**.
   b. Change the word *you* to the word **eou**.
2. Move the cursor to the top of the document.
3. Select **Options/Check Spelling**. The menu in Figure 2.6 will be displayed.
4. The first word that is flagged is the proper name *Daniel*. Press **ALT-G** to select **<Ignore All>**.
5. Works will stop on the proper names *Farkas* and *Springhurst*; press **ALT-G** for each.
6. When the checker stops on *Thaank*, ask for suggested spellings by pressing **ALT-S**. The cursor will be placed in the **Suggestions** List Box and you can highlight the correct spelling of the word.
7. Highlight *Thank* and press **ENTER** which selects the **<Change>** button. The old spelling is replaced and the checker moves on.
8. The word *eou* is flagged. Ask for suggested spellings by pressing **ALT-S**.

Works will not find any possible spellings so you will need to edit the word yourself. Press **ENTER**.

9. The cursor should now be on the **Replace with** Text Box. Press the **LEFT ARROW** and replace the *e* with a y and press **ENTER**.
10. Finish spell checking the document, making the appropriate selections.
11. Checking the spelling cannot be a substitute for proofreading. If there are words that are incorrect but not misspelled, the spell checker will not flag them. Consider the sentence: *There are too ways to skin a cat*. The word *too* is a valid word but is used incorrectly in this sentence.

Saving a Document as a File

When text is entered, two things happen: the text appears on the screen and it is stored in the computer's main memory, known as **RAM (Random Access Memory).** When the document is edited, the text is reorganized in **RAM** and then the screen is redrawn to reflect the changes. Since information is only temporarily stored in **RAM**, the letter must be saved to a data disk.

Anything saved on a disk is stored in a *file*. The file includes the text that you have entered, plus all of the formatting information that will enable Works to display and print the document according to your instructions. Since the document is saved in a file, the **Save** command is located on the File Menu.

1. Select **File/Save**. If this is the first time the file is being saved, the Save As Dialog Box (Figure 2.7) is opened and a highlight bar is on the filename. This gives you a chance to save the file using a more meaningful name than **WORD1.WPS**. If **ENTER** is pressed, the file is saved on the current directory, using the filename **WORD1.WPS.**
2. If your data disk is not in the drive listed after *Directory of* on the screen, you will need to change the current drive using the *Directories* List Box.
   a. Press **ALT-I**.
   b. Use the **UP** and **DOWN ARROW** keys, if necessary, to move the highlight to the name of the drive that contains your exercise disk.
   c. Press **ENTER**.
3. Once the correct drive is indicated, the cursor returns to the Save File As Text Box, and all you need to enter is the new filename. You should try

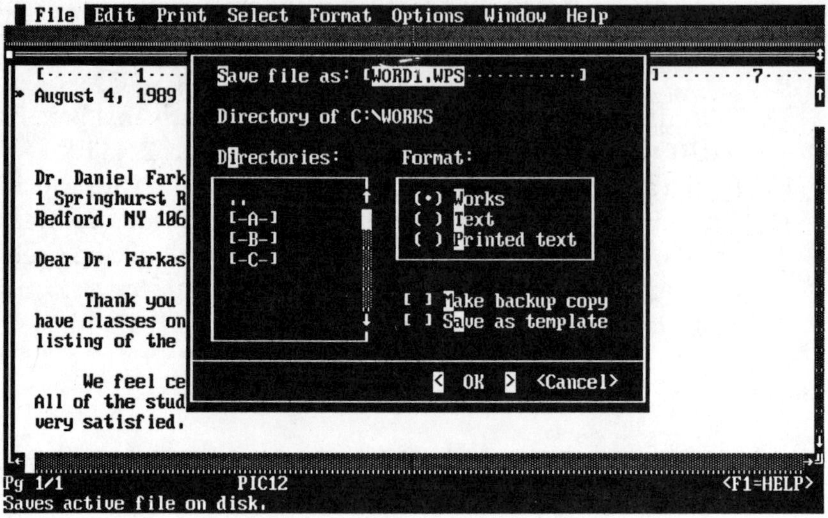

Figure 2.7. Save As Dialog Box

to use a meaningful name so you can easily recognize the file when you want to retrieve and use it in the future. DOS limits the name to eight characters and Works adds its word processor extension **.WPS** to the filename. Type the new filename: **Courses**

4. Press **ENTER**. After the file has been saved, the new filename will appear on the Message Line at the top of the screen.

Note As shown in Chapter 1, the **File/Save As** command can also be used to save a new file. After selecting **File/Save As**, follow steps 2–4 above.

Printing a Document

The Print Menu is divided into three sections (Figure 2.8). Each command is followed by an ellipsis, indicating that a Dialog Box requesting further information will appear when the command is selected.

1. Select **Print**.
2. This pulls down the Print Menu.

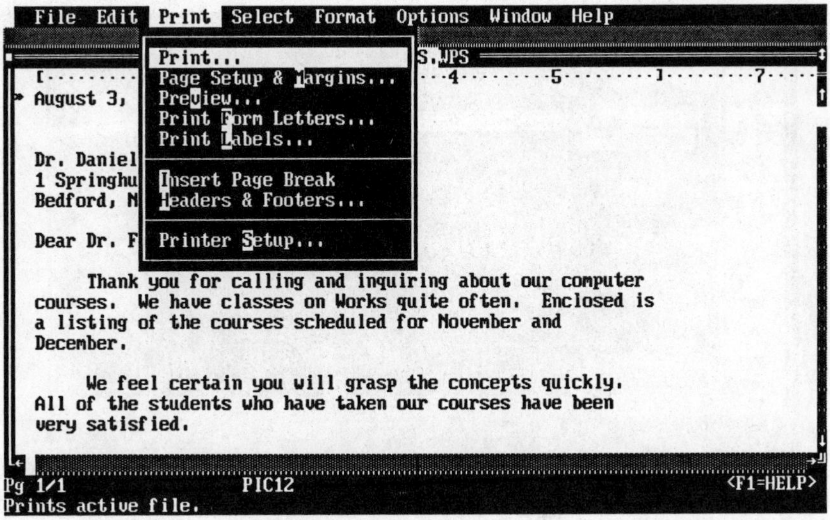

Figure 2.8. Print Menu

Checking the Printer Selection

Since this is the first time we are using Works to print, check that the printer options have been correctly set. If problems occur during printing, refer to this section for help in correcting them.

1. Select **Printer Setup**. Figure 2.9 represents the screen display. Your screen may have different information in the List Boxes since you are probably using a different printer.
2. In the Setup program, you selected the printer, model and the port to which the printer is attached.
   a. If the printer that you are using has changed since the Setup program was run and the new printer is **not** listed in the Printers or Model List Boxes, exit from Works, insert the Setup disk in Drive **A** and rerun the Setup Program. When asked whether you are creating a copy of Works or modifying an existing copy, select *Modify an existing working copy of Works 2.0*. Refer to Chapter 1 of this book for help in using the Setup Program.
   b. If you have more than one printer, and only one is listed in the Printer List Box, follow the directions in *Step a* to select the second printer. Once both printers have been selected in the Setup Program,

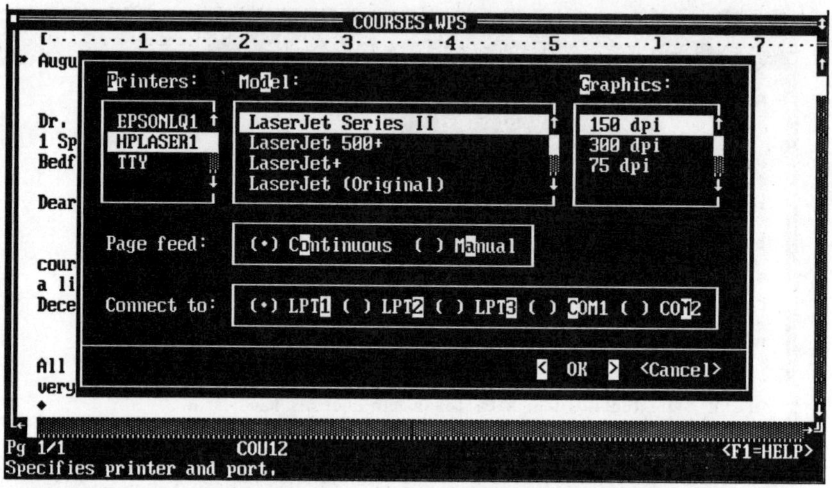

Figure 2.9. Printer Setup Dialog Box

Print/Setup is used to specify which printer is being used for the current task.

c. If you try to print and nothing happens, check that the printer cables are secure and the printer is turned on and is on-line. If the printer still does not respond, it is possible that you have selected the wrong printer port in the Connect to Option Box. Change the selected Connect to Option and try printing again.

3. The information for the Graphics and Page Feed Boxes was not supplied during setup. The defaults are probably adequate, but some changes may be necessary:
   a. The Graphics List Box indicates the density of print; you may want to change the default setting to increase or decrease the clarity of the printed copy, particularly when printing graphics.
   b. Select the Manual Option in the Page Feed Option Box if you must insert each sheet of paper into the printer individually. If this option is selected, you will be prompted to enter new sheets of paper.
4. When you are finished with the Printer Setup Dialog Box, press **ENTER**.

Print

To print the document:

1. Select **Print/Print.** The Dialog Box shown in Figure 2.10 is displayed.

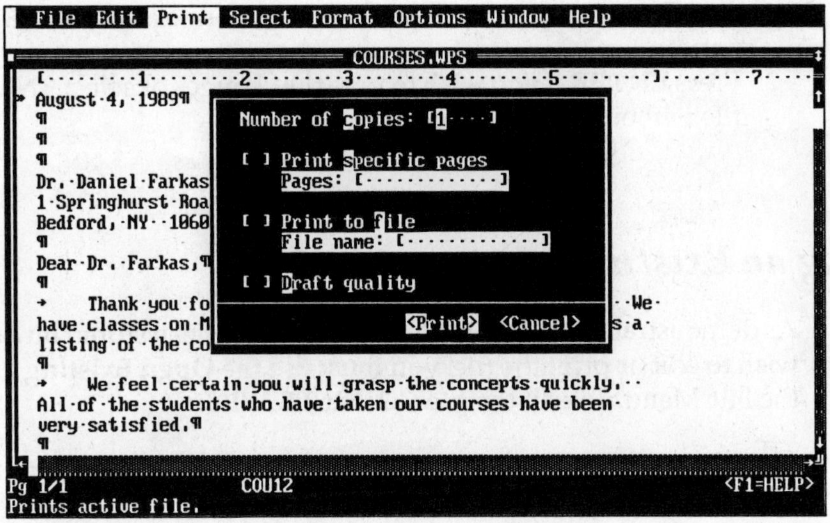

Figure 2.10. Print Dialog Box

The first three options in this box are common to all of the tools. The default settings currently displayed in the Print Dialog Box can be used.

2. Before selecting the **<Print>** button, make sure that your printer is ready to print. Check to see that:
   - The printer is turned on
   - The printer is on-line
   - The paper is correctly aligned in the printer
3. Since the **<Print>** button is in highlighted brackets, it is the active button. Press **ENTER** to print the document.

Closing the Current Word Processor Document

As many as eight files may be active at one time, so it is possible to create a new file without closing the current files. However, it is good practice to close files that are not being used by selecting **File/Close**.

1. Select **File/Close**. If you have saved your latest changes the **Close** command will be executed immediately and you will be returned to the Main Menu. If you have not saved the latest changes to your letter, a Di-

alog Box asking if you want to save changes to **COURSES.WPS** will appear.

2. Press **ENTER** if you wish to save the changes or select **<No>** to close the file without saving the changes.

Opening an Existing File

As demonstrated in Chapter 1, when a file has been stored on a disk and you wish to edit or print the file, you must use the **Open Existing File** option on the File Menu. To edit the file **COURSES.WPS**:

1. Select **File/Open Existing File** from the Main Menu.
2. Look at the information following *Directory of*. If it does not list the directory of your data files, then follow the steps below:
   a. Select the Directories List Box by pressing **ALT-I**.
   b. Highlight the directory that contains your data files by pressing the **UP/DOWN ARROWS**.
   c. Press **ENTER**.
3. Once the correct directory is selected a list of all Works files will appear in the Files List Box. Using the **ARROW** keys, highlight the **COURSES.WPS** file and press **ENTER**.

Note If you are sure of the exact spelling of the file you wish to open, type the directory followed by the filename in the File to Open Text Box. For example, if your data disk is in the A drive you would type **A:COURSES.WPS.**

Selecting Text

Using the method of deleting characters that has been shown, deleting more than a few words is slow and tedious. However, Works provides a function called *Selecting Text* that allows you to highlight a block of text and then specify the function you would like to perform on that block.

There are several methods of defining a block of text. The general procedure is:

- Move the cursor to the beginning of the area that needs work
- Press the **F8** key (Works calls **F8** the **EXTEND** key)

- Use the **ARROW** keys, **F8** key, or mouse to **EXTEND** the highlight
- Perform the desired function on the highlighted text

You can use the **ARROW** keys, **F8** key, or the mouse to select a logical block of text such as a word, a sentence, a paragraph or an entire document. Table 2.2 lists the methods to perform these special selections with the **F8** key or mouse.

Canceling a Selection

What happens if you start to select text, and then change your mind? To **CANCEL** a text selection:

1. First select the date on the first line of the document (or any text you wish to change):
   a. Move the cursor to the beginning of the date.
   b. Press **F8**; EXT will appear on the Status Line.
   c. Highlight the entire date.
2. Press **ESC**. *EXT* should disappear from the Status Line.
3. Press any **ARROW** key. The highlight bar should disappear and the cursor should return to the screen.

Deleting a Block of Text

To delete the paragraph shown in Figure 2.11 you could start at the beginning of the paragraph and press **DEL** until the entire paragraph has been deleted. However, it is much faster to select the paragraph and then delete it.

Table 2.2. Methods of Selecting Text

Selecting	**Press F8**	**Click Mouse**
Word	Two times	Right Button on word
Sentence	Three times	Both Buttons in sentence
Line	—	Left Button in left window margin
Paragraph	Four times	Right Button in left window margin
Entire Document	Five times	Double Click Buttons in left window margin

==
We feel certain you will grasp the concepts quickly.
All of the students who have taken our courses have been very satisfied.
==

Figure 2.11. Paragraph to be deleted

1. Tabs are represented by an arrow; if you cannot see the arrow that signifies a tab, select **Options/Show All Characters**.
2. Move the cursor to the tab mark of the paragraph in Figure 2.11.
3. Press **F8**.
4. Highlight the entire paragraph.
5. Press **DEL**.
6. Adjust the spacing by deleting extra blank lines between paragraphs.

Undoing the Last Command

If you have deleted text and IMMEDIATELY change your mind, Works provides an option called **Edit/Undo**. This command will also undo and of the operations listed below, provided it is the LAST action taken prior to selecting **Edit/Undo**:

- All typing from the last command you issued or since the last time you moved the cursor
- All commands on the Edit Menu, except Bookmark Names and the Undo command
- All format commands
- All changes made while using the spell checker
- All changes made while using the Replace command

1. Delete the date on the top of the document.
2. Select **Edit/Undo**. The date will return to the screen.

Inserting a New Paragraph

Now alter the existing letter to actually include a class listing by inserting the text shown in Figure 2.12 after the last paragraph in the letter. In this text

```
==============================
COURSE:     Microsoft Works
LOCATION:   Russell Hall, Room 405
TIME:       9:00 - 4:00
TEACHER:    Ms. Nancy Fisher
DATE:       December 10
==============================
```

Figure 2.12. Course data to be entered

use **CAPS LOCK** to capitalize letters in several words and **TAB** to align text in two columns.

1. Position the cursor on the blank line after the last line and add an extra blank line.
2. Press **TAB** once to indent the course listing.
3. Press **CAPS LOCK** once and the letters **CL** will appear on the Status Line; then type: **COURSE:**
4. Press **CAPS LOCK** again to turn off **CAPS LOCK**.
5. Press **TAB** to align the course information at position 15, type: **Microsoft Works**, and press **ENTER**.
6. Repeat steps 2–5 to enter the rest of the information in Figure 2.12.
7. Enter a blank line at the end of the listing.

Copying Text

To add another class listing shown in Figure 2.13, you can type the information as shown. However, since much of the information is the same as in the

```
==============================
COURSE:     Microsoft Works
LOCATION:   Russell Hall, Room 405
TIME:       9:00 - 4:00
TEACHER:    Ms. Karin Cieplicki
DATE:       December 17
==============================
```

Figure 2.13. Second course listing to be added

listing you just entered, you can take advantage of the Copy Command. Since you know how to select text, copying text is easy. All you need to do is:

- Select the text to be copied
- Choose **Edit/Copy**
- Move the cursor to the new location
- Press **ENTER**

1. Select the five lines of the course listing and the blank line below the listing.
2. Choose **Edit/Copy**. The following message is displayed on the Message Line: *Select new location and press* **ENTER**. *Press* **ESC** *to cancel.*
3. Press **DOWN ARROW** once to position the cursor directly below the text you are copying.
4. Press **ENTER** to perform the copy.
5. In the new course listing change the text:

Teacher:	*Ms. Nancy Fisher*
Date:	*December 10*

to

Teacher:	**Ms. Karin Cieplicki**
Date:	**December 17**

Moving Text

In Works the procedure for moving text is almost identical to that for copying text. The only procedural difference is that the **Edit/Move** command is used in place of the **Edit/Copy** command. Text which is moved appears only in the new location while copied text appears in the original and new locations.

Place the two class listings after the first paragraph in the document. Follow these instructions:

1. Select both class listings.
2. Choose **Edit/Move**.
3. Move the cursor to the blank line after the first paragraph.

4. Press **ENTER.**
5. Adjust the spacing as necessary.
6. Compare your document with the copy of the revised document (Figure 2.14) and make any corrections needed.

==

Today's Date

Dr. Daniel Farkas
1 Springhurst Road
Bedford, NY 10605

Dear Dr. Farkas,

Thank you for inquiring about our computer courses. We have classes on Microsoft Works quite often. Attached is a listing of the courses scheduled for December.

COURSE:	Microsoft Works
LOCATION:	Russell Hall, Room 405
TIME:	9:00 - 4:00
TEACHER:	Ms. Nancy Fisher
DATE:	December 10

COURSE:	Microsoft Works
LOCATION:	Russell Hall, Room 405
TIME:	9:00 - 4:00
TEACHER:	Ms. Karin Cieplicki
DATE:	December 17

If you have any questions, please feel free to telephone us at (914) 555-4328. Our office hours are Monday through Friday, 8:30 to 4:30.

Karen Johnson

==

Figure 2.14. Edited document

Saving a Document for a Second Time

There have been considerable alterations to the letter. It is wise to save the document before continuing. Since the document has already been saved once, there are two choices:

- Save the document using the same filename or
- Save the document using a new filename

Typically, you do not want to keep multiple revisions of the same document—this wastes space on the disk and, if you go back to the document after a few days, you may retrieve a document without the correct changes. At other times you may want to use your original as a *template*—the frame of a document that may be used over and over with some modifications or additions.

To save the file using the **same name:**

1. Select **File/Save.**
2. Works automatically will replace the previously saved file with the revised text.

To save the file using a **different name:**

1. Select **File/Save As.** The Dialog Box appears and the current filename is highlighted.
2. Type the new filename that you wish to use. Refer to the file naming rules, to make sure that your new filename is valid.
3. Press **ENTER.**

---

1. Add another class listing by copying one of the existing listings and changing the date and teacher.
2. Spell check the document.
3. Save the document as **CRS-LIST.WPS.**
4. Print the document.
5. Close the document.

1. *Move the cursor to the C in* Course. *Use* **F8** *to select the entire course listing. Select* ***Edit/Copy***. *Move the cursor beneath the second course listing and press* **ENTER**. *Correct the spacing as necessary.*
2. *Move the cursor to the beginning of the document. Select* **Options/Check Spelling**. *Use the procedures discussed in the section on spell checking to make any necessary spelling corrections.*
3. *Select* ***File/Save As***. *Type:* ***CRS-LIST*** *in the Save File As Text Box and press* **ENTER**.
4. *Select* ***Print/Print*** *and press* **ENTER** *to print the letter using the default settings.*
5. *Select* ***File/Close*** *to close the document.*

Here we introduced the basic word processing tasks: creating, editing, saving, and printing a document. In addition we introduced some of the more advanced concepts that demonstrate the power of Works. You moved from editing character by character to selecting and working with blocks of text. The procedures followed provide the basis for further exploration of the word processor and of the other Works tools. For example, the process of selecting a block of text and then acting upon it with a command is the first step in many of the more advanced word processing activities. We will also use the same procedure in some of the database and spreadsheet activities which will be explained later in this book.

Exercise

1. Enter the letter shown in Figure 2.15.
2. After you type the information on the **Green Room**, copy the block of information so that it is repeated immediately below itself. Figure 2.16 shows the block to be copied.
3. Change the second room listing to read:

Room:	**Blue Room**
Hall:	**Tamany Hall**
Seating Capacity:	**40**
Fee:	**$80**

September 5, 1989

Beverly Busman
123 Strawberry Lane
Putnam Valley, NY 10670

Dear Ms. Busman,

I received your letter regarding rental of a lecture hall. There are several rooms available for small private lectures. Below is a list of the rooms, their seating capacity, and rental fee. If you have any questions, please feel free to call my office to arrange a tour.

Room:	Green Room
Hall:	Tamany Hall
Seating Capacity:	50
Fee:	$100

Sincerely yours,

Yolanda Fiore

Figure 2.15. Document to be entered

Room:	Green Room
Hall:	Tamany Hall
Seating Capacity:	50
Fee:	$100

Figure 2.16. Block of text to be copied

4. Spell Check the document and then proofread the document using the editing techniques you have learned to correct any errors.
5. Save the document to your data disk.
6. Print the document.
7. Close the document.

3

Introducing the Spreadsheet

Now we're ready to take a look at another Works tool—the spreadsheet. If you've already worked through Chapter 2 on Word Processing, you'll have a head start since the information on the screen and all but one of the main menu headings are identical. If the spreadsheet is the first Works tool you're using, you'll be surprised at how quickly you can get Works to work for you. In this chapter you will learn how to:

- Move around the spreadsheet
- Enter text, numbers, and formulas
- Use one of Works' built-in functions
- Copy the contents of one cell to another cell or to a range of cells
- Change the appearance of text and values
- Change the width of cells

What Is a Spreadsheet?

A spreadsheet is an organized way to keep track of a lot of numerical information. Usually this information is financial, and oftentimes the information changes quickly. For those in business settings, spreadsheets have become an indispensable tool. For individuals who are involved with groups doing fund raising or budgeting, a spreadsheet is invaluable. For day-to-day home budgets or vacation planning, a spreadsheet can be quite useful.

This chapter introduces the Works spreadsheet. You will become familiar with some of the key vocabulary words used and you will have the opportunity to practice entering data into several spreadsheets. You will also begin to use the menus found on the Spreadsheet tool in Works.

Starting a Spreadsheet File

After starting Works, the Main Menu will be on the screen.

1. If the File Menu is not displayed, press **ALT**. **Create New File** should be highlighted.
2. Press **ENTER** to select **Create a New File.**
3. Select **<New Spreadsheet>.**

The Menu Bar

The Menu Bar, which provides the spreadsheet options, is across the top of the spreadsheet screen (Figure 3.1). Menu choices are selected, as you have done earlier, by pressing ALT to highlight one letter in each of the menu options, and then either typing the highlighted letter in the option you wish to select or using the **ARROW** keys and pressing **ENTER**.

The Formula Bar

Below the Menu Bar is the Formula Bar, which is blank at the moment. As you will see shortly, this area serves as a "holding zone" when you enter information into the spreadsheet. When you type in information it appears in the Formula Bar first so that you have the opportunity to examine it and make corrections before you "send" it off to its designated cell. You will see this in action in a few moments.

Below the Formula Bar in the center of the spreadsheet is the filename of the current spreadsheet **SHEET1.WKS**. Works automatically names the first new spreadsheet **SHEET1.WKS**, the second one **SHEET2.WKS**, and so

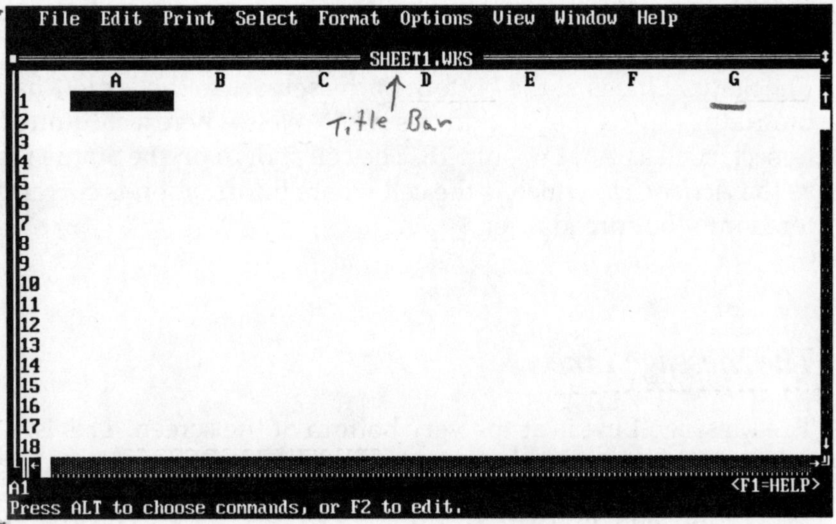

Figure 3.1. The Spreadsheet screen

on. You may give the spreadsheet a more meaningful filename when you save it.

Column Names

Below the Formula Bar is the row of *Column Names*. There are 256 columns in the spreadsheet; only columns A through G are currently displayed on your screen. To see additional columns, press the **RIGHT ARROW** key until you see the columns to the right. When you are done, press the **HOME** key to bring you back where you started.

Row Numbers

In the left margin of the spreadsheet are the *Row Numbers*. There are 4096 rows in the spreadsheet; only rows 1 through 18 are currently displayed on your screen. To see the subsequent rows, press the **DOWN ARROW** until you see the rows below row 18. When you are finished, press **CTRL-HOME** to bring you back where you started.

The Status Line

The Status Line is at the bottom of the screen. In the far left-hand corner of the Status Line is the cell address A1. A *cell* is where a column and a row intersect, such as A1, D35, or F18. The cell shown on the Status Line is known as the *Active Cell,* which is the cell where information is currently being entered into the spreadsheet.

The Message Line

The Message Line is at the very bottom of the screen. This is where Works sends you messages as you enter and modify information. Sometimes these messages will tell you the options that you have and sometimes these messages will tell you how to handle a problem.

Moving Around the Spreadsheet Screen

One of the differences between the word processor and the spreadsheet is that it is possible to move the cursor around the spreadsheet screen before you enter any information. There are some keys that act differently when used on a blank screen than when used on a screen that contains data. To begin, we'll examine those cursor movement keys which achieve the same results on both an empty and a full spreadsheet. Then, after you have entered some information in the first spreadsheet, we'll take another look at moving around the spreadsheet screen.

When you move around a spreadsheet, usually you do so in one of three ways: *cell-to-cell, screen-to-screen,* or with *global movement.* We will save the discussion of the global movement key combinations until we have entered information in some cells, because as long as the screen is blank the program treats cell A1 as both the beginning and the end of the spreadsheet file.

Cell-to-cell movement is accomplished by using the **ARROW** keys on your keyboard. Pressing these keys will move the cursor one cell in the direction of the arrows.

Screen-to-screen movement is accomplished by using some of the special keys on your keyboard. These keys, and the movements that they perform, are listed in Table 3.1.

Table 3.1. Key Movements

Key	Movement
PGDN	Down one screen
PGUP	Up one screen
CTRL-PGDN	Right one screen
CTRL-PGUP	Left one screen

Scrolling the Screen with a Mouse

When you want to move the cursor to a certain cell address on the screen, you simply position the mouse on the cell and click. Scrolling the screen using the mouse is more complex. Here we list the vertical and horizontal movements available to you:

Vertical movement:

- To move one row down, place the mouse on the down arrow on the vertical scroll bar and click once
- To move one row up, place the mouse on the up arrow on the vertical scroll bar and click once
- To move one screen down, place the mouse on the vertical scroll bar anywhere below the elevator and click
- To move to row 1, place the mouse on the elevator on the vertical scroll bar and click once
- To move many pages down, place the mouse on the elevator, hold down the button, and drag the elevator down; the spreadsheet will be adjusted relative to the point the elevator is positioned on the vertical scroll bar
- To move many pages up, place the mouse on the elevator, hold down the button and drag the elevator up; the spreadsheet will be adjusted relative to the point the elevator is positioned on the vertical scroll bar

Note There currently isn't any quick way to page up using the mouse in the spreadsheet tool.

Horizontal movement

- To move one row to the left, place the mouse on the left arrow on the horizontal scroll bar and click

- To move one row to the right, place the mouse on the right arrow on the horizontal scroll bar and click
- To move one screen to the right, place the mouse on the horizontal scroll bar anywhere to the right of the elevator and click
- To move one screen to the left, place the mouse on the horizontal scroll bar anywhere to the left of the elevator and click
- To move to column A, place the mouse on the horizontal elevator, hold the left button down and drag the elevator to the end of the horizontal scroll bar

To practice cursor movement, try the following exercise. You can check your answers with the results that follow.

1. Create a new spreadsheet file.
2. Use screen-to-screen movements to move two screens to the right. What is the current address of the cursor?
3. Move three screens down. Where is the cursor now?
4. Move right one screen and then up one screen. Where is the cursor now?

---

1. *File/Create New File/New Spreadsheet*
2. *CTRL-PGDN, CTRL-PGDN. O1.*
3. *PGDN, PGDN, PGDN. O55.*
4. *CTRL-PGDN, PGUP. V37.*

Entering Data in a Spreadsheet

When you enter information into a spreadsheet, you enter either text, numbers, or formulas. Numbers and formulas are often referred to as *values*. Text that is used for headings is often referred to as *labels*. Labels can appear anywhere on the spreadsheet but are often used across the top of the spreadsheet as column headings or down the left-hand side of the spreadsheet. For example, in the list below, *Supplies* and the data below would be referred to as labels.

<u>Supplies</u>

Paper
Pens
Pencils

Entering Text

Works handles text very differently than numbers or formulas. When you enter text it is automatically *left justified*. This means that the text starts at the left edge of the cell. You will learn later how to change this justification, should you choose to do so. Also, Works automatically places a quotation mark in front of any text. You will not see the quotation mark in the cell itself, but it appears in the Formula Bar. This quotation mark signifies that the content of the cell is text rather than numbers or formulas.

1. If you have not already done so, select **Create New File/New Spreadsheet.**
2. Use the **RIGHT**and **DOWN ARROWS** to move the cursor to cell *B3*.
3. Type: **Monday** and press **ENTER**.

The characters *"Monday* appear in the Formula Bar but the characters *Monday* will appear in cell *B3.*

4. Move the cursor to cell *C3* and type the following labels. This time, after you type each label, press the **RIGHT ARROW** instead of **ENTER**. This will enter the information in the cell and then move your cursor over to the next available cell in one step.

Cell	*Label*
C3	**Tuesday**
D3	**Last Year**

Entering Months as Text

Works applies a special format to any text that is the name of a month. This format (the Time/Date format) shortens the name to a three letter abbreviation and will *right justify* it (displays it in the right end of the cell). Works also assigns a numerical value to each date. You will not see numbers on the screen when you enter the name of a month in a cell, but if you include that cell in a mathematical computation the numerical value will be used.

1. Enter the name of a month as the label in cell *E3*. Type: **January** and press **ENTER**. (Figure 3.2).

January has been shortened to the first three letters *Jan*. In addition, the abbreviation *Jan* is right justified in the cell and it is **not** preceded by a quotation mark in the Formula Bar.

If you want the entire name of a month to appear in a cell, you have to tell Works to treat it as conventional text and not as a special Time/Date value. Works uses a quotation mark to precede all text, so if you type a quote before you type the name of a month, the program will display exactly the characters you enter. Let's try this now.

2. Move the cursor to cell *E4*.
3. Type: **"January** and press **ENTER**.
4. Enter the labels **"February** in cell *F3* and **"March** in cell *G3*.

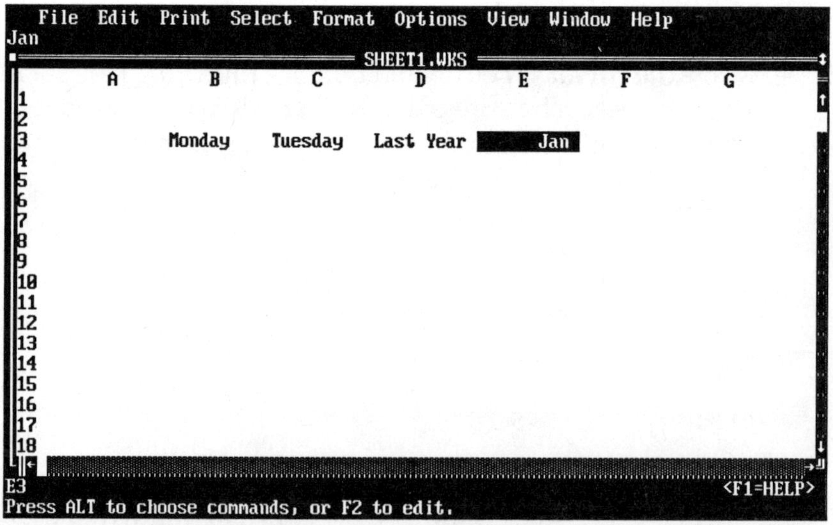

Figure 3.2. Entering months in the spreadsheet

Entering Numbers

When entering numbers, do not enter what is known as the *format* characters such as commas. For example, when entering the value 1,000, you will type 1000. If you enter a number with a comma, the number will be displayed without the comma. Then, after all the values have been entered, you can tell Works to *format* them with commas, dollar signs, or percentage signs. Numbers are also right justified. You will learn how to format cells later in this chapter, but for now, let's just enter some numbers and formulas and see how the unformatted values appear.

1. In cell *B6* type: **200**
2. In cell *C6* type: **287.89**
3. In cell *D6* type: **1,234.56**

The **,** does **not** appear on the screen.

Entering Formulas

Formulas can contain several components. The first component for any formula is an equal sign (=) which tells Works to treat the data in the cell as a formula. The formula may contain numbers and/or cell addresses and a mathematical operator such as a plus or minus sign.

1. In cell *E6* type: **=C6+D6**

This formula permits us to **add** the values in two cells.

2. In cell *F6* type: **=E6*2**

This formula permits us to **multiply** the value in cell E6 times 2.

3. In cell *B8* type: **=B6/3**

This formula permits us to **divide** the value in cell *B6* by 3, and carries the new value to six decimal places.

Entering Numbers as Text

There may be times that you want to enter a numeric date such as 1989 as a label. If you do not enter a number as a label, it will be right justified and therefore look different than your other labels. Let's see how the number differs when it is treated as text.

1. In cell *C8* type: **1989**

This entry will be right justified.

2. In cell *D8* type: **"1989** and press **ENTER**.

This entry is left justified.

If you have entered all of the values and labels correctly, your spreadsheet should resemble Figure 3.3.

Closing the Spreadsheet

Now that you have seen the ins and outs of entering labels and values, you are ready to create your first spreadsheet. If you wish to continue with the following activity now, you will want to start on a new spreadsheet.

1. To leave the current spreadsheet, select **File/Close.** Works will ask you if you want to *Save changes to: SHEET1.WKS?*

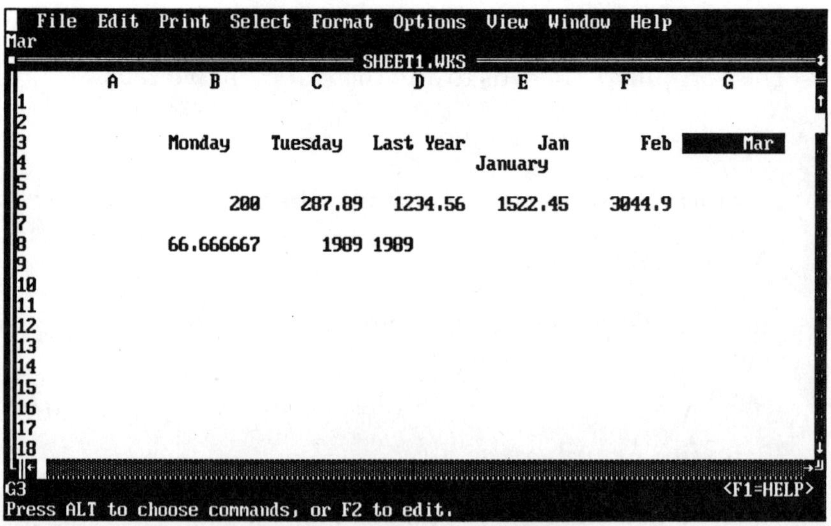

Figure 3.3. Finished spreadsheet

2. Since you were just practicing, you can select **<NO>**.

Be aware that throughout our spreadsheet we will be referring to **SHEET1.WKS** and your spreadsheet will be **SHEET2.WKS**.

Correcting Errors

There are several ways to correct errors you make while entering information. They are:

- Use the **BACKSPACE** key to erase what you are typing **before** you have entered it into a cell by pressing an **ARROW** key or **ENTER**.
- Move your cursor to the cell in which you have made the mistake. Type the correct text and then press **ENTER**. The information you just typed will replace the incorrect information.
- Move your cursor to the cell in which you have made the mistake and press **F2** to access Works' EDIT mode. When you do this, the word *EDIT* will appear on the Status Line.

When this happens, the cell contents are available to you on the Formula Bar as if you had just typed them. You may use your **BACKSPACE** key to erase incorrect characters or you may use your **ARROW** keys to move your cursor to the location in which you would like to change information. Then delete and insert the necessary characters.

Creating a Spreadsheet for Budgeting Expenses

Let's try setting up the first spreadsheet. In this exercise, you will set up a simple budget which could be used to keep track of monthly business expenses. While completing this spreadsheet, you will create, format, save, and print a simple spreadsheet. In the process you'll learn how to correct errors and learn your first shortcut—a method of copying information from one cell to another. The completed budget spreadsheet is shown in Figure 3.4.

The first task in setting up any spreadsheet is to set up the labels which will identify the values to be entered. Use the techniques for entering labels introduced previously. While entering the data you'll also consider strate-

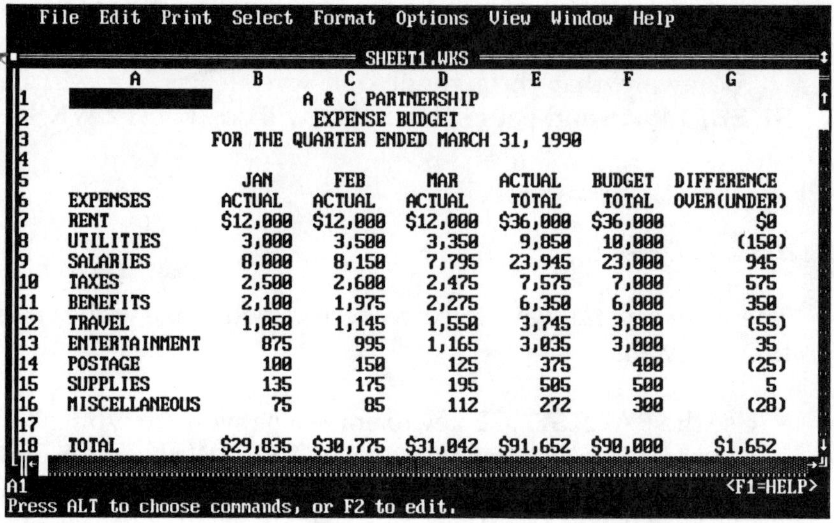

File Edit Print Select Format Options View Window Help

SHEET1.WKS

	A	B	C	D	E	F	G
1			A & C PARTNERSHIP				
2			EXPENSE BUDGET				
3		FOR THE QUARTER ENDED MARCH 31, 1990					
4							
5		JAN	FEB	MAR	ACTUAL	BUDGET	DIFFERENCE
6	EXPENSES	ACTUAL	ACTUAL	ACTUAL	TOTAL	TOTAL	OVER(UNDER)
7	RENT	$12,000	$12,000	$12,000	$36,000	$36,000	$0
8	UTILITIES	3,000	3,500	3,350	9,850	10,000	(150)
9	SALARIES	8,000	8,150	7,795	23,945	23,000	945
10	TAXES	2,500	2,600	2,475	7,575	7,000	575
11	BENEFITS	2,100	1,975	2,275	6,350	6,000	350
12	TRAVEL	1,050	1,145	1,550	3,745	3,800	(55)
13	ENTERTAINMENT	875	995	1,165	3,035	3,000	35
14	POSTAGE	100	150	125	375	400	(25)
15	SUPPLIES	135	175	195	505	500	5
16	MISCELLANEOUS	75	85	112	272	300	(28)
17							
18	TOTAL	$29,835	$30,775	$31,042	$91,652	$90,000	$1,652

A1 <F1=HELP>

Press ALT to choose commands, or F2 to edit.

Figure 3.4. Completed budget spreadsheet

gies for good spreadsheet design. Table 3.2 reviews and summarizes entering data.

The first task is to enter a two-line title to the spreadsheet. All spreadsheets have a *default column width*. In Works, the default column width is 10. If a label is longer than the column width allows and the adjacent cell is blank, the excess will overflow into the adjacent columns. This is called *cell overflow* and is often used when entering spreadsheet titles. If the adjacent cell is not empty, you must increase the width of the column in order to display a label of more than 10 characters. We discuss how to increase column widths later.

1. Move the cursor to cell *C1*; type: **A & C Partnership**
2. Press the **DOWN ARROW** to move to cell *C2*.
3. Type: **EXPENSE BUDGET** and press **ENTER**.

Table 3.2. Entering Data

1.	Move the cursor to the cell that should contain the information.
2.	Type the information. It will appear in the Formula Bar.
3.	Press an **ARROW KEY** to enter the information into the cell and position the cursor for the next label or value to be entered. When entering the last piece of data, you may simply press **ENTER** and the cursor will remain in the current cell.

4. Press the **DOWN ARROW** and **LEFT ARROW** keys to move to *B3*.
5. Type: **For the Quarter Ended March 31, 1990**

You've already learned how to enter labels and values. The Self-Check exercise that follows contains the information you need to enter the column and row labels and the values for your budget spreadsheet. Since your goal is to create a workable spreadsheet, you will also see some good design practices. For example, since our column labels are much longer than the data to be contained in the column, you'll be instructed to put the first part of a label in one cell and the second part in the cell directly below it.

1. First, follow the instructions below to enter the row and column labels. When completed, your spreadsheet should resemble Figure 3.5.
   a. In cell *A6*, enter **Expenses**.
   b. Enter **Actual** in cell *B6* and **"Jan** in cell *B5*.
   c. In cell *C6* type: **Actual** and in *C5* type: **"Feb**
   d. In cell *D6* type: **Actual** and in cell *D5* type: **"Mar**
   e. In cell *E6* type: **Total** and in cell *E5* type: **Actual**
   f. In cell *F6* type: **Total** and in cell *F5* type: **Budget**

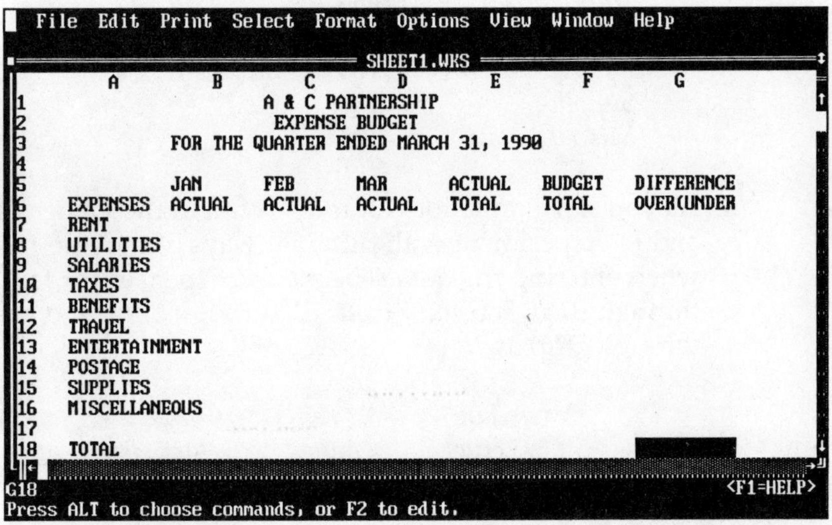

Figure 3.5. Spreadsheet with labels

g. Type: **Over(Under)** in cell *G6* and **Difference** in cell *G5*.
h. Move your cursor to cell *A7*, and in cells *A7 through A16*, type the names of the different expense categories listed below.

Rent
Utilities
Salaries
Taxes
Benefits
Travel
Entertainment
Postage
Supplies
Miscellaneous

i. Then move to cell *A18* and type: **Total**

2. Enter the values as indicated below:

a. The **January Actual** expenses in cells *B7* through *B16* are:

Rent	**12000**
Utilities	**3000**
Salaries	**8000**
Taxes	**2500**
Benefits	**2100**
Travel	**1050**
Entertainment	**875**
Postage	**100**
Supplies	**135**
Miscellaneous	**75**

b. As you have done for column B, type in the values for columns C and D. Experiment with different ways of moving from cell-to-cell when entering the data. The **Actual** expenses for January (cells *B7* through *B16*), February (cells *C7* through *C16*), and March (cells *D7* through *D16*) are:

	Jan Actual	*Feb Actual*	*Mar Actual*
Rent	**12000**	**12000**	**12000**
Utilities	**3000**	**3500**	**3350**

Salaries	8000	8150	7795
Taxes	2500	2600	2475
Benefits	2100	1975	2275
Travel	1050	1145	1550
Entertainment	875	995	1165
Postage	100	150	125
Supplies	135	175	195
Miscellaneous	75	85	112

c. As you have done for columns B, C, and D, type in the values for column F which are the Budgeted numbers.

	Budget Total
Rent	36000
Utilities	10000
Salaries	23000
Taxes	7000
Benefits	6000
Travel	3800
Entertainment	3000
Postage	400
Supplies	500
Miscellaneous	300

If you have entered the data correctly, your spreadsheet should resemble Figure 3.6. Check your data and correct any errors. If your spreadsheet does not match Figure 3.6, review the steps for entering labels and values in Table 3.2. The hints which follow may also help you understand how your spreadsheet looks.

- *Did you remember to type a quotation mark (") before typing the names of the months? If not, they will be right-justified in the cell and only the first three letters of each month will be entered.*
- *The column labels and values do not line up because they are automatically positioned differently in the cell. We discuss how to correct that later in the chapter.*

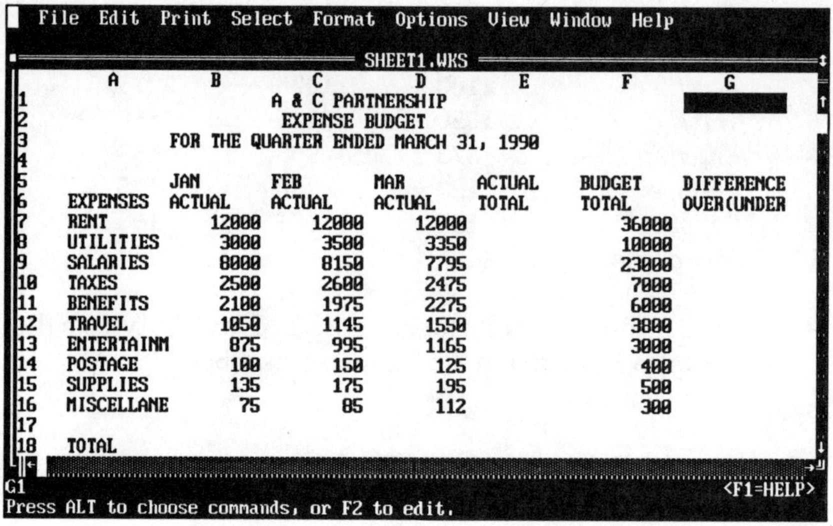

File Edit Print Select Format Options View Window Help

SHEET1.WKS

	A	B	C	D	E	F	G
1			A & C PARTNERSHIP				
2			EXPENSE BUDGET				
3		FOR THE QUARTER ENDED MARCH 31, 1990					
4							
5		JAN	FEB	MAR	ACTUAL	BUDGET	DIFFERENCE
6	EXPENSES	ACTUAL	ACTUAL	ACTUAL	TOTAL	TOTAL	OVER(UNDER
7	RENT	12000	12000	12000		36000	
8	UTILITIES	3000	3500	3350		10000	
9	SALARIES	8000	8150	7795		23000	
10	TAXES	2500	2600	2475		7000	
11	BENEFITS	2100	1975	2275		6000	
12	TRAVEL	1050	1145	1550		3800	
13	ENTERTAINM	875	995	1165		3000	
14	POSTAGE	100	150	125		400	
15	SUPPLIES	135	175	195		500	
16	MISCELLANE	75	85	112		300	
17							
18	TOTAL						

G1 <F1=HELP>

Press ALT to choose commands, or F2 to edit.

Figure 3.6. Budget spreadsheet with labels and values

Changing Column Widths

As you view your results, you will notice a problem. Some labels are wider than the column width. Column width determines the number of characters that fit within a cell. The default setting in Works sets your column width at 10. You can change that to any width between 0 and 79. If you enter text wider than a column's width, the excess text is displayed in the cells to the right, if those cells are empty. If the cell to the right is not empty, Works displays only the text or values that fit in the cell. However, Works displays ###### if a number or a date exceeds its cell width. To make columns wider, you need to place your cursor on the longest label and determine how many additional spaces you will need. Then you need to use the **Format/Column Width** command to change the width of each column.

1. Place your cursor in *A13* highlighting *Entertainment*, our widest label.
2. Select **Format/Column Width.**

The default width is **10**. To fit the widest of these labels in column A, and to leave one extra space between it and column B, increase the width by four.

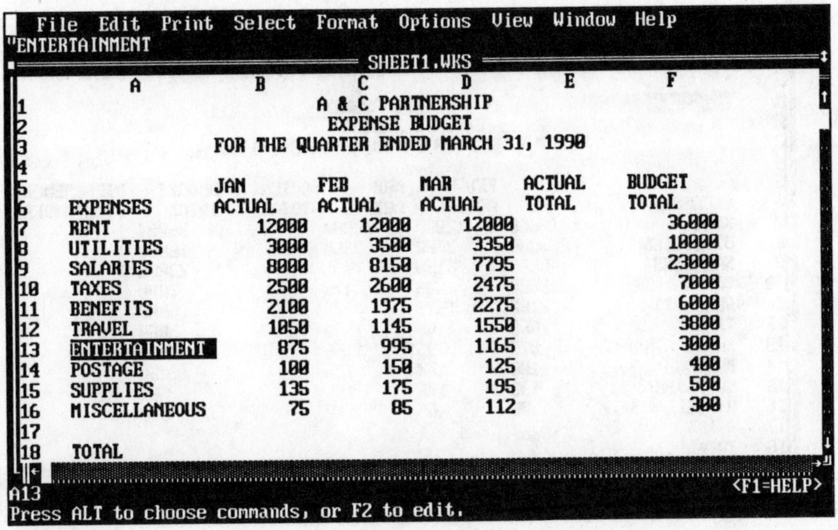

Figure 3.7. Changing column widths

3. Type: **14** and press **ENTER** (Figure 3.7).

We would like to make columns B through F narrower, so that we can see all of them on the screen at one time. To do this, you must move the cursor to each column and select **Format/Column Width**, and then enter the desired width.

1. Move your cursor to cell *B7*.
2. Select **Format/Column Width**.
3. Type: **9** and press **ENTER**.
4. Repeat this process for columns C through F.

Note There is a shortcut available in Works to change the width of adjacent columns to the same value in one step. We'll discuss this later in the chapter.

5. For the G Column, you need to increase the column width so the title fits within the column. Change the column width to 11.
6. Press **HOME**. Now all of the labels should be visible on your screen (Figure 3.8).

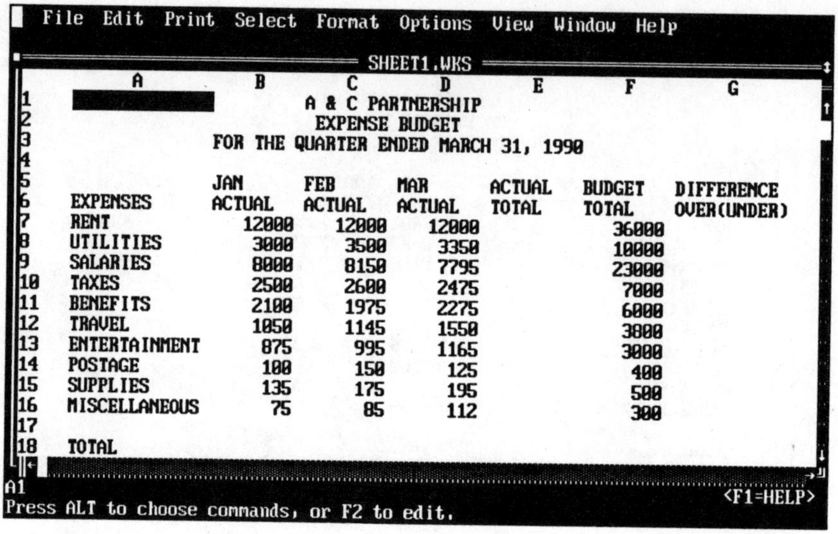

Figure 3.8. Column widths set to proper width

Moving Around a Spreadsheet

Now that you have filled several cells with information, we'll take another look at moving the cursor around the spreadsheet screen. If you try moving the cursor from cell-to-cell and from screen-to-screen with the keys that were discussed earlier in the chapter, you will find that they achieve the same results as they did when the screen was blank. Now, however, you also can use the global movement keys. Try some of these now.

1. Use the **ARROW** keys to move your cursor to cell *F18* if it is not there already.
2. Press **HOME**. As you probably expected, this returns the cursor to column A of the same row (i.e., cell *A18*).
3. Now press **END**. The cursor moves to cell *G18*, although you might have expected it to stop in cell *E18* since E is the last column with an entry in row 14. The **END** key, however, always moves the cursor to the last column that contains an entry in any row.
4. Press **CTRL-HOME**. Even though there is no information in cell *A1*, the program considers it the beginning of the spreadsheet. Where does the cursor go when you press **CTRL-END**?

Just as **END** moves the cursor to the last column that contains an entry in any row, **CTRL-END** moves the cursor to the intersection of the last row that contains any data and the last column that contains any data (i.e., in our current spreadsheet, cell G18).

Entering a Formula

Now that you've entered the raw data, you're ready to perform the calculations that will give you the information you need. When performing calculations on data in a spreadsheet, you always want to refer to the cell containing the data, rather than to the actual value of the data. In this way if the data changes, the calculation will automatically be up-dated. You do this by entering a *formula*. In the sections below you'll look at several ways to enter formulas. Table 3.3 reviews and summarizes the key movements described here.

Typing Cell Addresses into a Formula

One way to enter a formula into a cell is to type all of the required information. For example, to see the **Actual Total** amount for Rent in cell *E7*, take the *value* for one month's rent, which is in cell *B7*, and multiply it by **3**, since the rent remains constant. Here's how to do this:

1. Move the cursor to cell *E7*.
2. In cell *E7*, type: **=B7*3**

The formula appears at the top left of your screen in the Formula Bar. If you see that you have made a mistake, use your **BACKSPACE** key to erase what you have typed and then retype it.

Table 3.3. Key Movements

Key	Movement
HOME	To column A of the current row
END	In the current row, to the right-most column that has data in it on any row
CTRL-HOME	To cell *A1*
CTRL-END	To the intersection of the last filled row and the last filled column in the spreadsheet

3. Press **ENTER**.

If you have done this correctly, the value **36000** automatically appears in cell *E7* (Figure 3.9). You could use this method to enter formulas if the same values were in every column. In our first row, the rent is the same for each month. As this is not the case for all our other expenses, let's look at another method for entering formulas using the actual values in each column.

Using Pointing to Enter a Formula

It is uncommon for your values to be the same in each column. Therefore, it is unlikely you will very often want to use a formula that will simply take a number and multiply it by three. Instead, you will want to take whatever the content of the cell is, and add it to the content of the subsequent cell, and so forth. You are also probably wondering how to get the formula in one cell, and then duplicate the formula for the rest of the column. Since spreadsheets are designed to save you from such repetitive typing, we will show you how to begin to use some of the time-saving features built into Works.

One time-saving feature is known as *pointing*. Rather than typing the

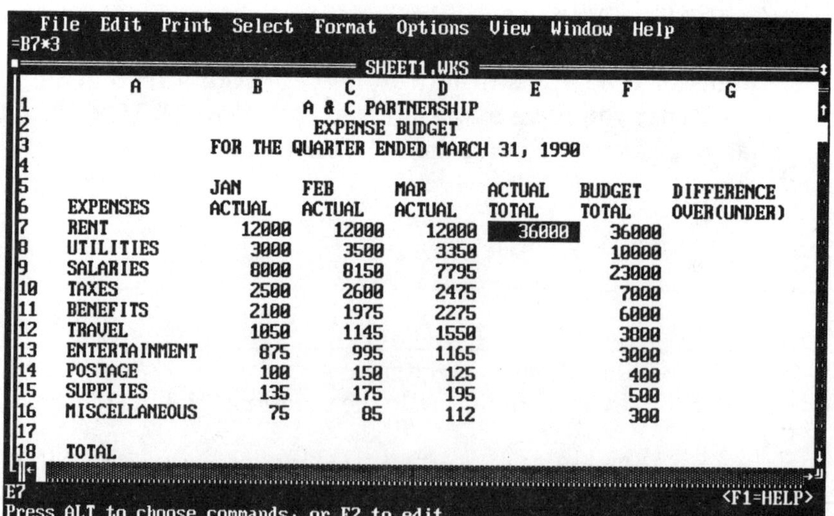

Figure 3.9. Entering a formula

formula, you will type part of the formula and use the cursor to *POINT* to the other information that you wish to include. Specifically, you still will type the mathematical symbols (= and +), but each time a cell address should be added to the formula, you will use the cursor to POINT to the cell rather than typing the cell name. Here's how to do this (Figure 3.10):

1. First, to redo the previous formula in *E7*, move the cursor to cell *E7*, the cell where the formula will go.
2. Begin the formula with an equal sign (=) so that Works will know that you are entering a **value,** not a **label.** Type: =
3. Now use the **LEFT ARROW** to move the cursor to cell *B7* (January), the first cell that you want to add in our formula. The word *POINT* has appeared at the bottom of your screen (Figure 3.11).
4. Type a plus sign (+). This tells Works that you are going to add something else to the formula. The cursor automatically moves back to cell *E7* and Works waits for you to continue. Move your cursor to *C7* (February).
5. Type a plus sign (+). This tells Works that you are going to add something else to the formula. The cursor automatically moves back to cell *E7* and Works waits for you to continue. Move your cursor back to *D7* (March).
6. Press **ENTER.** Your total will automatically appear (Figure 3.12).

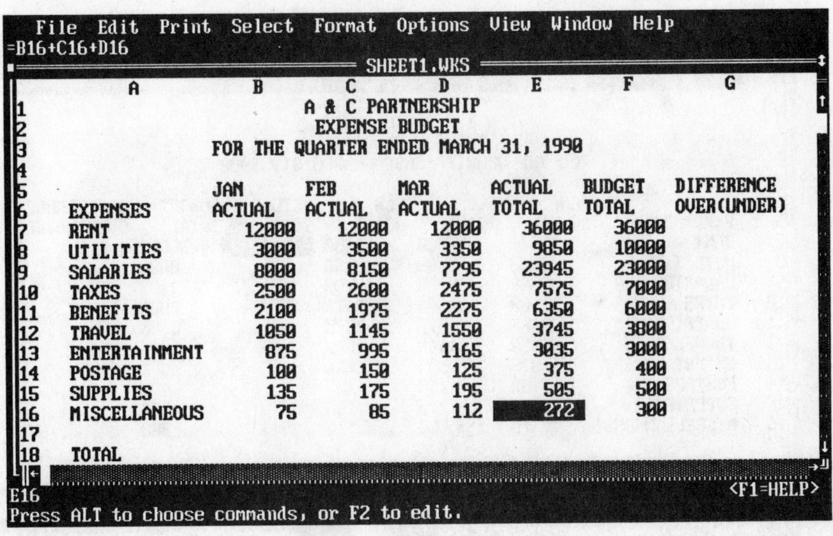

Figure 3.10. More formula

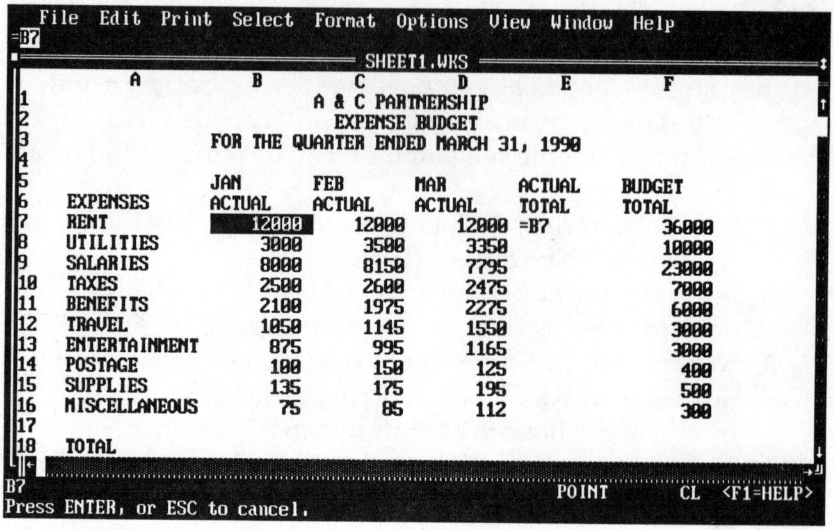

File Edit Print Select Format Options View Window Help
=B7
SHEET1.WKS

	A	B	C	D	E	F
1			A & C PARTNERSHIP			
2			EXPENSE BUDGET			
3		FOR THE QUARTER ENDED MARCH 31, 1990				
4						
5		JAN	FEB	MAR	ACTUAL	BUDGET
6	EXPENSES	ACTUAL	ACTUAL	ACTUAL	TOTAL	TOTAL
7	RENT	12000	12000	12000	=B7	36000
8	UTILITIES	3000	3500	3350		10000
9	SALARIES	8000	8150	7795		23000
10	TAXES	2500	2600	2475		7000
11	BENEFITS	2100	1975	2275		6000
12	TRAVEL	1050	1145	1550		3000
13	ENTERTAINMENT	875	995	1165		3000
14	POSTAGE	100	150	125		400
15	SUPPLIES	135	175	195		500
16	MISCELLANEOUS	75	85	112		300
17						
18	TOTAL					

B7 POINT CL <F1=HELP>
Press ENTER, or ESC to cancel.

Figure 3.11. Using pointing

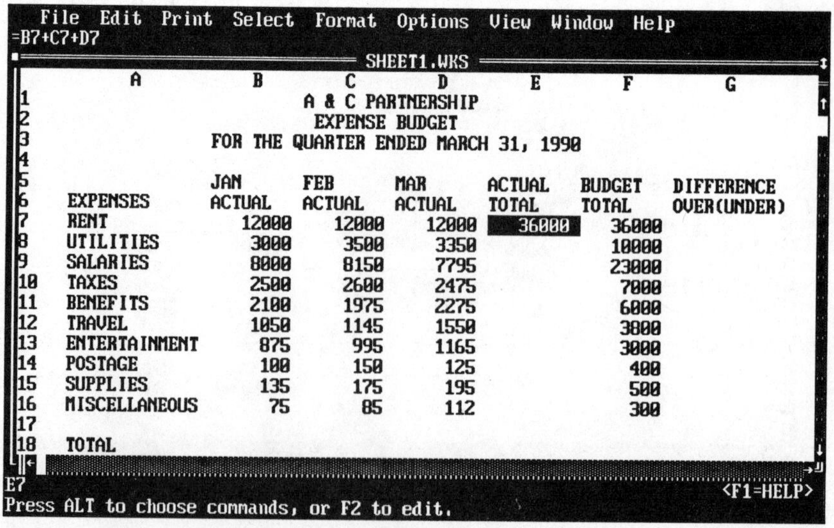

File Edit Print Select Format Options View Window Help
=B7+C7+D7
SHEET1.WKS

	A	B	C	D	E	F	G
1			A & C PARTNERSHIP				
2			EXPENSE BUDGET				
3		FOR THE QUARTER ENDED MARCH 31, 1990					
4							
5		JAN	FEB	MAR	ACTUAL	BUDGET	DIFFERENCE
6	EXPENSES	ACTUAL	ACTUAL	ACTUAL	TOTAL	TOTAL	OVER(UNDER)
7	RENT	12000	12000	12000	36000	36000	
8	UTILITIES	3000	3500	3350		10000	
9	SALARIES	8000	8150	7795		23000	
10	TAXES	2500	2600	2475		7000	
11	BENEFITS	2100	1975	2275		6000	
12	TRAVEL	1050	1145	1550		3800	
13	ENTERTAINMENT	875	995	1165		3000	
14	POSTAGE	100	150	125		400	
15	SUPPLIES	135	175	195		500	
16	MISCELLANEOUS	75	85	112		300	
17							
18	TOTAL						

E7 <F1=HELP>
Press ALT to choose commands, or F2 to edit.

Figure 3.12. Completed formulas

The formula for cells *E8 through E16* and *E18* is exactly the same as the one in cell *E7*, except that the rows are different. Use pointing to enter a formula into each of these cells.

The formula in cell E8 *should be* =B8+C8+D8. *Following rows should have the same formula, with the new row number substituted for the 8. If you did not get these formulas, be sure that you:*

1. *Move the cursor to the cell that will contain the formula and type an equal sign (=)* ***before*** *pointing to the first cell to be included.*
2. *When the pointer is on a cell to be included in the formula, type the plus sign if another cell address is to be added to the formula or* **ENTER** *if the formula is complete. You must press a mathematical operator or* **ENTER** *before moving the cursor to the next cell.*
3. *If the notation* CIRC *appears on the bottom of the screen, you have probably included the cell containing the formula in the formula. To correct this, re-enter the formula.*

The ability to point the cursor provides you with three benefits:

- Speed
- Accuracy
- The ability to see exactly what cells are being used in the formula(s) you are creating

Copying Cells

Sometimes you have information in one part of the spreadsheet that could be used in other cells. For example, the first formula at the top of column E is really the same formula that was used all the way down that column. The only difference is that the formula has been **adjusted** to reflect the actual **row** that it is in. (The formula in cell *E7* is =*B7*+*C7*+*D7*. The formula in cell *E8* is =*B8*+*C8*+*D8*. The formula in cell *E9* is =*B9*+*C9*+*D9*.)

This is also true for the formulas in column G. So even though pointing at cells is a vast improvement over typing and retyping the information, proceed one step further to make the entering of formulas even easier.

In this operation, you will create one formula to total the columns (in cell

B18) and then you will **COPY** this formula across to the other columns on the spreadsheet. Let's try!

1. Use pointing to enter the following formula in cell *B18*:

   =B7+B8+B9+B10+B11+B12+B13+B14+B15+B16

2. Select **Edit/Copy**.

The Message Line says *Select new location and press* **ENTER**. *Press* **ESC** *to cancel.*

3. Since you want the exact same formula in cell *C18*, move the cursor to cell *C18*. Press **ENTER**.

The formula has been correctly copied over to column C and the cell references have been *relatively adjusted* by Works. Relative adjustment is discussed in detail in Chapter 6.

4. Select **Edit/Copy** again.
5. Move the cursor to cell *D18* and press **ENTER**.

---

1. Copy the formula from *C18* to *E18* and *F18*.
2. Place a formula in cell *G7* to calculate the difference between the Actual Expenses and the Budgeted Expenses.
3. Copy the formula from *G7* through to *G16*.
4. Calculate the total in *G18*.

Compare your spreadsheet with Figure 3.13.

Enhancing the Spreadsheet

Earlier, you observed that the labels in this spreadsheet are all left justified. It would be nicer to line them up above the values in their respective columns. Also, since you are dealing with currency, you might wish to have some dollar signs on the budget. Changes to both the appearance and the

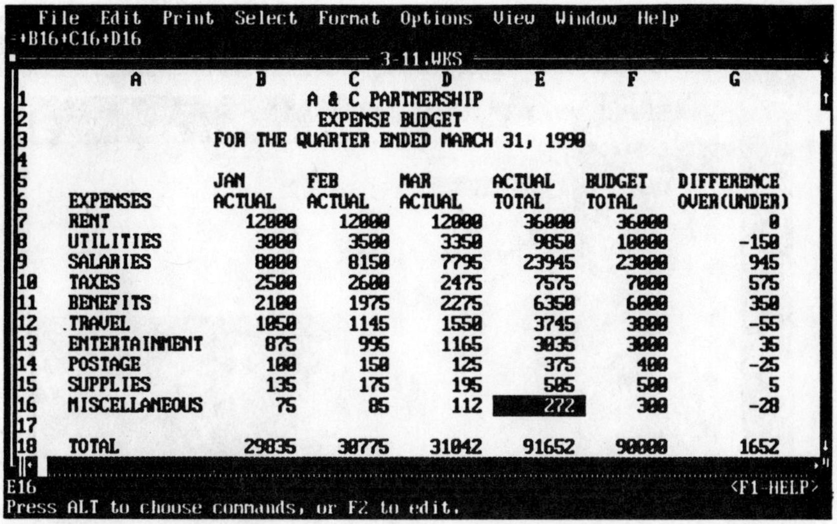

Figure 3.13. Copied formulas

alignment of the labels and values in a cell are made using the **Format** command. Here's how to do this.

Formatting Labels

First, you need to identify the specific cells to be formatted. Next, you must decide which format you would like to have. This process will introduce us to new vocabulary, the word **range**. In a spreadsheet, a range is one cell or a rectangular block of cells (Figure 3.14).

In addition to being able to format one cell at a time, you can format a range of cells, by selecting the range first, and then specifying how to format it. This is similar to selecting a block when using the word processor. In fact, to select a range, use Function Key **F8**, just as you selected a block of text in the word processor.

1. Move the cursor to cell *B5* and press **F8**.

The word *EXT* appears on the Message Line. **EXTEND** means that Works is waiting for you to define the range with which you are going to work.

2. Use your **ARROW** keys to **EXTEND** the highlight across to column G and then down to row 6. The far left corner of the Status Line says that the range has been defined as **B5:G6** (Figure 3.15).

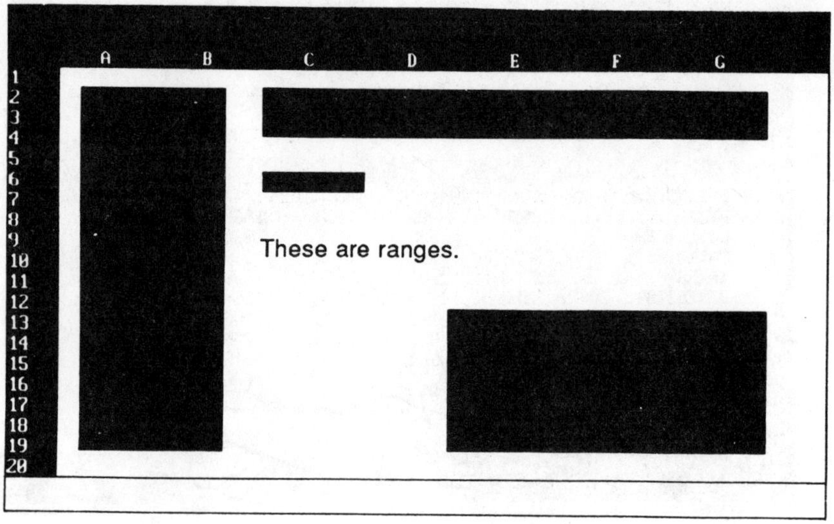

Figure 3.14. Range of cells

Note Remember, if you start to **EXTEND** the highlight and then change your mind, you can press **ESC** to quit the EXTEND mode.

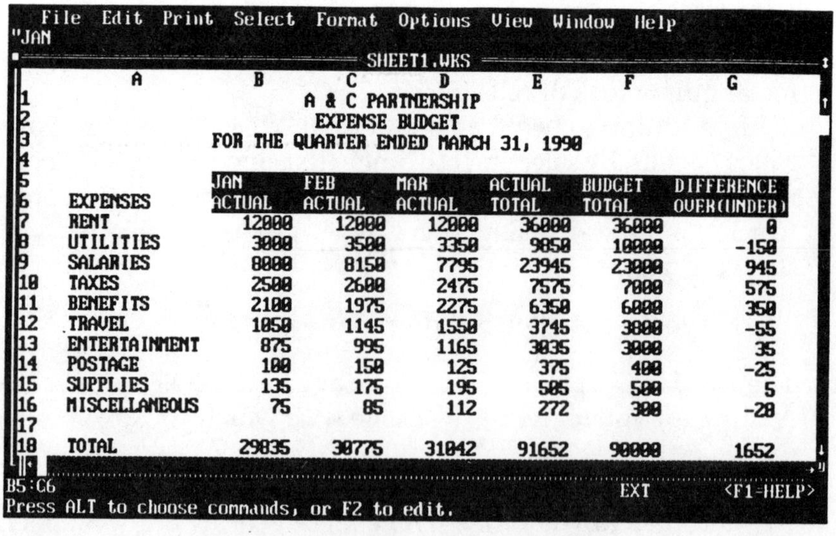

File Edit Print Select Format Options View Window Help
"JAN

SHEET1.WKS

	A	B	C	D	E	F	G
1			A & C PARTNERSHIP				
2			EXPENSE BUDGET				
3		FOR THE QUARTER ENDED MARCH 31, 1990					
4							
5		JAN	FEB	MAR	ACTUAL	BUDGET	DIFFERENCE
6	EXPENSES	ACTUAL	ACTUAL	ACTUAL	TOTAL	TOTAL	OVER(UNDER)
7	RENT	12000	12000	12000	36000	36000	0
8	UTILITIES	3000	3500	3350	9850	10000	-150
9	SALARIES	8000	8150	7795	23945	23000	945
10	TAXES	2500	2600	2475	7575	7000	575
11	BENEFITS	2100	1975	2275	6350	6000	350
12	TRAVEL	1050	1145	1550	3745	3800	-55
13	ENTERTAINMENT	875	995	1165	3035	3000	35
14	POSTAGE	100	150	125	375	400	-25
15	SUPPLIES	135	175	195	505	500	5
16	MISCELLANEOUS	75	85	112	272	300	-28
17							
18	TOTAL	29835	30775	31042	91652	90000	1652

B5:G6 EXT <F1=HELP>
Press ALT to choose commands, or F2 to edit.

Figure 3.15. Extending ranges

3. Select **Format/Style** (Figure 3.16).
4. Select **Right** in the **Alignment** Option Box and press **ENTER**. The labels should all be right justified.

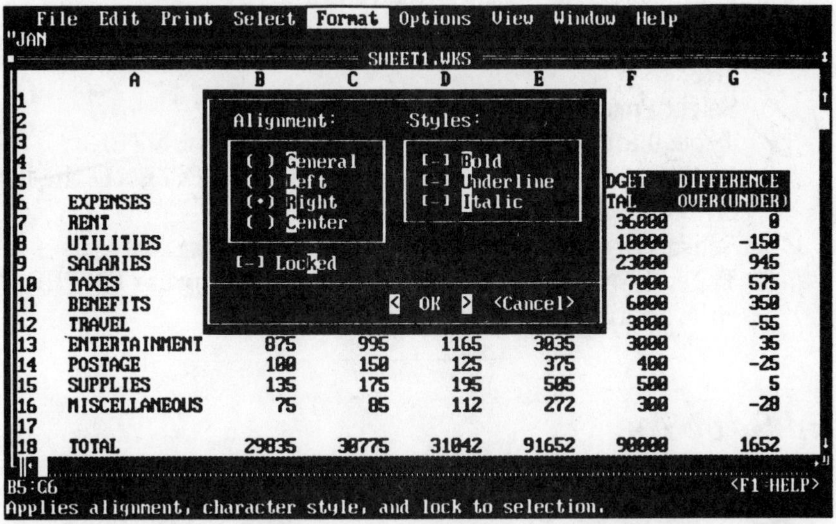

Figure 3.16. Changing the alignment of labels

Formatting Values

Values also may be formatted to change their alignment in the cells, but typically values in a spreadsheet remain right justified. With values you use the **Format** command to change their appearance. The procedure to do this is almost the same as the one to change the label justifications. First you indicate the range that you are interested in changing, and then you tell Works how you would like to format that range. In most instances, financial information is formatted either in currency notation, or in comma notation. These are identical except that currency places a dollar sign ($) in front of the value, and comma does not. In this example, let's format all of the values in rows 7 and 18 with dollar signs. Then let's format all the values in rows 8 through 16 in comma notation. Here's how to do it:

1. Move the cursor to cell *B7*.
2. Press **F8** and **EXTEND** the highlight for all of the values in row 7. Notice the left side of the Message line reads *B7:G7*.
3. Select **Format/Currency**.

A Dialog Box permits you to choose how many decimals you would like to include after each value.

4. Type the number **0** and press **ENTER**. Now all the values in row 7 have a dollar sign preceding them.
5. Move the cursor to cell *B18*. Press **F8** and **EXTEND** the highlight to cell *G18*.
6. Select **Format/Currency**.
7. Type: **0** for Number of Decimals and press **ENTER**.
8. Move the cursor to cell *B8*. Press **F8** and **EXTEND** the highlight to cell *G16*.
9. Select **Format/Comma.**
10. Type: **0** for the Number of Decimals and press **ENTER.** Now your results should resemble Figure 3.17.

Save and Save As...

As we have discussed, it is important to save your work fairly frequently. The usual advice is to save your work every 15 minutes, so that if you should make a serious mistake, or if the power should fail, you will not lose all your work. Let's save our spreadsheet.

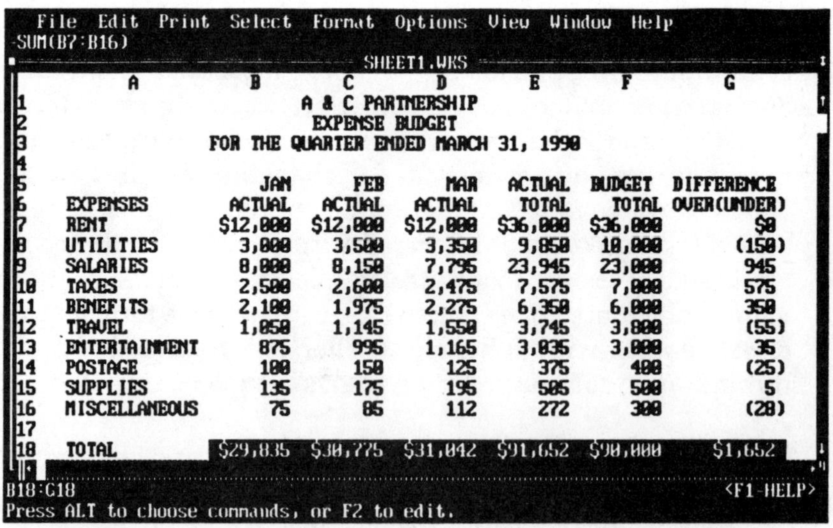
File Edit Print Select Format Options View Window Help
-SUM(B7:B16)
SHEET1.WKS

	A	B	C	D	E	F	G
1			A & C PARTNERSHIP				
2			EXPENSE BUDGET				
3		FOR THE QUARTER ENDED MARCH 31, 1990					
4							
5		JAN	FEB	MAR	ACTUAL	BUDGET	DIFFERENCE
6	EXPENSES	ACTUAL	ACTUAL	ACTUAL	TOTAL	TOTAL	OVER(UNDER)
7	RENT	$12,000	$12,000	$12,000	$36,000	$36,000	$0
8	UTILITIES	3,000	3,500	3,350	9,850	10,000	(150)
9	SALARIES	8,000	8,150	7,795	23,945	23,000	945
10	TAXES	2,500	2,600	2,475	7,575	7,000	575
11	BENEFITS	2,100	1,975	2,275	6,350	6,000	350
12	TRAVEL	1,050	1,145	1,550	3,745	3,800	(55)
13	ENTERTAINMENT	875	995	1,165	3,035	3,000	35
14	POSTAGE	100	150	125	375	400	(25)
15	SUPPLIES	135	175	195	505	500	5
16	MISCELLANEOUS	75	85	112	272	300	(28)
17							
18	TOTAL	$29,835	$30,775	$31,042	$91,652	$90,000	$1,652

B18:C18 <F1-HELP>
Press ALT to choose commands, or F2 to edit.

Figure 3.17. Formatted values and labels

1. Select **File/Save.**

A Dialog Box appears because this is the first time you are saving this spreadsheet, and Works assumes that you want to give it a more meaningful name than **SHEET1.WKS** (Figure 3.18).

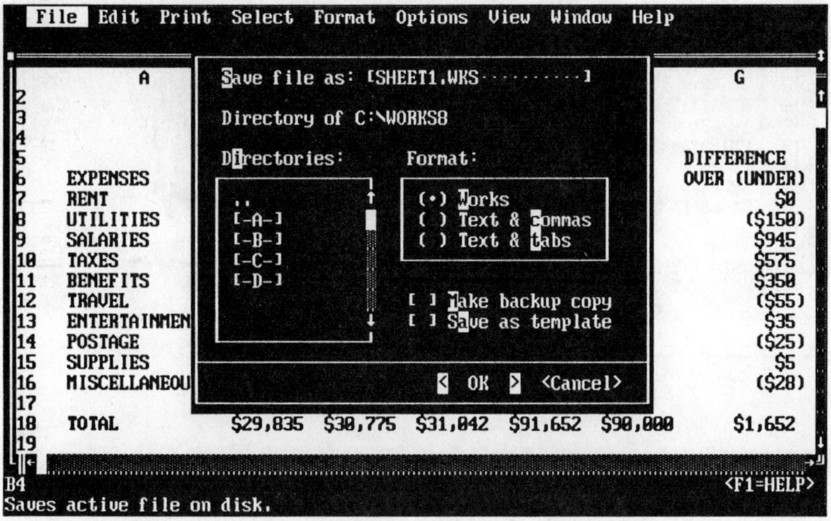

Figure 3.18. Save Menu

2. If the *Directory Of* (the second line of the Save Menu) is not the drive containing your exercise disk, there are two ways to save the file on the correct drive. The first method is the one you used in Chapters 1 and 2. You selected the appropriate drive from the Directories List Box and then typed the new filename in the File Name Text Box. You may also use the following procedure.

If you are saving your data in Drive A, type: **A:BUDGET1** If you are saving your data in Drive B, type: **B:BUDGET1** (Figure 3.19).

Note This procedure does not permanently change the current default drive.

Note Type the drive name and filename, but do not type the file extension. The spreadsheet extension (**.WKS**) will be added automatically by Works.

3. Press **ENTER.**

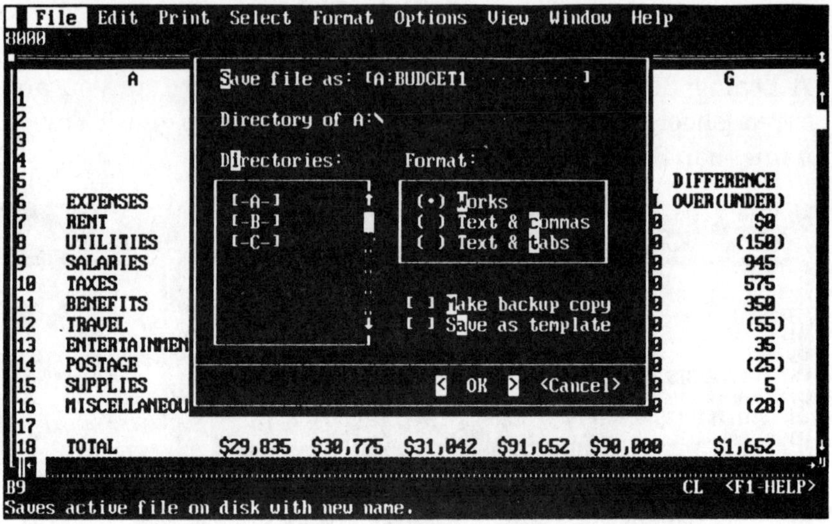

Figure 3.19. Changing the Save filename

Note Hereafter, each time you save your file using **File/Save,** it automatically will be saved as **BUDGET1.WKS** on the drive that you chose.

Should you wish to change the name of your file again (or the drive on which it will be saved), you will have to Select **File/Save As** to do so.

Printing the Spreadsheet

There are many options available to you within the Print Menu. For the moment, however, we will ignore most of them and just print out our newly created spreadsheet **BUDGET1.WKS.** Here is how to do that:

1. First, you have to tell Works the range of cells to print.
   a. Move the cursor to cell *A1*.
   b. Press **F8** and **EXTEND** the highlight to cover cells *A1* through *G18*.
2. Select **Print/Set Print Area.**

This sends a signal to Works telling it to print the range of cells that you have highlighted. If you do not set a print area, the entire spreadsheet will print.

3. Select **Print/Print.**

This will cause a Dialog Box to appear on your screen. We will use the default selections provided by Works (Figure 3.20).

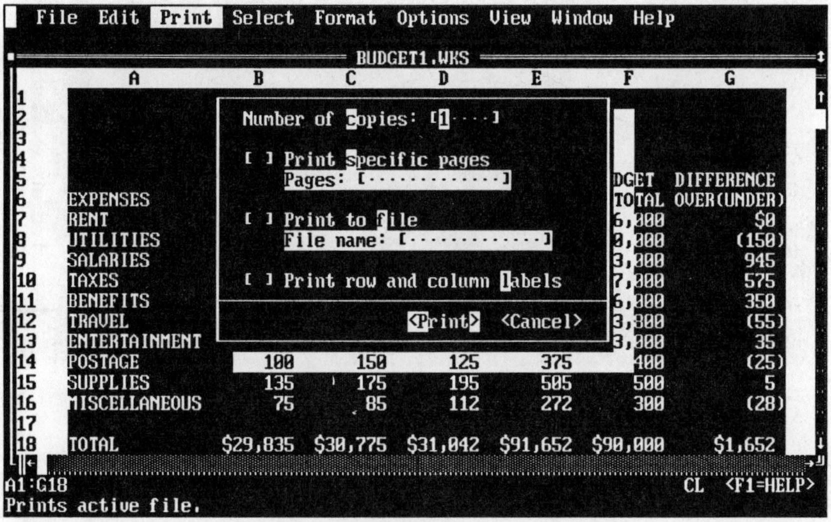

Figure 3.20. Default print settings

4. Be sure that your printer is turned on and it is on-line, and that the paper is aligned properly.
5. Press **ENTER** and your printer will produce your output.

There is one problem when you print this spreadsheet. It is too wide to fit on a standard piece of paper. Therefore,Works automatically divides it into chunks and prints it out on two pages. You probably aren't happy with the way this looks, however. One way to get around this problem is to change the margins for printing. Follow these steps to print your entire spreadsheet on one piece of paper.

Note Notice on your screen that the range of cells to be printed is still highlighted. Also, Works will remember the last print area set. This means that you do not have to go back to **Print/Set Print Area**.

1. Select **Print/Page Setup and Margins**.

This will cause a Dialog Box to appear on your screen (Figure 3.21).

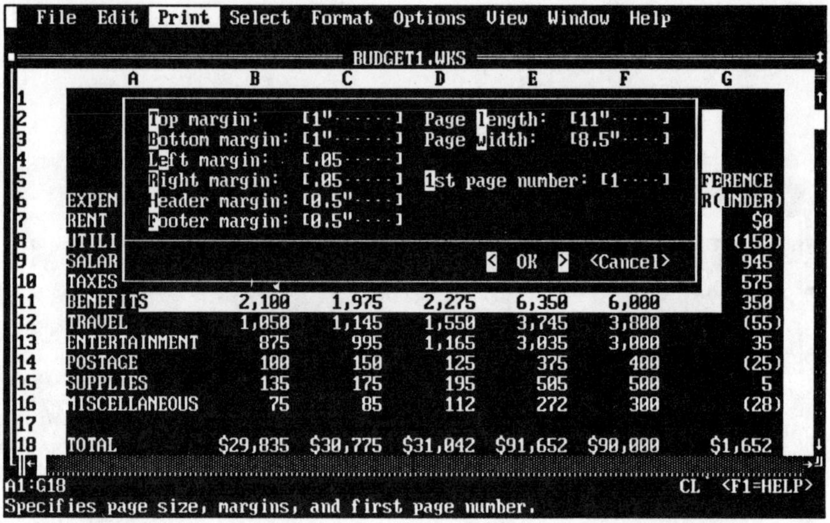

Figure 3.21. Changing the left and right print margins

2. **TAB** down to the **Left Margin** Text Box or press **ALT-E** to move to the **Left Margin** Text Box.
3. Type: **0.5"**
4. Now change the **Right Margin** Text Box to **0.5"**
5. Press **ENTER**.
6. Select **Print/Print** and then press **ENTER**.

You have now successfully completed your first spreadsheet. You have entered data, formatted it, printed, and saved the spreadsheet. Next, we discuss some shortcuts to save time when creating spreadsheets.

The Extend Key

In this chapter, we introduced you to the term **range**. In a spreadsheet, a range is a cell or a rectangular block of cells. To select a range, the Function Key **F8** was used to refer to a range of cells. When using the **F8 key**, the word **EXTEND** appears on the screen, and the arrow keys allowed us to point to a group of cells. This was used when referring to labels and values to be formatted. The **F8** key can also be used when erasing cells, changing column widths, or when we need to perform repetitive steps on a range of cells. Let's examine how to use the **F8 key** on the completed spreadsheet.

Let's first erase some formulas. Then look at how to place a formula in one location and then duplicate it to a range of cells.

1. Place the cursor in cell *E7* and press **F8.** The word *EXT* appears on the Message Line. Works is waiting for us to define the range.
2. Use your **ARROW** keys to **EXTEND** the highlight down the column to cell *E18*. Notice the far left corner of the Status Line says that the range has been defined as *E7:E18* (Figure 3.22).
3. Select **Edit/Clear.** The range has been erased.

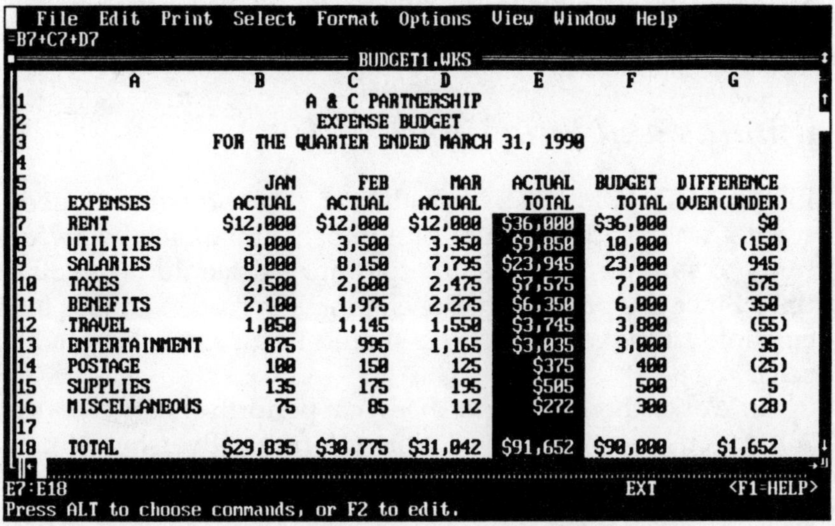

File Edit Print Select Format Options View Window Help
=B7+C7+D7
BUDGET1.WKS

	A	B	C	D	E	F	G
1			A & C PARTNERSHIP				
2			EXPENSE BUDGET				
3		FOR THE QUARTER ENDED MARCH 31, 1990					
4							
5		JAN	FEB	MAR	ACTUAL	BUDGET	DIFFERENCE
6	EXPENSES	ACTUAL	ACTUAL	ACTUAL	TOTAL	TOTAL	OVER(UNDER)
7	RENT	$12,000	$12,000	$12,000	$36,000	$36,000	$0
8	UTILITIES	3,000	3,500	3,350	$9,850	10,000	(150)
9	SALARIES	8,000	8,150	7,795	$23,945	23,000	945
10	TAXES	2,500	2,600	2,475	$7,575	7,000	575
11	BENEFITS	2,100	1,975	2,275	$6,350	6,000	350
12	TRAVEL	1,050	1,145	1,550	$3,745	3,800	(55)
13	ENTERTAINMENT	875	995	1,165	$3,035	3,000	35
14	POSTAGE	100	150	125	$375	400	(25)
15	SUPPLIES	135	175	195	$505	500	5
16	MISCELLANEOUS	75	85	112	$272	300	(28)
17							
18	TOTAL	$29,835	$30,775	$31,042	$91,652	$90,000	$1,652

E7:E18 EXT <F1=HELP>
Press ALT to choose commands, or F2 to edit.

Figure 3.22. Extending ranges to erase

The **EXTEND** key permitted us to erase a range of cells in one step rather than repeating the operation many times. When you copied a formula, you ran across a similar problem. You had to enter the formula once, and then had to use **Edit/Copy** to copy the formula to each cell. Next, examine how to enter the formula once and duplicate it to a range of cells.

1. With the cursor in *E7*, enter a formula to add up cells *B7*, *C7*, and *D7*. Hint: Remember, formulas must start with an = sign and need a mathematical operand such as +, -, *, or / between cell entries.
2. Leaving your cursor in *E7*, press **F8** and extend the range to *E16*.
3. Select **Edit/Fill Down,** and the formula in *E7* will duplicate and adjust

relatively from *E7* through *E16*. Notice that if you would have extended the range through to *E18, E17* would have a formula in it. Since you want *E17* to be blank, you will have to copy the formula to *E18* as a separate step.

As you were copying the formula, you probably noticed that you can copy something to the right as well as down. The Edit Menu permits you to choose **Fill Right** or **Fill Down.** With either, you must **EXTEND** the range first by using the **F8** key. Also, when you copy the contents of a cell or range to another part of the spreadsheet, Works copies the cell styles and alignments and adjusts relative references.

Using Formulas and Functions

In the **BUDGET1.WKS** spreadsheet, you probably noticed how awkward it was to add columns of numbers. Imagine how awful it would be to try to sum up 100 cells in a column. This could take you quite a bit of time. Since the purpose of developing a spreadsheet was to simplify calculations, it makes sense there should be an easier way to add groups of cells.

In Works, there are 57 *functions* that perform common spreadsheet tasks. A function is a built-in calculation or formula. By using a function, you can avoid having to type in mathematical operators (+, -, *, /). To use a function, you type its name, and then tell it what values to act upon. For example, to add up a column of values, you will use the **SUM** function. Again, to make sure Works knows you are entering a formula and not a label, all functions are preceded by an equal sign (=).

Let's erase the totals in row 18 and use the **SUM** function to total the columns.

1. Place the cursor in *B18*, and press the **F8** key.
2. Use the **ARROW** key to **EXTEND** the range through *G18*.
3. Choose **Edit/Clear** to erase all the old totals.
4. In *B18*, type the formula

=SUM(B7:B16)

This formula tells Works to add the range of information from cell *B7* through *B16*.

5. Press **F8** to **EXTEND** the range from *B18* through *G18*, and choose **Edit/Fill Right** to copy the total across all columns.

Your spreadsheet should now resemble Figure 3.23.

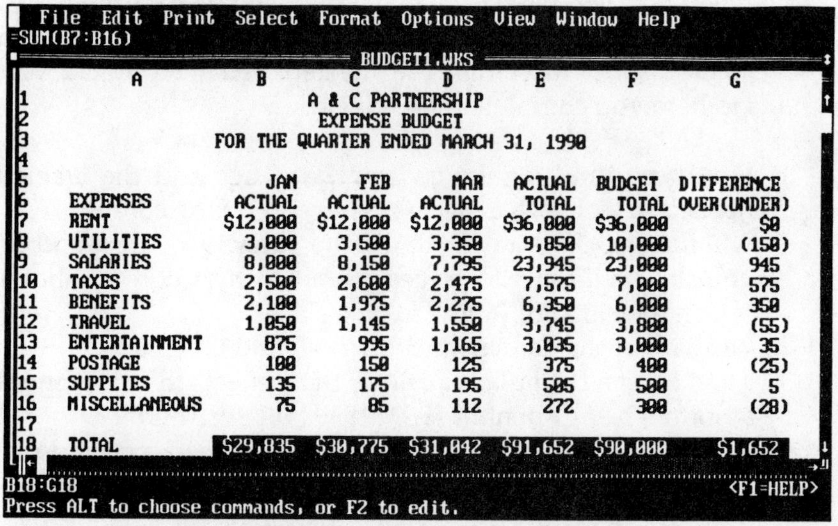

	A	B	C	D	E	F	G
1			A & C PARTNERSHIP				
2			EXPENSE BUDGET				
3		FOR THE QUARTER ENDED MARCH 31, 1990					
4							
5		JAN	FEB	MAR	ACTUAL	BUDGET	DIFFERENCE
6	EXPENSES	ACTUAL	ACTUAL	ACTUAL	TOTAL	TOTAL	OVER(UNDER)
7	RENT	$12,000	$12,000	$12,000	$36,000	$36,000	$0
8	UTILITIES	3,000	3,500	3,350	9,850	10,000	(150)
9	SALARIES	8,000	8,150	7,795	23,945	23,000	945
10	TAXES	2,500	2,600	2,475	7,575	7,000	575
11	BENEFITS	2,100	1,975	2,275	6,350	6,000	350
12	TRAVEL	1,050	1,145	1,550	3,745	3,800	(55)
13	ENTERTAINMENT	875	995	1,165	3,035	3,000	35
14	POSTAGE	100	150	125	375	400	(25)
15	SUPPLIES	135	175	195	505	500	5
16	MISCELLANEOUS	75	85	112	272	300	(28)
17							
18	TOTAL	$29,835	$30,775	$31,042	$91,652	$90,000	$1,652

Figure 3.23. Totals using the SUM function

This chapter has provided you with an introduction to the spreadsheet module found in Works. For many people, the concepts of setting up a spreadsheet are new and sometimes seem unfamiliar for a while.

Hopefully, you have begun to see that a spreadsheet is a powerful tool that can quickly and efficiently provide you with a way to keep track of complex financial calculations. Our examples, while simple in some respects, are in many ways typical of the work that one does with a spreadsheet. There is always the initial determination about how the rows and columns are to be labeled. Then one usually begins to place values and formulas into the spreadsheet. Finally, there are all of the minor adjustments such as formatting cells to better present the information that they contain, or erasing some cells to clean the spreadsheet up a bit.

You also had the opportunity to see how we can become more and more efficient with our continued spreadsheet mastery. Initially we had to type in the cell addresses for our formulas. Then we began to point to the cells that we wished to include. Finally, we were able to incorporate one of the many functions that come with the Works spreadsheet into our formulas. As you have seen, each one of these steps provides us with greater power for less work.

Exercise

In this exercise, you are going to put together a spreadsheet that will reflect a departmental budget for 2 years worth of expenses. The supervisor wishes to have the budget reflect the percent of change for each category, in addition to the actual dollar differences. When you are finished, your spreadsheet should resemble the one depicted in Figure 3.24. Here are some hints to help you complete the exercise:

1. First type in all of the column headings and the labels that will be needed in Column A. You will have to widen column A so that they all will fit. Also, if you wish to use the dates 1988, 1989, and 1990 as labels, you should be sure to precede them with a quote symbol in the cells in which they are not followed by a slash.
2. Next, enter the values for columns B and C.
3. Then enter a formula for cell D8 that reflects the difference between the amounts being spent in 1989/1990 and 1988/1989.
4. When you are sure that the formula is correct, copy it down column D.
5. Next, enter a formula that reflects the percent of change. This can be done by dividing the actual amount of the change by the original amount. In this case the original amount is the 1988/1989 figure.
6. When you are sure that the formula is correct, copy it down column E.

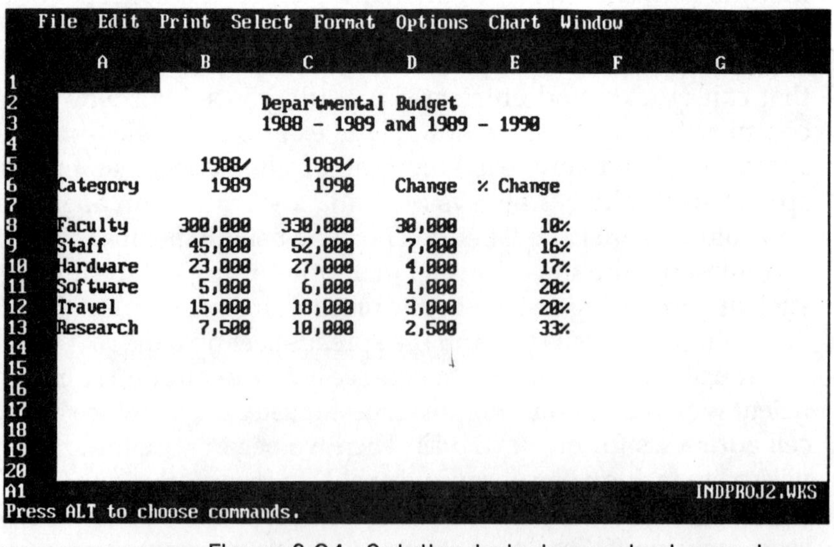

Figure 3.24. Solution to independent exercise

7. Now format the values in columns B, C, and D so that they all have commas in them and no decimal points.
8. Next, format the values in column E so that they are percents with no decimal points.
9. If you wish to be fancy, you could format all the labels above columns B, C, D, and E so that the labels are right justified.
10. Finally, save your spreadsheet as **INDPROJ1.WKS** and print out a copy of it.

4

An Introduction to the Database Manager

The third Works tool is the Database. The Database screens and many of the commands are similar to those that you encountered in the spreadsheet, since one way of storing information in a database is in columns and rows similar to those used in spreadsheets. In this first look at the database you will learn how to:

- Design a database file
- Enter information into the database
- View information in the database
- Change the width of the fields displaying information
- Search for information in the database
- Print information in the database

What Is a Database?

A database is an organized way to keep track of a lot of information. One of the most familiar examples is the telephone book, in which people are able to access data about particular individuals in a quick and efficient fashion.

Databases can be used to keep track of any information that you might now keep in a filing system—personnel records, inventories, customer bills, patient records, stock transactions, the data for the groups which you belong to, or even information about your record collection.

A database, although in some respects similar to a spreadsheet, is in many ways quite different. If the work that you are doing has a great deal of numerical information in it, and if there are lots of relationships among that information, then a spreadsheet is the logical tool for you to be using. However, if you are dealing primarily with information about people, places, or things, then a database is the correct choice. In addition, the Works database can function with the word processor or spreadsheet for efficient information management.

Starting a Database File

If you have just loaded Works into your computer's memory, select **Create New File**, and then select the third option, **New Database**, from the Dialog Box.

If you already are using Works, select **File/Create New File** to open the Dialog Box. Then select **New Database**.

Designing a Database

When you begin to use a database, the first thing that you must decide is what information you wish to include. To demonstrate this process, this chapter introduces the Works database by developing a database for a small painting company.

When contemplating setting up the database, begin by thinking about the kind of information that you would like to have about each client. Probably you would want to have their names, addresses, and phone numbers, as well as information for tracking the progress of the work—the date for assessing the cost of the job, the estimate, and whether or not a contract was sent and signed. You might also want information about the painting job—the names of the painters assigned, color, type, and amount of paint, etc., but it would be better practice to keep this information in a separate database.

Each one of these different categories is known in the world of database management as a *field*. A possible list of fields for our database might include:

Title:
First Name:
Last Name:
Address:
City:
State:
Zip:
Home Phone:
Work Phone:
Date of Estimate:
Estimate:
Contract Sent:
Contract Signed:

The information is broken down to the smallest unit that might be used. For example, Title (Mr., Ms., etc.), First Name, and Last Name were three separate fields, because just the person's first name, or just their title and last name might be used in a letter created by merging the database with a letter written in the word processor (for more about that topic see Chapter 8 on Integrating Works). A single Works database may include as many as 256 fields.

An entire collection of fields for one client is called a *record*. Each record includes a full set of fields, although some of the fields may be blank in an individual record. Each database may have up to 4096 records.

The entire set of records for the painting clients is called a *file*.

A Tour of the FORM Screen

Most databases, including Works', allow you to view the information contained in your database in two ways—one record at a time, or in a grid of columns and rows where each row represents a record and each column represents a field. When you create a new database in Works, the FORM screen appears. This is the screen that shows the database one record at a time. You can design a database either from the FORM screen or from the LIST screen which displays the database in columns and rows. You will use the FORM screen to create the CLIENTS database. Let's look at the FORM screen (Figure 4.1).

Across the top of the FORM screen is the Menu Bar. If you have already used the Spreadsheet, you will notice that the top Menu selections in the database are identical to those in the spreadsheet. Immediately below the Menu Bar is the default name of the database file DATA1.WDB.

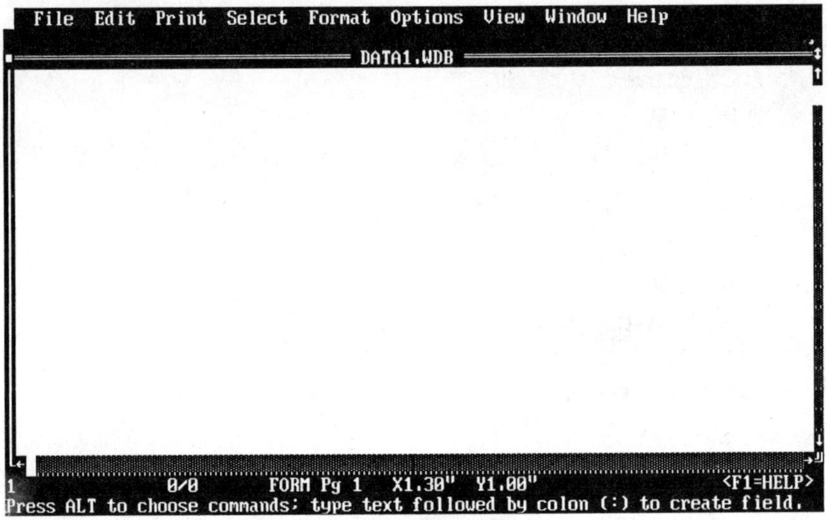

Figure 4.1. FORM screen

The Status Line is at the bottom of the screen. It contains more types of information than the Status Line in the other tools. In the far left corner of the Status Line, the *1* indicates the record currently on the screen, in this case the first record. Once fields have been created, the current field name will also be indicated. The *0/0* indicates the number of Displayed records/Total records; this number becomes important later when only some of the records in the database are selected for a particular task. In the center of the Status Line is the word *FORM* indicating the current view. Since Forms may be multipage, *Pg 1* indicates that this is the first page of the form. This is followed by the X and Y coordinates which indicate the current location of the cursor. Additional information will appear on the Status Line as different commands are used.

At the very bottom of the screen is the Message Line. Works assumes that you are going to begin by creating the database. Therefore, this line tells you how to create fields. It also reminds you that you must press **ALT** in order to begin selecting commands.

Entering Field Names

A field consists of the field name and the field contents. To design the database, you enter the field names and their maximum sizes. Entering field names onto the FORM screen is quite simple. To demonstrate the process, you'll set up the CLIENTS database, but to limit your data entry time, only fields for the client's name, complete address, home telephone, and estimate will be included.

Here are the field names that will be used:

First Name:
Last Name:
Address:
City:
State:
Zip:
Home Telephone:
Estimate:

Now, let's enter these field names into your database. You may place the field names anywhere you want on the form as long as the fields don't overlap. The following instructions just list the fields down the left-hand side of the screen.

1. With the cursor positioned at the top left corner of the screen, type the first field's name followed by a colon (**:**). A field name may be from 1 to 15 letters. It is very important that you always type a colon after entering a field name, as this is what tells Works that the field name is complete. Type: **First Name:**

   As you type the characters, they appear on the second line of your screen in the *Formula Bar* and on the screen at the point of the cursor (Figure 4.2). At this point, the information is in a holding zone on the database, and you have the opportunity to review it. If there are any errors, use the **BACKSPACE** key to erase them and then type the correct information.

2. When your entry is correct, press **ENTER**.

   A Dialog Box appears asking for information about the Width and Height of the field. The *default width is 20* and the *default height is 1* line.

3. It's necessary to estimate how long the longest entry in the First Name field will be. Try a length of 12. If that proves to be too short, it can be changed later. Type: **12** in the Width Box.
4. The Height indicates how many lines the field will include. The second line is only used when the first is filled. Therefore, more than one line is most useful when you have notes, comments or other fields with running text. For these exercises, a height of 1 will always be used. Press **ENTER** to accept the Width of 12 and Height of 1.

Figure 4.2. Entering a field name

As soon as you press **ENTER**, the cursor moves, usually down to the next line.

5. Press the **DOWN ARROW** once to leave a blank line between fields to increase readability.
6. To enter the second field, type: **Last Name:** and press **ENTER**. When the Dialog Box appears, press **ENTER** again to accept the default Width and Height.

Continue adding the fields. Remember to type the colon (:) at the end of each field name. Skip a line between each field name to improve readability.

Field Name	Width	Height
Address:	20	1
City:	15	1
State:	2	1
Zip:	5	1
Home Phone:	13	1
Estimate:	10	1

Your FORM should now resemble Figure 4.3. When you review the FORM screen, be sure that each field name ends with a colon. If it doesn't, Works won't recognize

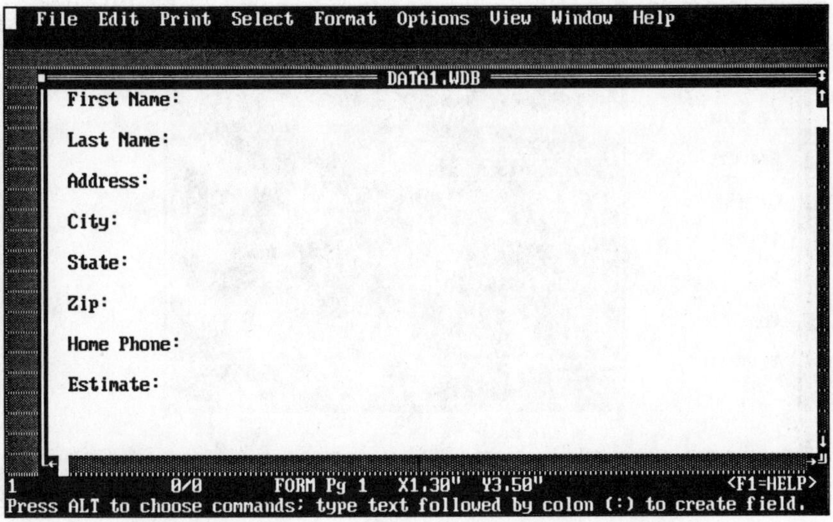

Figure 4.3. Completed FORM screen

it as a field and won't let you add data. If you omitted the colon or misspelled a field name, follow these steps to correct your error:

1. *Move the cursor to the field name.*
2. *Retype the field name and the colon, and press* **ENTER**.

Don't worry if your fields are positioned differently on the screen.

Saving a Database

To ensure that the structure of the database won't accidentally be lost, let's save the database structure even before adding any data.

1. Select **File/Save.** Since this is the first time that you are saving a new database, the Save File As Dialog Box appears (Figure 4.4). Just as with the other tools, Works assumes that the first time you save a file, you will want to give it a name other than the one that has been assigned by the program (**DATA1.WDB**). Once you save a database, if you select **File/Save** again Works will automatically save the database using the existing name and will replace the preceding version of the file.

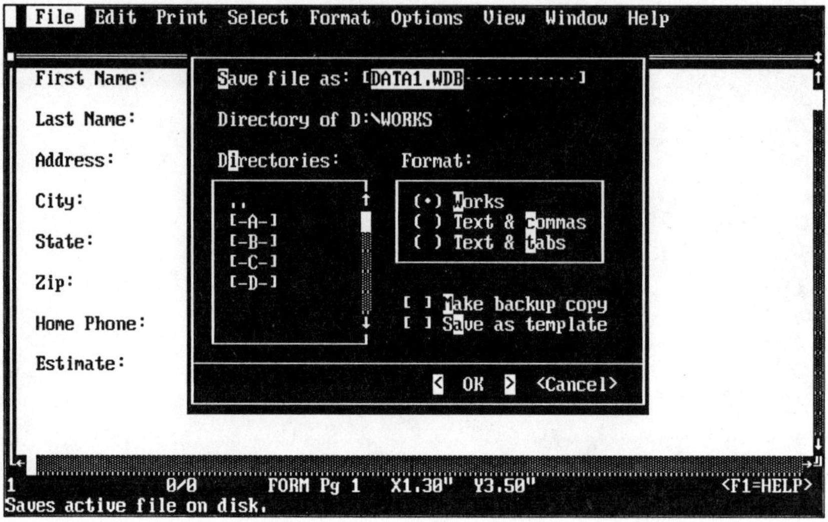

Figure 4.4. Save As Dialog Box

2. Look at the second line of the Dialog Box which begins *Directory of*. Be sure that it indicates the name of the drive containing your data disk (A: or B:). If it doesn't, highlight the correct drive from the *Directories* List Box and press **ENTER**.
3. For the filename, use **CLIENTS**. Works automatically will add the extension **.WDB** (Works Database) to the filename. Type: **CLIENTS.** Remember not to type a period after the filename, as it stops Works from adding the **.WDB** extension.
4. Press **ENTER**.

Entering Data

Now that you've completed and saved the design of the database, let's enter some information into the database so that you can begin to get a feel for how it works. You may enter data on either the FORM or LIST View screens. Start by using FORM View.

Although you can't see it, when you enter a field name and size, Works reserves space for the field contents beginning two spaces to the right of the field name. (The colon and first space are considered part of the field name.) You can view and select the area allocated for the field contents by either:

- Using the **ARROW** keys to move the cursor to the right of one of the field names or
- Clicking the mouse on the area to the right of the field name.

To enter data,

1. Select the *First Name:* field.
2. Type the data for the *First Name*: field: **Robert**

You may use either uppercase or lowercase letters when entering data. It is best to type the entries as you would like them to appear in reports, labels, and letters. As when you entered the field names, the letters that you type will appear simultaneously in the holding zone at the top of the screen and on the screen. Use the **BACKSPACE** key to correct any typing errors.

3. Press **TAB** to enter the data and move to the next field. If you accidentally skip a field, or want to return to a field, use **SHIFT-TAB** to move through the fields backwards.
4. Now enter the data for the remaining fields. After you enter the information for the final field, however, press **ENTER** instead of **TAB** so that you don't move immediately to the next record.

Note Don't worry for now if you notice errors after you have moved the cursor to a different field. Methods for editing data will be discussed a little further on in the chapter.

Last Name:	**Downey**
Address:	**52 Wilmot Circle**
City:	**Bedford**
State:	**NY**
Zip:	**10542**
Home Phone:	**(914)234-7821**
Estimate:	**2400**

Entering Numbers as Text

When entering data, simply type the information, without worrying about whether it contains letters, numbers, or both. However, just as in the

Spreadsheet, Works treats values and text differently. It considers all the entries except Zip and Estimate as text, since Zip and Estimate are considered to be numeric entries since they only contain numerals. The differences between the treatment of values and text is discussed at length in the beginning of Chapter 3 on the Spreadsheet.

Note In spreadsheets, text entries are often referred to as *labels*. In databases, the term *label* refers to descriptive text that is entered on every record in a database. Therefore, it should not be used to refer to field entries that are text.

To see the effects of this difference in the database:

1. Move the cursor to *Bedford*. *Bedford* is left justified in the field on the FORM screen and is preceded by the label prefix character (") on the Formula Bar (Figure 4.5).
2. Now move the cursor to the Estimate field entry, *2400*, and notice the position of the entry (see Figure 4.6).
   The estimate is right justified because, just as in the Spreadsheet, all numeric entries are automatically right justified. The same is true for the zip code only you can't see the justification because the field size is the exact length of the zip code. There are other ways in which Works treats numeric data differently from text. Some of these differences would

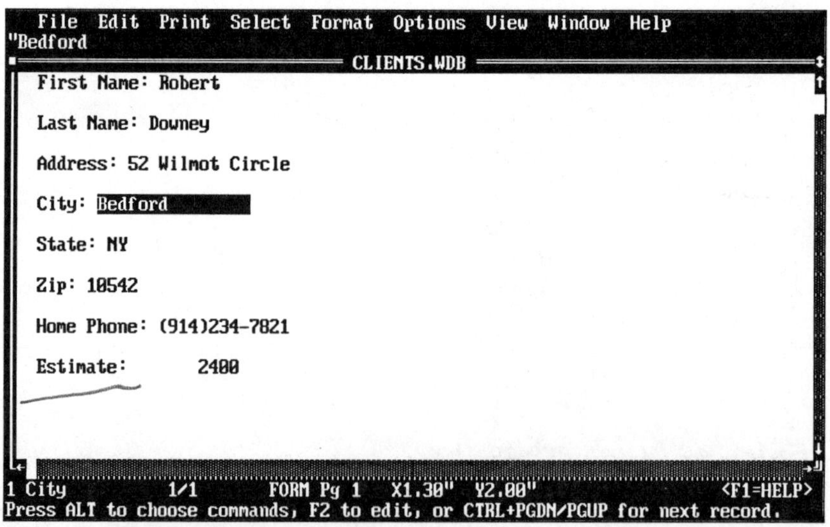

Figure 4.5. Text data on the screen and in the Formula Bar

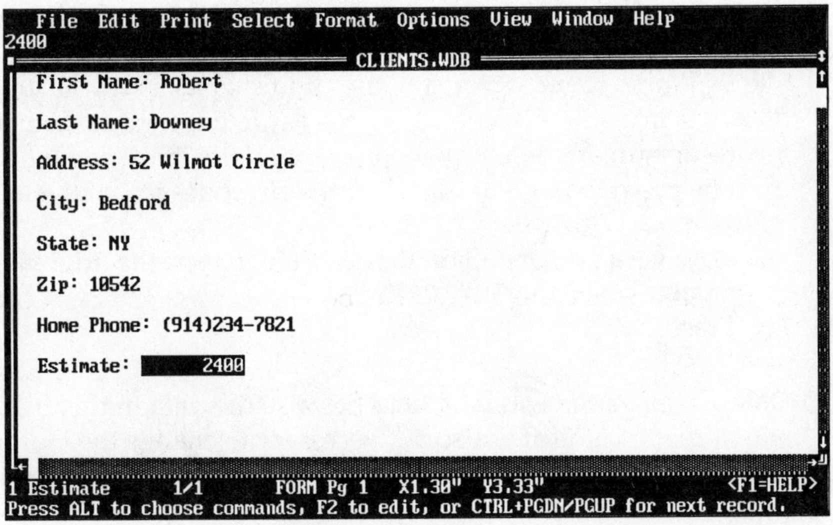

Figure 4.6. Numeric data on the screen and in the Formula Bar

have serious consequences for the zip code data. For example, if you attempt to enter a zip code beginning with a zero, such as 03456, Works will eliminate the leading zero, changing the entry to 3456.

3. Try that now. With your cursor on the Zip field, type: **03456**
   Press **ENTER** and view the screen and the Formula Bar (Figure 4.7).

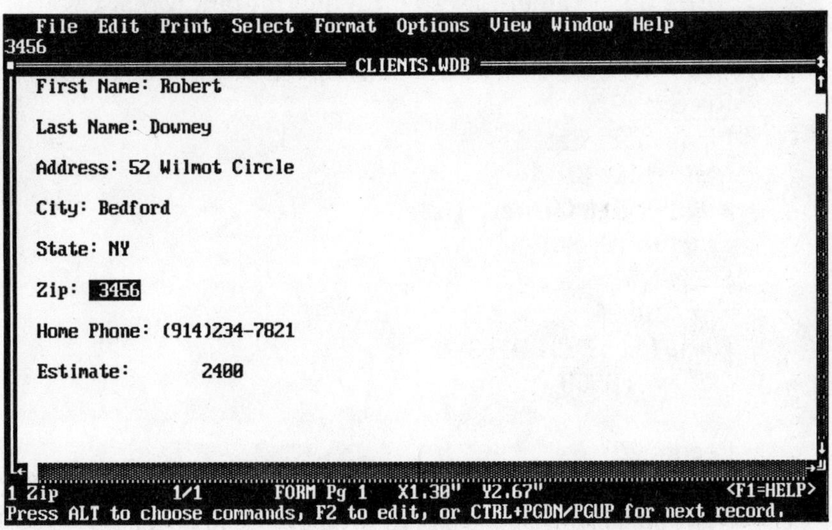

Figure 4.7. Leading zeros and dropped in numeric entries

To enter numeric data as text, you must type a quotation mark at the beginning of the entry ("03456). As in the Spreadsheet tool, the quotation mark allows Works to recognize a string of numerals as text instead of numeric data. It is important that the data in a particular field are either text in every record or numeric in every record. Therefore, since some of the zip codes must be preceded by a quote, all of the zip codes must be entered as text.

4. With your cursor still on the Zip field, retype the original zip code with a quote preceding it: **"10542**
5. Press **ENTER.**

Note Do not change the Estimate field because the data in this field will be used as a numeric value. It is also not necessary to change the Home Phone field. Works considers the telephone number to be text and not a numeric value because it is not simply a string of numbers, but contains a hyphen and a set of parentheses.

6. Press **TAB** until the cursor moves to the first field on record 2. You can check that you are on the second record by looking for the number 2 in the left corner of the Status Line.
7. Enter the data for the next few records. While entering the data, you'll see some of the problems often encountered in data entry and ways of solving them. Press **TAB** to move from field to field after typing the information. Remember to type the quotation mark (") prior to each zip code entry.

Record #2:
First Name: **Peter**
Last Name: **Brody**
Address: **456 Gilbert Street**
City: **South Salem**
State: **NY**
Zip: **"10590**
Home Phone: **(914)763-7676**
Estimate: **3200**

Record #3:
First Name: **"April**
Last Name: **Marcus**
Address: **Snake Hill Rd.**

City: **White Plains**
State: **NY**
Zip: **10605**[Don't forget the quote ("10605)]
Home Phone: **(914)764-3201**
Estimate: **1800**

Note If you try to enter a name such as Marc, April, or June, which is the same as the beginning or all of the name of a month, Works assumes you are entering a month, and enters only the first three letters of the name (Mar, Apr, Jun). To enter the name, or partial name, of a month as text, type a quote at the beginning of the entry (e.g., "Marc, etc.) (see the Entering Labels Section in Chapter 3 on the Spreadsheet).

Changing Field Widths in FORM View

1. Enter Record 4, and look carefully at how it appears on the screen.

Record #4:
First Name: **Jerome**
Last Name: **Adams**
Address: **15 Martine Ave., Apt. 3M**
City: **White Plains**
State: **NY**
Zip: **10608**
Home Phone: **(914)681-5674**
Estimate: **900**

Did you notice a problem when you entered the address? Although you typed an apartment number, it is not displayed on the FORM screen because Jerome's address is longer than the 15 spaces you allotted when creating the Address field.

The address isn't lost. It's just not visible on the screen. Move the cursor to the address entry. The full address can be seen in the Formula Bar (Figure 4.8). When creating the database, you tried to make each field wide enough to contain the widest entry. However, sometimes you guess wrong. Luckily, it's easy to increase the width of a field.

2. Move the cursor to the Address field contents.
3. Select the command **Format/Field Size**.

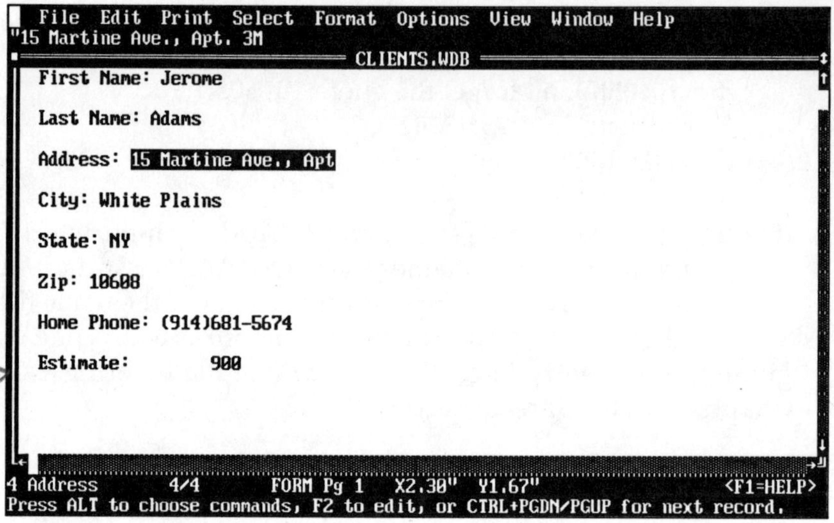

Figure 4.8. Address on the form and on the Formula Bar

4. Type the new width: **25** and press **ENTER**.

The entire address should now be visible on the screen.

Enter the data for the remaining six records. Remember to change field widths and precede the data with the label prefix character (") when necessary.

Record #5:
First Name: **Robert**
Last Name: **McDonald**
Address: **43 Lakeshore Drive**
City: **South Salem**
State: **NY**
Zip: **10590**
Home Phone: **(914)763-9008**
Estimate: **1200**

Record #6:
First Name: **John**
Last Name: **Miller**

Address: **P.O. Box 1118**
City: **Yorktown Heights**
State: **NY**
Zip: **10598**
Home Phone: **(914)592-7683**
Estimate: **900**

Record #7:
First Name: **Susan**
Last Name: **Lippman**
Address: **Whipporwill Drive**
City: **Darien**
State: **CT**
Zip: **06820**
Home Phone: **(203)224-6785**
Estimate: **800**

Record #8
First Name: **Marc**
Last Name: **Patterson**
Address: **Sheridan Hill Drive**
City: **Greenwich**
State: **CT**
Zip: **06830**
Home Phone: **(203)744-3489**
Estimate: **2500**

Record #9
First Name: **Suzanne**
Last Name: **Miller**
Address: **96 Summer Hill Rd.**
City: **Bedford**
State: **NY**
Zip: **10542**
Home Phone: **(914)234-3916**
Estimate: **5000**

Record #10
First Name: **William**
Last Name: **Tippett**

Address: **Fox Hollow Run**
City: **Westport**
State: **CT**
Zip: **06880**
Home Phone: **(203)254-8136**
Estimate: **1300**

The only trouble spots that you should have encountered are:

1. *In Record 6, Yorktown Heights is too wide for the field. Use* ***Format/Field Width*** *to change the field width to 16.*
2. *In Record 8, Marc must be preceded by a " or only the month, Mar, will be entered in the field.*
3. *In all records, the zip code entry should be preceded by a quotation mark.*

For now, if you made a mistake, move back to the field and retype the entry. If you accidently entered text in the blank line between fields, Works will consider this entry to be a label and it will appear on each form. Move the cursor to the label and select Edit/Delete Label. The next section contains information on shortcuts for moving through the database.

The data in your database is precious and is worth saving on a regular basis. Therefore, save the database before going futher.

1. Select **File/Save**. The database will automatically be saved using the same name, **CLIENTS.WDB**.
2. While it's saving the file, Works indicates the percent saved in the lower left side of the Status Bar.

Viewing Records in the Database

The next step is reviewing the records you have entered. In FORM View each record is displayed as a separate form, and may be viewed simply by using a combination of keys.

1. To move to the **previous** record in FORM View, press **CTRL-PGUP**. **CTRL-PGUP** will move you back through the database, so that you may see one or several of the previous records. Try this now, until you are looking at the first record in the database, that of Robert Downey.

2. To move to the **next** record, press **CTRL-PGDN**. Try this now until you have reached Robert McDonald's record.
3. As you may have expected, there is a quicker way to move to the very beginning of your database. Just press **CTRL-HOME** and you will return instantly to the first record in the database, that of Robert Downey.
4. Similarly to move to the last record in the database in FORM View,
    a. Press **CTRL-END.** The record *after* the final one in your database is displayed in anticipation that you want to enter a new record.
    b. Press **CTRL-PGUP** to view the final record.

LIST View

Works also provides us with the ability to see a list of many records at once, in what is known as LIST View. As you will see, this is easy to do.

1. Before changing to LIST View, place your cursor on the Last Name field in record 10.
2. Select **View/List**. Your screen should resemble Figure 4.9. The cursor is in the same field and record as it was in FORM View. That record is at the top of the screen.
3. Press **PGUP** to display the entire database. If some of the data in the Zip field is right justified and some is left justified, don't worry about it. A

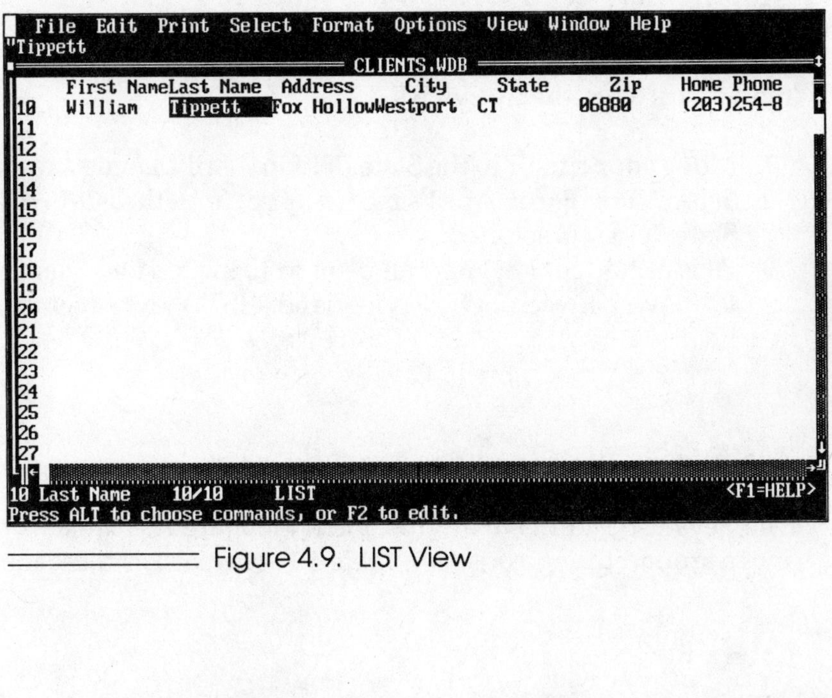

Figure 4.9. LIST View

quick method for correcting this is indicated in the Self-Check exercise in a later section on Editing Data.

The LIST View of the database has features of both the database FORM screen and the spreadsheet screen. Its appearance resembles the Works spreadsheet, and the intersection of a row and a column is also called a *cell*. In the database, however, the rows and columns have specific meanings. Each *row* represents a *record* and each *column* represents a *field*. As in the spreadsheet only 18 records and a limited number of fields are visible at one time.

Some of the data are not visible on the screen. That's because LIST View has its own field width which may be different than that set in FORM View. The default field width (like the column width on the spreadsheet) is only 10 characters wide. Therefore, many of the addresses and cities are not fully visible. The field width can be changed in a similar manner to that used in the spreadsheet and that process will be covered after LIST View is explored further.

The Menu Bar headings are identical to those in the database FORM View, although a few of the commands in the **Edit**, **Select**, **Format**, and **Options** menus are different. The Status Line also contains similar information, but the X/Y coordinates and page number are omitted.

Moving Between FORM View and LIST View

You used the View command to switch to LIST View. There are two ways of moving between the two views.

1. Move your cursor to the State field in April Marcus's record.
2. Select **View/Form**. April's record appears on the FORM screen with the State field still selected.
3. **F9** is a shortcut key that can be used to switch between views. Press **F9** to move between FORM View and LIST View several times. Stop in LIST View.

Moving Around the List

The keys used to move around LIST View are the same as those used to move around the spreadsheet. Table 4.1 summarizes these movements. For

Table 4.1. FORM screen movement keys

Keys	Movement
ARROW	One field or record in the direction of the arrow.
	Screen-to-Screen Movements
PGDN	Down one screen
PGUP	Up one screen
CTRL-PGDN	One screen to the right
CTRL-PGUP	One screen to the left
	Global Movements
CRTL-HOME	Beginning of database.
CRTL-END	End of database (*Note*: End of the database is defined as the intersection of the last field containing any data and the last record containing any data.)
HOME	First field in the current record
END	Last field in the current record (*Note:* Last field is defined as the right-most field that contains information for any record, even if that field is blank for the current record.)

a more detailed explanation see the section Moving Around a Spreadsheet in Chapter 3.

Record-to-record or *field-to-field* movement is accomplished by using the **ARROW** keys on your keyboard. Each one of the four arrows points in a particular direction. Pressing these keys will move the cursor in their respective directions.

Screen-to-screen movement allows you to jump an entire screen by pressing one of the special keys on your keyboard or a combination of keys.

Sometimes you want to move from the beginning to the end of a record or the end of a file. Special keys or key combinations can be used to accomplish these *global movements*.

Changing Field Width in LIST View

While LIST View is certainly an improvement, since many records can be viewed at one time, the current setup of the screen has some problems. One problem is that the various fields in the database are all smashed together on the screen. While the information is visible, it is rather difficult to read it clearly. Let's see how to improve this. The procedure for changing the width of a field is identical to the one used earlier when changing cell width in the spreadsheet. Let's use the Address column as an example.

1. Move your cursor anywhere in the field you wish to widen, the Address field.
2. Select **Format/Field Width.** The Dialog box with the default width of 10 is displayed.
3. To make the width 25, type: **25** (Figure 4.10) and press **ENTER.**

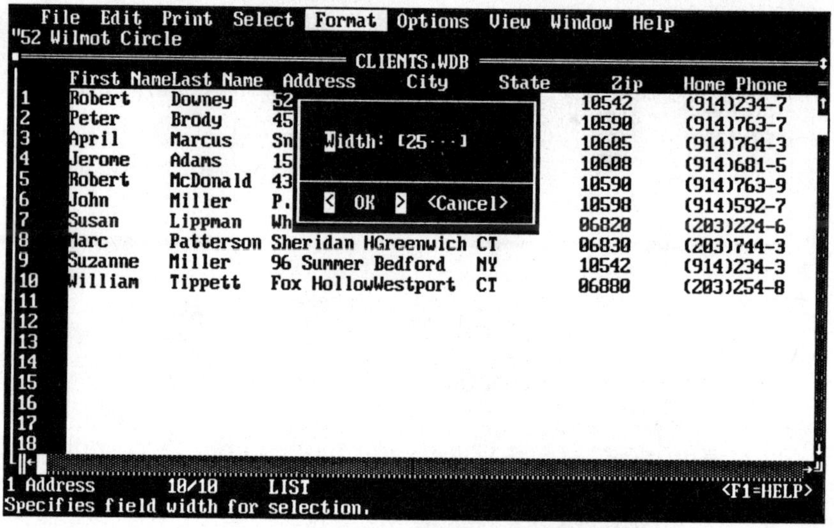

Figure 4.10. Width Dialog Box

Change the field widths of the remaining columns until each width is one wider than the longest entry in the field or than the field name whichever is longer.

Figure 4.11 shows the first six fields of LIST View with the field widths changed. For the First Name, State, and Estimate fields the lengths used were equal to the field names since these were longer than the longest entry in the field.

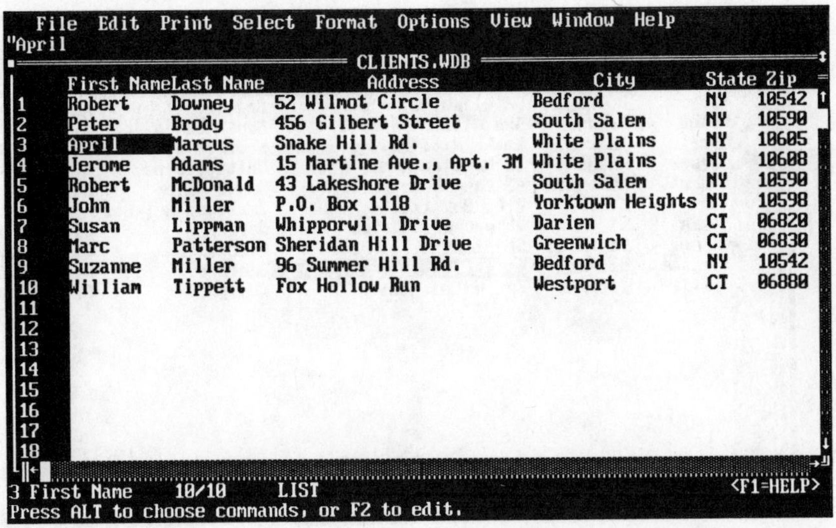

Figure 4.11. LIST View with modified field widths

Editing Data

One of the challenging aspects of database management is keeping a database current and accurate. Since the data in a database frequently change, it is important to be able to edit these data quickly and comfortably. The methods for editing data are the same as those used in the spreadsheet. The same editing procedures are used in both FORM View and LIST View.

There are two main ways to edit data. The first, which you have already used, is to simply retype the entire entry. The second is to use the Edit Key **F2** to change just the incorrect part of the data. Once Edit Mode is invoked, editing proceeds as in the word processor. Any text typed is inserted to the left of the cursor, and the **DEL** or **BACKSPACE** keys are used to delete text.

To edit Suzanne Miller's address:

1. Switch to LIST View if that is not the current view so that your screen matches the ones shown on the following pages.
2. Move the cursor to the field containing her address.
3. Press **F2,** the **EDIT** key.

The cursor should appear in the Formula Bar at the end of the entry, and the Status Line should indicate that you are in *EDIT* mode (Figure 4.12).

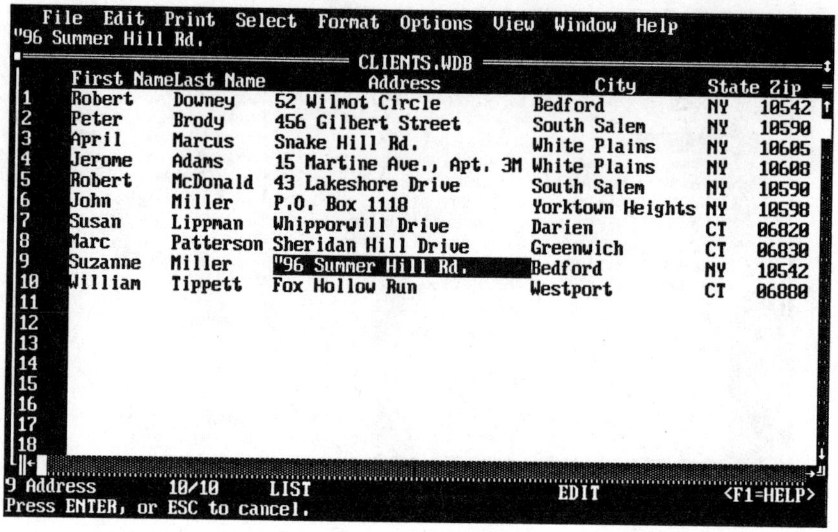

Figure 4.12. Edit Mode

4. To change *Rd.* to Road, use the **LEFT ARROW** key to move the cursor under the *d* in *Rd.*
5. Type the correction: **oa**
6. Use the **RIGHT ARROW** key to move the cursor under the period and press **DEL** to delete it.
7. Press **ENTER** to indicate that you have finished editing.
8. The data have been changed in the database as well as on the screen. Press **F9** to see that the data have been changed in FORM View as well.
9. While in FORM View, press **CTRL-HOME** to move to record 1 and change Robert Downey's home phone to *(914)234-7829.*
   a. Move the cursor to the Home Phone field.
   b. Press **F2**.
   c. Press **BACKSPACE** to delete the final *1*.
   d. Type: **9** and press **ENTER**.

Note If you press **ESC** before pressing **ENTER**, the editing changes are canceled and the entry appears as it did before you started editing. Once you press **ENTER**, the original data are replaced by the changes. The only way to return to the original data is to edit the field and type the original data again.

General guidelines for editing data and shortcuts for moving around the edit screen are indicated in Table 4.2.

Table 4.2. Edit mode

If the amount of data in the field that has an error is **small** or most of it is incorrect, replace the contents of the cell by:

1. Moving the cursor to the field to be changed.
2. Typing the new information and pressing **ENTER.**

If the data entry to be changed is long and you only want to change one or two characters or add or delete characters, edit the data by:

1. Moving the cursor to the field to be edited.
2. Pressing the **EDIT** key (**F2**).
3. Using the following keys to move the cursor to the part of the Formula Bar that you wish to change:

Key	Movement
LEFT/RIGHT ARROW	One space in the direction of the arrow
HOME	To the beginning of the Formula Bar
END	To the end of the Formula Bar

4. Type the new information. Delete any remaining information by using **BACKSPACE** to delete characters to the left of the cursor or **DEL** to delete the selected character.
5. Press **ENTER** to enter the changes or press **ESC** to cancel them.

1. If you are in FORM View return to LIST View so that you can quickly scan the data.
2. Look carefully at the records in your list to see if you entered any data incorrectly. Then use the guidelines in Table 4.2 to make the necessary changes.

One likely error that you may have made is failure to enter all of the zip codes as text data. For example, in Figure 4.13, the zip codes for records 1, 4, 5, and 6 were entered as values.

1. *To check the accuracy of your Zip field entries, move to the Zip field and use* ***Format/Field Width*** *to change the width to* ***10***.

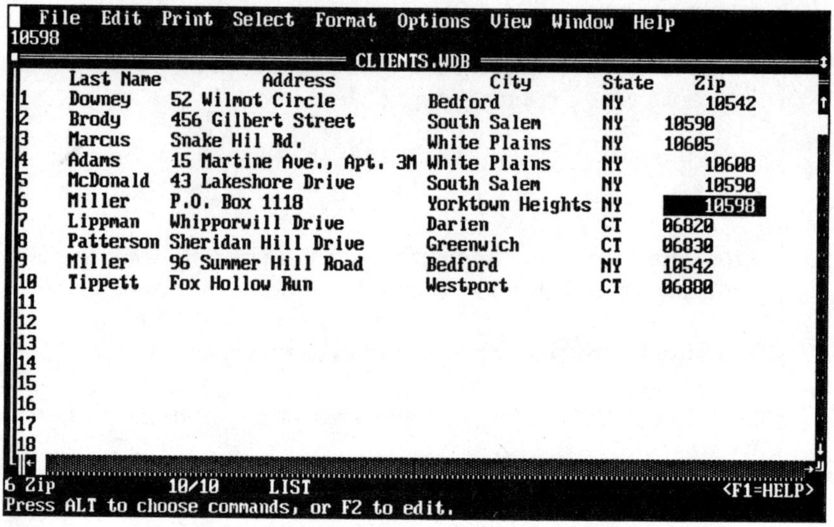

Figure 4.13. Zip codes entered as text and as values

2. *If any of the entries are right-justified:*
   a. *Move the cursor to the incorrect entry.*
   b. *Press* **F2**.
   c. *Press* **HOME** *to move the cursor to the beginning of the Formula Bar.*
   d. *Type a quotation mark (") and press* **ENTER**.
3. *Change the field width back to* **6**.

The database is now edited.

1. Save it again using the **File/Save** command.
2. If you want to take a break, select **File/Exit**. If not, continue with the next section.

Searching for Data

Once you have assembled information in a database, the next step is to be able to use the database so that you may find specific information you need. That might mean looking for a particular client's address or telephone number or finding everyone who lives in Connecticut or has an estimate over $2,000 in the **CLIENTS** database. There are several ways to find records containing specific information. The first method, using the **Select/Search** command, finds records that contain specific data.

Initiating a Search

There are several options that can be employed in a search. They are the same in LIST View and FORM View, except that in LIST View you can limit the search to only part of the database. Let's use LIST View:

1. With the **CLIENTS.WDB** database in LIST View, select **Select/Search.** The Search Dialog Box will appear (Figure 4.14). It contains space to enter data for which you are searching and an option to find records matching the data one at a time or simultaneously.
2. Type the name **Brody** in the Search For Text Box. The Next record Check Box will be selected. Press **ENTER** to initiate the search.

Note Works is not case sensitive; therefore, you could enter **brody** or **BRODY** and it would find the data just as well.

Your cursor immediately moves to the last name **Brody.** Now that you've found the record for Brody, you can edit it, use the data, view the entire form, etc.

A Search for Several Records

Often more than one record contains the data for which you are searching. There are several ways to deal with this situation. In the first example, as-

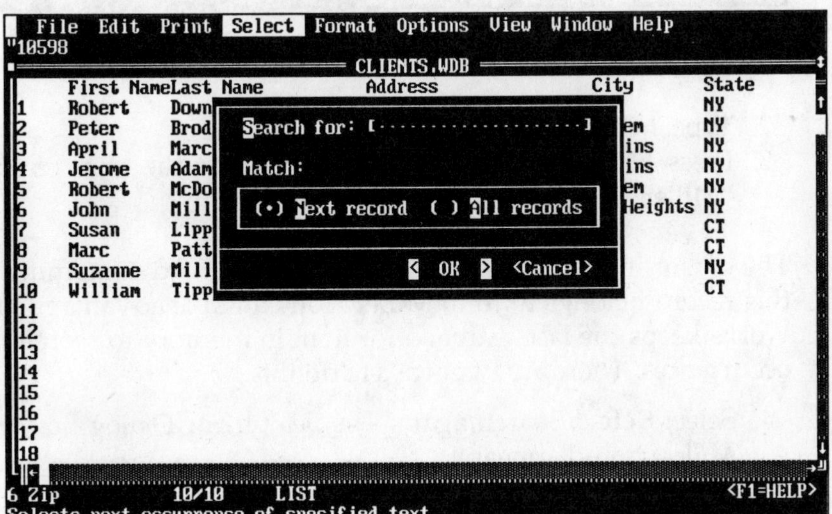

Figure 4.14. Search Dialog Box

sume that you want to find Suzanne Miller's record. Since the information entered in the Search For Text Box must be contained in only one field, let's begin by searching for Miller.

1. With your database in LIST View, move your cursor up to Home position, by pressing **CTRL-HOME**. Now select **Select/Search**. The Search For Dialog Box will appear. It contains the information for which you previously searched (Figure 4.15).

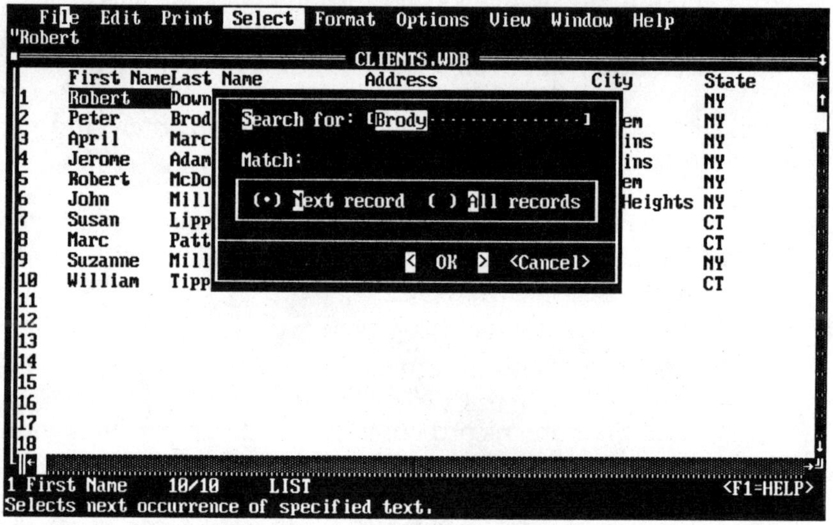

Figure 4.15. Search Dialog Box with data

2. Type: **Miller**
3. Press **ENTER** to search the database for the next record containing "Miller."

The cursor immediately moves to the first record containing "Miller," but this record belongs to John Miller. You can take advantage of the fact that Works keeps the last searched for item in memory to search for additional occurrences. There are two ways to do this.

4. Select **Select/Search** again. The Search For Dialog Box with the name *Miller* should appear.
5. Press **ENTER** to repeat the search.
6. The highlight will move to the next example of "Miller", in this case the record for which you were searching. This time let's look for all of the

records containing "CT" and use a shortcut method for repeating the search.

7. Select **Select/Search**, type: **ct** in the Search For Text Box, and press **ENTER**.

When a Next Record search is initiated, Works begins at the point of the cursor and searches towards the end of the database. If nothing is found it wraps around to the beginning of the database and continues searching.

8. Press the Repeat Search key **F7** to repeat the search.
9. Continue pressing **F7** until all occurrences of **ct** are found.

Note

Works will continue cycling through the database finding the next record meeting the search criteria. The only way to know if all of the records have been found is to keep track of the first occurrence found and then discontinue the search when this record is found again.

10. To see what the Next Record search looks like in FORM View:
    a. Switch to FORM View.
    b. Select **Select/Search**. *CT* appears in the Search for Text Box even though it was entered in LIST View.
    c. Press **ENTER**.
    d. Press **F7** to continue the search. The records containing CT will be displayed one at a time.
11. Switch back to LIST View.

Searching for All Records

The Next Record search finds occurrences of the searched for information, one at a time. Often you want to display all the records containing specific information.

12. To display all of the **Bedford** records simultaneously:
    a. Select **Select/Search**.
    b. Type: **Bedford**
    c. **TAB** to the Match Check Box. Press the **RIGHT ARROW** to move the mark to *All records*.
    d. Press **ENTER** to display all records containing Bedford (Figure 4.16).

The search for All Records is more powerful than the search for the next record. It not only searches for the matching records, but selects those records.

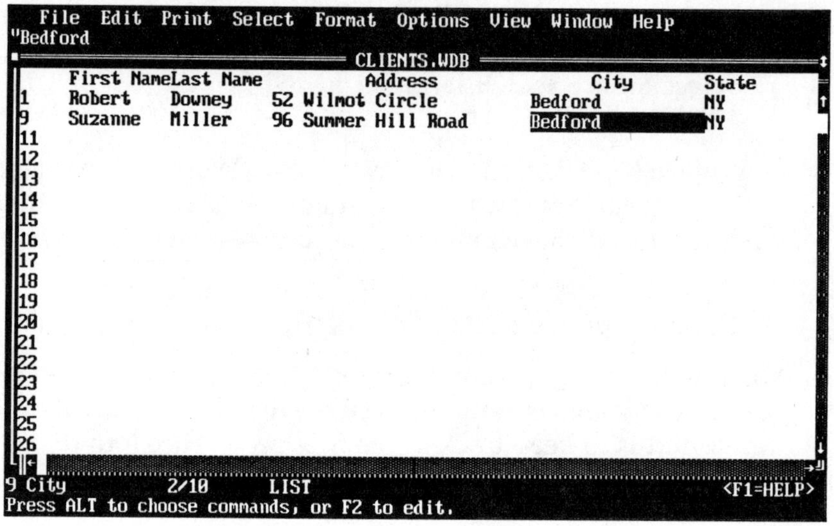

Figure 4.16. Selecting all records containing Bedford

Look at the Status Line. In all previous exercises the number of records displayed has equalled the total number of records. Now the number of records displayed/total records shows *2/10*. This means that only two of the ten records have been selected. All commands issued subsequent to this will only effect the selected records until a new selection is made. For example:

13. Press **F9** to switch to FORM View. Record #1 should be displayed.
14. Press **CTRL-PGDN** to display the next record. Instead of displaying record #2, record #9, which is the next record containing Bedford, is displayed.
15. Press **CTRL-PGDN** again. Since no other records in the database contain Bedford, a blank record will be displayed.

Just as Works only displays the selected records, if you now attempted to print, create a report or use the database with the word processor to print labels or form letters, only the data from the displayed records would be used.

Redisplaying Hidden Records

Works refers to records that are no longer displayed as hidden records. Before searching for other data not contained in the currently displayed records or using information from hidden records, the records must be redisplayed.

1. Select **Select/Show All Records.**
2. Scroll through the database. All records are now displayed as indicated by the *10/10* now appearing on the Status Line.

Selecting Only Part of the Database

Sometimes you only want to search for records in part of the database. For example, suppose that you entered six new records and only wanted to search within those new records or you only wanted to search for information in one or more fields of the database. These limited searches are done by selecting the part of the database that you want searched and then initiating the search. A limited search can only be done in LIST View.

There are several techniques for selecting the database.

- Any area of the database can be selected by using the **F8** and **ARROW** keys to EXTEND the highlight to any group of adjacent cells; these techniques are covered in Chapters 2 and 3 on the word processor and spreadsheet
- To select a group of consecutive records, highlight one field in each record and then use the **Select/Record** command to extend the highlight to the entire record
- To select one field or a group of consecutive fields, highlight the field in one record and then use the **Select/Field** command to extend the highlight to the field in all records

Try using these techniques to search only parts of the database.

1. Change to LIST View if you are not already there.
2. Move the cursor to the First Name field in Record #5.
3. Press **F8** to begin highlighting. *EXT* will appear on the Status Line.
4. Use the **DOWN ARROW** key to highlight the First Name field in Records #6–#10.
5. Select **Select/Record.**
6. Search for: **bedford**
7. Press **F7** to continue the search. No other records are found as the other occurrence of Bedford is in Record #1 which was not selected.

Using the Mouse to Select Fields or Records

To use the mouse to select one or more records:

1. Move the cursor to the record number of the first record to be selected.

2. Press the Left Button and drag the mouse down to highlight the numbers of all additional records.

The same procedure would be used to select one or more adjacent fields, except that you would click and drag on the field names instead of the record numbers.

Limitations of the Select/Search Command

As it has been used in this chapter so far, the **Search** command finds all occurrences of the information throughout the database. This can cause Works to find data you had not intended to be found. Let's find the record of someone with the first name of Marc.

1. Return to LIST View.
2. Select **Select/Search**.

When the Search Dialog Box is displayed, the last searched for information, *bedford*, remains displayed, but the Match Option Box has switched back to *Next record*.

3. Type: **marc** and press **ENTER** to search for the *Next record*.
4. Press **F7** and continue searching until no new occurrences are found.

Were you surprised that both **Marc** and **Marcus** were found? Information in the Search For Text Box is matched even if it matches only part of a field. If you want to select only exact matches, you must use the **Query** command, which will be covered in Chapter 7 on additional database commands.

Since the **Select/Search** command finds all the places in the database where the characters entered in the Search For Text Box occur, it cannot be used to find data that falls within a certain range (e.g., greater than $1000, or between the letters A and Z) or data that contain specific information in more than one field (e.g., a first name of Richard and a last name of Smith). The **Query** command must also be used to locate these records.

---

1. Search for all of the records containing **South Salem**, finding one record at a time.
2. Display all of the records from **NY** at the same time.
3. Now display all of the records from **CT**. Look at the Select Menu and see if you can think of a shortcut for doing this.

4. Find all of the phone numbers beginning with the **234**. Limit the search to the Home Phone field.
5. Search for **Marc** in the First Name field only.

---

1. *Select **Select/Search** and enter **South Salem** in the Search for Text Box. Press **F7** to repeat the search until all matches are found.*
2. *Select **Select/Search**. Enter **NY** in the Search for Text Box and change the Match Option box to All Records.*
3. *Select **Select/Show All Records**. Then repeat the procedures in step 2, substituting CT for NY. In this database, since all the records contain either NY or CT in the State field, the **Select/Switch Hidden Records** is a shortcut to the same result.*
4. *Select **Select/Show All Records**. Move the cursor to the Home Phone field and select **Select/Field**. Use **Select/Search** to find **234**. Press **F7** to repeat the search.*
5. *Highlight one entry in the First Name field. Use **Select/Field** to highlight the entire field. Use **Select/Search** to search for **Marc**.*

Sorting Records

Another way to find groups of related records is to sort the database. A database may be sorted into alphabetical or numerical order, using the contents of any field in the database. A second and third sort field may also be selected, but these only sort records that have identical entries in the first sort field. For example, when sorting by last name, the first name is typically chosen as a second sort field so that records containing the same last name can be sorted in a logical order.

Once the **Sort** command is issued, all following commands, such as **Print**, act upon the sorted database. Furthermore, when you save the file, it is saved in its sorted order. To keep both the sorted and unsorted files, use **File/Save As** to save the sorted file with a new name.

Let's sort the database by the Zip field, so that a printout will be in order for mailing purposes. Since sorting records is another way of selecting records, that command is on the **Select** menu.

1. Select **Select/Sort Records**.

The SORT Dialog Box will be displayed (Figure 4.17). Works has placed the

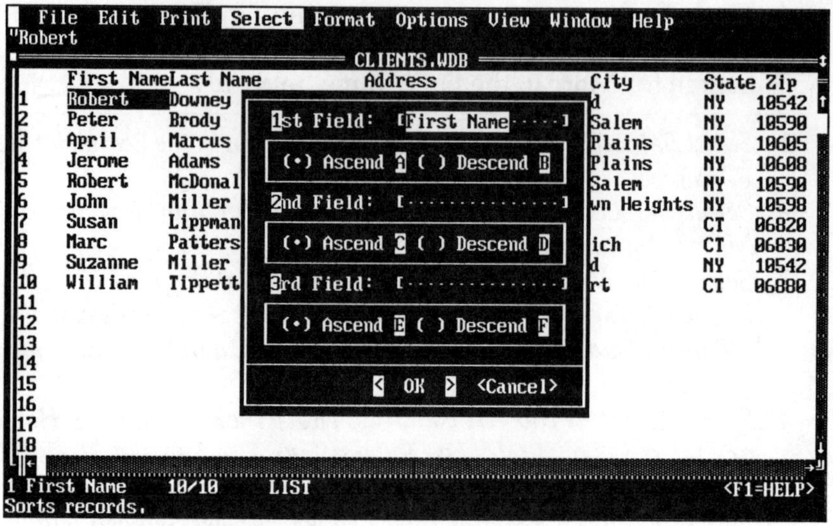

Figure 4.17. SORT Dialog Box

name of the first field in the database, First Name, into the 1st Field Text Box, because people frequently want to sort a database on the first field.

2. To sort on Zip instead of First Name, type: **Zip**
3. Press **ENTER** to sort in ascending order on the Zip field.

Note Works sorts all text entries first and then all numeric entries. If you omitted the " (quotation mark) before some of the zip codes when you entered them, they will appear at the end of the list. Edit those entries to include the ".

4. Use **File/Save As** to save the sorted database with the name **CLIENZIP**. If you haven't used the **Save As** command before, follow these instructions:
   a. When the **Save File As** Dialog Box appears, type the new name: **CLIENZIP** in the Save file as Text Box. The extension **.WDB** will automatically be added.
   b. Press **ENTER**. The new filename **CLIENZIP.WDB** will replace **CLIENTS.WDB** at the top of the screen.

---

1. Sort the database on last name and first name.
2. Save the sorted database using the name **CLIENTAZ**.
3. Close **CLIENTAZ** and open **CLIENZIP**.

1. *Select* ***Select/Sort****. Enter* ***Last Name*** *in the 1st Field Text Box and* ***First Name*** *in the 2nd Field Text Box.*
2. *Use the* ***File/Save As*** *command to save the file using the name* ***CLIENTAZ.***
3. *Use* ***File/Close*** *to close the current file and* ***File/Open Existing File*** *to reopen* ***CLIENZIP.***

Printing

There are three options available to you, should you wish to print the information in your database: the first one permits you to print information from FORM View, the second one allows you to print a list of information, and the third one permits you to print fairly intricate reports. We'll look at the first two options here and discuss creating reports in Chapter 7 on the advanced database.

To print a form:

1. Display FORM View.
2. Be sure that your printer is turned on, is on-line, and has paper properly aligned in it.
3. Select **Print/Print.**

The Print Dialog Box is displayed (Figure 4.18). It contains more options than in the other tools. In addition to the typical options to print only specific pages or to print to a file, the following options may be used:

Page breaks between records: This option is turned on when the Dialog Box first appears. However, if you want to print many records, it may be preferable to turn this option off. If you do so, it is necessary to specify how much space Works should leave between records.

Print which records: Prints either the current record only or all records in the database. To print a blank form, move the cursor to a blank record before opening the Print Menu and then select *Current record only.*

Print which items: Prints either the field contents, field names and labels, or prints the field contents only.

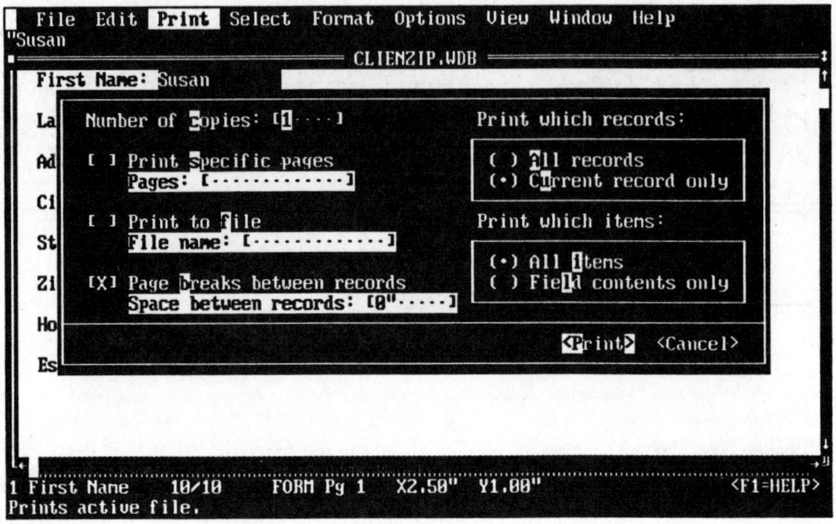

Figure 4.18. Print Dialog Box accessed from FORM View

4. Select the options that you want to use and press **ENTER**.

It is also very easy to print a listing of the database using the default settings.

1. Display your database using LIST View.
2. Select **Print/Print.**

The Print Dialog Box will appear (Figure 4.19).

3. Press **ENTER** and see what happens.

As many fields as will fit across the page and still leave the default margins appear on the first page. Additional fields are printed on succeeding pages.

Changing Margins for Printing

If the entire database is only slightly too wide to fit on one page, you can increase the space available by changing the print margins as you did with the spreadsheet, or by decreasing the width of the fields. Let's try using both of these strategies to fit more of the database on the page. Before changing field widths, save your database again so that you can return to the original field

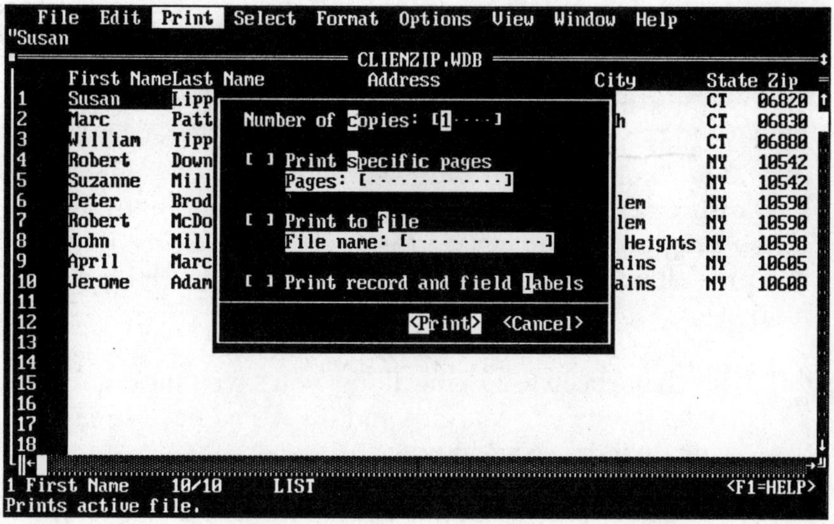

Figure 4.19. Print Dialog Box accessed from LIST View

widths by retrieving the old database rather than changing the field widths back.

1. Select **File/Save As** to save the database using a new name.
2. If you made your fields wide enough for either the longest entry or the longest field name, the widths of the First Name and State fields are bigger than necessary. Use the **Format/Field Width** command to change the width of the First Name field to **8** and the width of the State field to **3**.
3. Select **Print/Page Setup & Margins**.
4. Enter the value **.2** in the *Left Margin* and the *Right Margin* Text Boxes.
5. Select **Print/Print** and press **ENTER**.

The name and address now fit on the first page of the printout. Often this is the best that you can do. However, sometimes you only need to print some of the fields from a database. This can be done by hiding the unnecessary fields.

Note

The procedure for hiding the fields is very simple. However, redisplaying them can be a tedious procedure. Therefore, it is highly recommended that you save the database immediately before hiding the fields, and then open the original database.

Hiding Fields in List View

You might remember that earlier you changed the width of some of the fields in LIST View by using **Format/Width**. Permissible field widths range from **0** to **79** characters. If you set the width at **0** while in LIST View, the field disappears from the screen but the information from the field remains in the program's memory and is visible in FORM View. To demonstrate this procedure, let's print the current database with the Home Phone field hidden.

1. If you have been following along, you saved the database in the section on Changing Print Margins and there's no need to save it again. If you didn't do it then, save it now.
2. To hide the Home Phone field:
   a. Move the cursor anywhere in the Home Phone field.
   b. Use the **Format/Width** command to set the field width to **0**.

Can you see the cursor on the screen? It's still in the hidden Home Phone field so it's not visible.

   c. To redisplay the cursor, press the **RIGHT** or **LEFT ARROW**. The cursor should reappear in the next field.

Note

Hidden fields function differently than hidden records. Hidden records do not appear in either FORM View or LIST View and are not affected by any actions taken while they are hidden. Hidden fields sometimes appear and sometimes don't depending on the particular action. For example, they remain hidden when you print the database, but are copied if you copy the bordering fields to a new file.

3. Now that the field is hidden, print the database again. If you have forgotten how to do this, look back at the section on printing.

The printout should now be only one page unless you are using a large font size.

Reopening the Current File

There are two ways to redisplay the hidden file. The easiest, particularly when changes have been made to a number of fields, is to open the file as you saved it immediately before changing field widths.

1. Select **File/Open Existing File**.
2. Move the cursor to the Files List Box and select the current file, **CLIENZIP.WDB**.
3. A message will appear warning that if you open the file you will lose any changes made since the file was last saved (Figure 4.20). Since this is exactly what you want to do, press **ENTER** to open the file.

CLIENZIP.WDB will appear as it was when last saved.

Redisplaying Hidden Fields in LIST View

Reopening a file is a useful way to return a file to its state at the time it was last saved. However, what should you do if you forgot to save the file before hiding fields, or if you accidentally saved the condensed list without changing the filename, and you want to redisplay the hidden fields? The field will be redisplayed once it has a field width greater than zero. The apparent difficulty with this is that the cursor must be in a field before the field width can be changed. Let's see how this is done.

1. Hide the Home Phone field again.
2. Select **Select/Go To**. The Go To Dialog Box with a list of the names of all

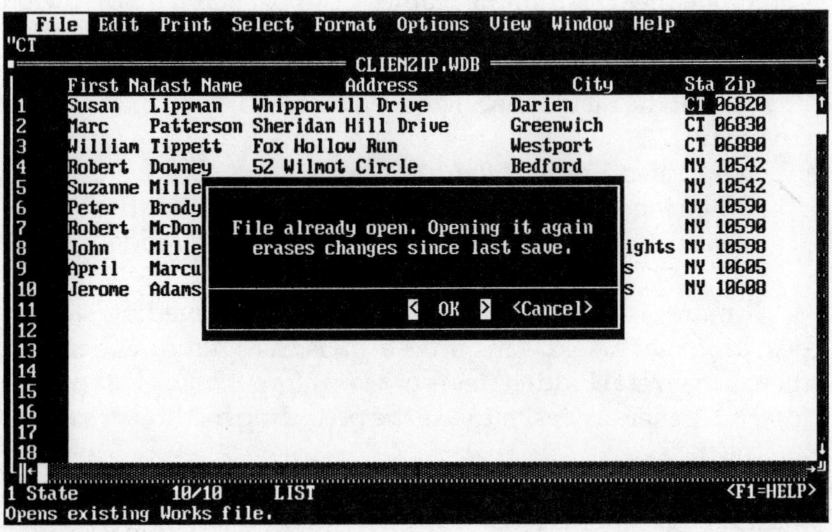

Figure 4.20. Reopening the active file—A warning

of the fields in the database appears (Figure 4.21). This is a Dialog Box that we haven't seen before, but the methods of making selections within it are the same as with any other Dialog Box in Works.

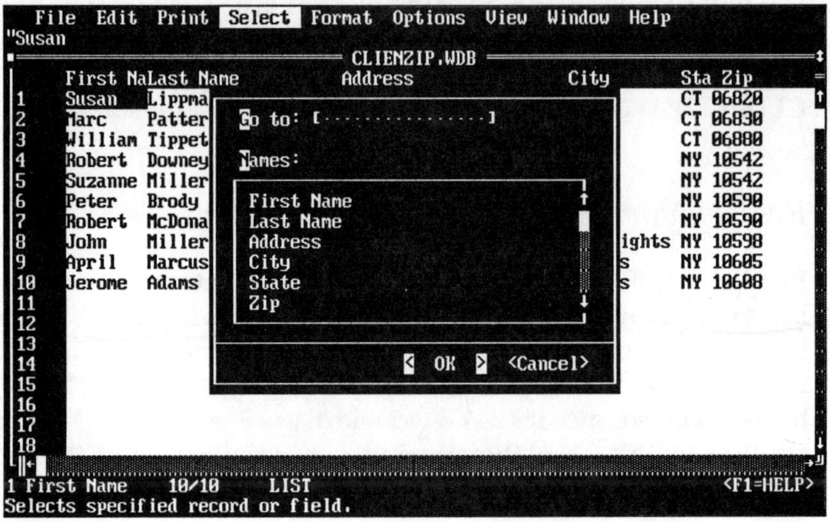

Figure 4.21. Go To Dialog Box

3. Move the cursor to the Names List Box. Scroll down the box to display the name of the hidden field, Home Phone.
4. Press **ENTER**. Nothing appears to have happened. However, if you look at the Status Line, *Home Phone* is indicated as the current field (Figure 4.22).
5. Now select **Format/Field Width**.
6. When the Width Dialog Box appears, enter a width of **14**, which was the width of the Home Phone field before it was hidden.

If more than one field were hidden, the preceding steps would be repeated for each field. This procedure is easy, but can be time consuming if there are several hidden fields or if you forget how wide a field was. Therefore, it is generally easier to use the preceding method of saving and reopening the file.

If you've worked through this chapter, you should be comfortable performing basic database tasks—creating a database, entering, editing, searching for and sorting data, and printing the database. You've even learned some tricks, such as hiding fields so that they won't be printed.

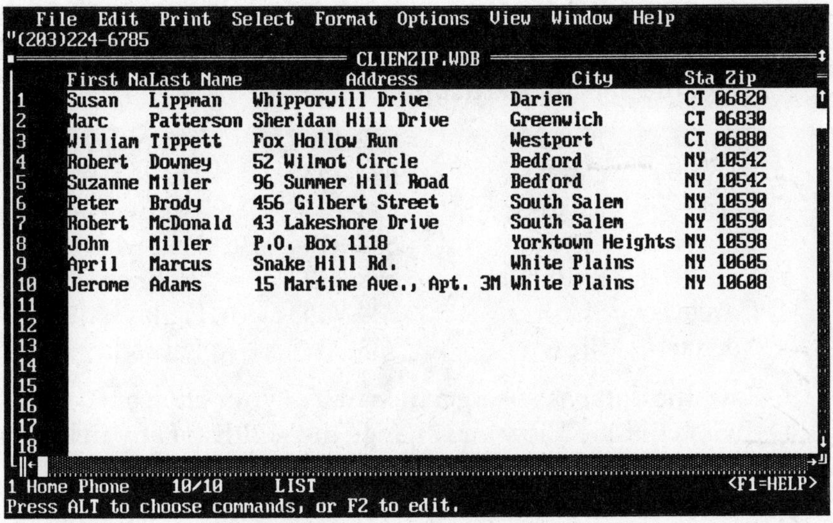

Figure 4.22. Status Line can locate the hidden cursor

Practice these tasks by creating a database of your own. When you feel comfortable with the basics, Chapter 7 on additional database commands will help you make finer selections of data by using the Query commands. Reporting, which allows you to add comments and summary calculations to your database printouts, will also be covered as well as some of the other options that display more of the power of the Works database.

Exercise

As you have seen earlier in this chapter, the essence of using a database is to set up the proper fields, enter the data, and be able to search for the needed data. This exercise will permit you to set up the necessary fields, change the field widths when necessary, and search and retrieve the information you desire.

In this exercise you want to set up a small database for your music school so that you can give individual instructors a list of their students, the students' home phone numbers, and the day of the lesson.

1. Create a database with fields for the students first and last names, their telephone number, day of instruction, and the instructor's name. In this chapter, field names were entered one after another in a list. Since Works allows you to enter them anywhere on the FORM, place them in

a different arrangement. For example, you might want to put the first and last names on the same line.

2. Enter the data for the database:

Sue	Hutchinson	632-1768	Thursday	Smith
Bob	Cohn	681-7432	Thursday	Zash
Paul	Keating	234-7645	Wednesday	Smith
Robert	Cohn	682-9134	Friday	Zash
Phil	Humber	576-3482	Wednesday	Zash
Daniel	Shapiro	234-7693	Friday	Emberley
Michael	Brown	763-2387	Thursday	Emberley

3. Save the database using a filename of your choice.
4. Switch to LIST View and change the widths of any fields that are not at least one space wider than the widest item in that field.
5. Save your database again and print out a copy.
6. Search for all of the students who are taking lessons on Thursday, one record at a time.
7. Now select all of the records for the instructor named Zash. Print out the list.
8. Sort the database by instructor and print it once again.

5

A Second Look at the Word Processor

In Chapter 2 we discussed basic document preparation skills—entering, editing, saving, printing, and retrieving documents. We also explored the power of word processing by learning some advanced editing commands involving selecting blocks of text and moving and copying. Here we will learn how to enhance and customize the appearance of documents by:

- Centering and right justifying text
- Bolding, underlining, and italicizing text
- Applying multiple enhancements to text
- Removing enhancements from text
- Changing tab settings and line spacing
- Searching for and replacing text
- Forcing text to start on a new page
- Adding headers and footers

The appearance of the text in your word processor documents can be altered by using the Format Menu commands. Text can be displayed using bold, underlining, or italic, or with a superimposed strikethrough character (dashed line). In addition, individual characters or groups of characters can be printed as superscripts or subscripts.

The Format Menu options also allow you to center, justify, or right or left align a paragraph. Works defines a paragraph as text of any length followed by a paragraph mark. Each time you press **ENTER**, a paragraph mark is inserted in the text.

When the format is changed without first selecting existing text, all new text will appear in the new format. Previously typed text can be reformatted by selecting the text and then using the Format Menu to change the format.

The letter in Figure 5.1 shows the enhancements that you will be applying to the text. Each section of this chapter will give you instructions for entering the letter and enhancing the text.

The method you use for applying enhancements or formats to text dif-

==================================

August 21, 1989

Dear Mr. Humphrey,

Enclosed is a listing of our Personal Computer Workshops. For further information, please call 323-4343.

CLASS LIST
FOR 1989

Workshop	Program Used	Dates	Cost
Integrated	*Works*	3/1,3/2	$150.00
Word Processing	*Word*	3/11,3/12	$200.00
Spreadsheet	*Excel*	4/6,4/7	$200.00
Database - 1	*Paradox*	5/1,5/2	$200.00
Database - 2	*dBase III+*	6/1,6/2	$200.00

==================================

Figure 5.1. Enhancements made to the completed document

fers when you are enhancing existing text or selecting the enhancement before you enter the text. Also the method is different for paragraph formats and text formats. Special formats for paragraphs and for blocks of text can be selected from the Format Menu. In addition, Works has supplied *shortcut keys* that are key combinations which correspond to most formats on the Format Menu.

Paragraph Formats

Paragraph formats affect the entire paragraph containing the cursor. A paragraph is defined as any text ending in a paragraph mark. Some of the paragraph formats you can use are:

- Center justification: Select **Format/Center** or use the **CTRL-C** shortcut key to center a paragraph between the left and right margin
- Right alignment: Select **Format/Right** or use the **CTRL-R** shortcut key to align a paragraph on the right margin
- Justified: Select **Format/Justified** or use the **CTRL-J** shortcut key to align text with both the left and right margins; this produces a straight, rather than ragged, right margin
- Double space: Select **Format/Double Space** or use the **CTRL-2** shortcut key to double space the text
- Normal Paragraph: Select **Format/Normal Paragraph** or use the **CTRL-X** shortcut key to reset the justification to the left margin and reset spacing to single spacing

The general procedure for applying a paragraph format to an existing paragraph is:

- Move the cursor anywhere on the paragraph to be formatted
- Press a shortcut key OR select the format of your choice from the Format Menu

The general procedure for selecting a paragraph format before you enter the paragraph is:

- Press a shortcut key OR select the format of your choice from the Format Menu

- Type the paragraph
- Reset the paragraph format to normal by selecting **Format/Normal Paragraph** or pressing **CTRL-X**

Right Aligning Text

Many documents have text that is aligned on the right margin. This is known as right alignment. In this letter you will enter a date and right align it. Right Aligning text is a **paragraph** format.

1. Create a new word processor file.
2. Select **Format**. The menu shown in Figure 5.2 is displayed.

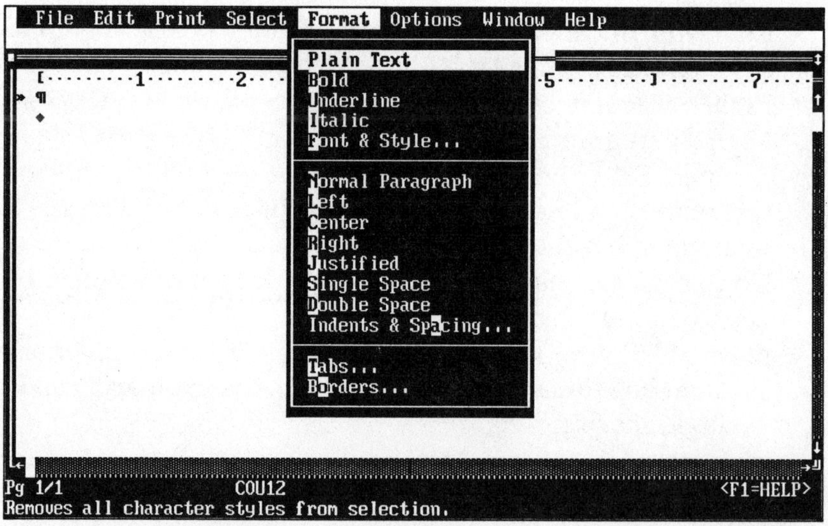

Figure 5.2. Format Menu

3. Select **Right**.
4. Enter today's date on the first line.
5. Press **ENTER**. Any text you enter will be right justified until you specify otherwise. On the Format Menu there is an option, **Normal Paragraph**, which turns the right justification off.
6. Select **Format/Normal Paragraph.**
7. Leave a blank line and then enter the paragraph shown in Figure 5.3.

```
===========================================
Dear Mr. Humphrey,

    Enclosed is a listing of our Personal Computer
Workshops. For further information, please call 323-4343.
===========================================
```

Figure 5.3. First paragraph of the document

Centering Text

Centering is another paragraph format, so the steps are similar to those you used to right align the date line.

1. Enter a blank line after the paragraph.
2. Select **Format/Center**.
3. Enter the line: **CLASS LIST**
4. Press **ENTER**.
5. As with the Right Align Option, centering must be turned off. Select **Format/Normal Paragraph.**

Center the line **FOR 1989** on the line directly below *CLASS LIST* and leave a blank line after it.

Position the cursor on the blank line following CLASS LIST. Follow steps 2–6 in the Centering Text section, typing: ***FOR 1989*** *in step 3.*

Tab Settings

Each new word processor file has default tab settings at 0.5-inch intervals. In Chapter 2 we used the default tabs. However, we can set the tab stops at the exact positions desired. To enter the list of classes, programs used, and the dates the classes meet, let's change the tab settings to the column positions of our choice. In addition, we can change the alignment of the tab. Setting new tabs will not affect any text above the cursor. The possible tab alignment settings are:

- Left: Text begins at the tab; this is the default setting
- Right: The cursor moves to the tab; all text is entered to the left of the tab
- Decimal: Text is aligned so that the decimal point is at the tab position; if no decimal point is typed, it works the same way as a right tab
- Center: Text is centered around the tab position
- Leaders: A leader is a character, such as a period, which will be printed between the last character typed before pressing **TAB** and the tab stop; for example:

  Word wrap.......56

The general procedure for establishing new tab settings is:

- Select **Format/Tabs**
- Type the new position of the tab
- If the tab is not a left tab, the alignment should be changed to Center, Right, or Decimal
- If a leader character is desired, select the character.

Now let's look at the default tab settings:

1. If it has not been selected already, select **Options/Show All Characters** so that you will be able to see the tab characters once they are used.
2. Press the **TAB** key several times. Arrows will appear indicating tab stops at 0.5 inch intervals.

Note Under the default settings, 0.5 inches equals five spaces or characters because 1 inch is assumed to equal ten characters. The reason the default unit for all settings is in inches is because the number of characters per inch changes as you change fonts. By setting tabs and margins in inches, the spacing will remain consistent regardless of the font used.

3. Press **BACKSPACE** to erase all of the TAB marks.

Setting Tab Stops

Now let's set a left tab at 2.5 inches, and a center tab at 5 inches:

1. Select **Format/Tabs**. The TABS Dialog Box will appear (Figure 5.4). The cursor should be in the **Position** Text Box.
2. Type: **2.5**
3. Press **ENTER**. Since the **<Insert>** button is the active (highlighted) button, pressing **ENTER** sets the tab.

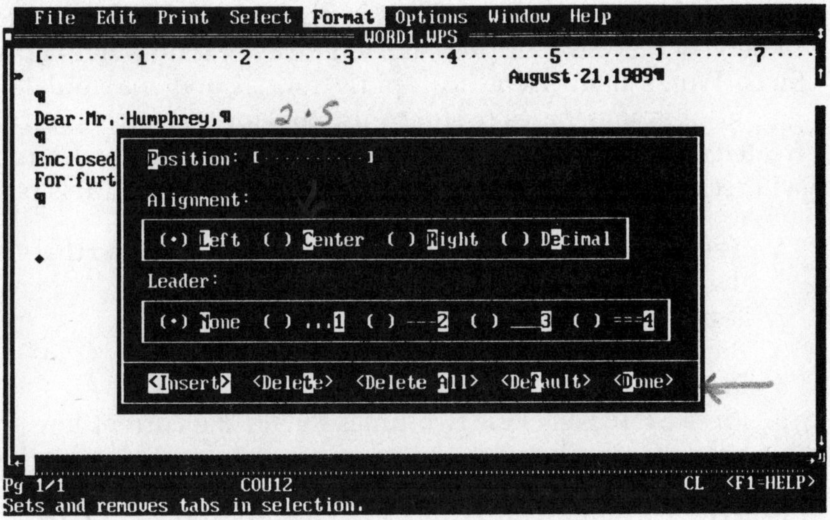

Figure 5.4. Tabs Dialog Box

An *L* (for left tab) now will appear on the ruler between the 2 and 3 markers.

[.........1.........2....L....3.........4.........5.........]

4. To set a Center Tab at 5 inches:
   a. Type: **5** and DO NOT press **ENTER**.
   b. Set the Alignment to **Center**.
   c. Press **ENTER**. A C appears in place of the **5** marker.
5. When you have completed setting new tabs you must signify this by selecting **<DONE>**.
6. Press **TAB**. The cursor moves directly to the new tab setting.

Note

Whenever a tab is set, all of the default settings to the left of the new setting disappear. Therefore, although tabs were set at 0.5, 1.0, 1.5, and 2.0 by default, they were removed when a new tab was set at 2.5 inches. If you were going to type any new paragraph requiring a tab at 0.5, it would be necessary to reset the tab.

Using the SHIFT-ENTER Keys

Now you're ready to enter the information for the chart. At the end of each line of the chart rather than pressing **ENTER**, press the **SHIFT-ENTER** key combination. The **SHIFT-ENTER** key combination affects wordwrap in the same way that **ENTER** does alone; however, it does not end a paragraph. Since Works allows you to rapidly format and manipulate entire paragraphs, it is sometimes useful to use this for text such as tables which are treated as one unit. If **Options/Show All Characters** has been activated, you will see a down arrow inserted each time **SHIFT-ENTER** is pressed.

1. Be sure that all tab characters have been deleted and that the cursor is at the left margin.
2. Type: **Workshop** at the left margin.
3. Press **TAB** and type: **Program Used**
4. Press **TAB** again and type: **Dates**
5. Press **SHIFT-ENTER** two times to end the current line and leave one blank line, without beginning a new paragraph.
6. Use tabs to type the remaining three lines of the table (Figure 5.5). Press **SHIFT-ENTER** at the end of the first three lines. At the end of the last line, press **ENTER** to end the table and paragraph.

=======================================

Integrated	Works	3/1-3/2
Word Processing	Word	4/11-4/12
Spreadsheet	Excel	6/6-6/7

=======================================

Figure 5.5. First three lines of table

Changing Existing Tab Stops

Suppose that after creating the table, you decide that you want to add a column. To do this, you need to move the Dates column so that there is enough room for the new column. To avoid having extra tab stops, you should clear the old tab position after adding the new tab.

1. Use the **File/Save** command to save your file. Use the filename **CLASS.WPS**.
2. Move the cursor anywhere in the table.
3. Select **Format/Tab**.
4. Create a **Center** tab at **4.5** inches.

5. To delete the **Center** tab that exists at **5** inches:
   a. Enter the position of the tab to be removed: **5**
   b. Select the **<Delete>** button by pressing **ALT-T** or tab to the **<Delete>** button and press **ENTER**.
6. Now add a new tab setting with the following attributes:
   Position: **6**
   Alignment: **Decimal**

Note Instead of typing the **TAB** position, use the **CTRL-LEFT ARROW** or **CTRL-RIGHT ARROW** keys to move the cursor to the desired location. The cursor moves along the ruler at the top of the screen.

7. Leave the Tabs Dialog Box by selecting **<Done>**.
8. Be sure that **Options/Show All Characters** has been activated. It is difficult to position the cursor correctly to add the new column unless you can see the characters indicating the current end of line.
9. Position the cursor at the end of the heading line of the table (under the down arrow code). Press the **TAB** and type: **Cost**

Note If the cursor is to the right of the down arrow code rather than under it, the tab will be entered on the line below the one it should be.

10. Press **DOWN ARROW** twice to move to the next line of text.
11. Add the costs to the last column of the table (Figure 5.6). Be sure your cursor is under the down arrow code when you **TAB**. When you have finished, the table will resemble Figure 5.6.

Bolding, Underlining, and Italicizing Text

Bolding, underlining, and italicizing are all options on the Format Menu. The procedure for applying these enhancements to text is slightly

Workshop	Program Used	Dates	Cost
Integrated	Works	3/1-3/2	**$150.00**
Word Processing	Word	4/11-4/12	**$200.00**
Spreadsheet	Excel	6/6-6/7	**$200.00**

Figure 5.6. Table with a new column

different than those you used to right justify text. These enhancements can be done to any length of text—a character, a word, or several paragraphs.

The general procedure for applying a format to an **existing block of text** is:

- Move the cursor to the beginning of the text you wish to enhance
- Press **F8**
- Extend the highlight to cover the entire text you wish to enhance
- Press a shortcut key OR select the format of your choice from the Format Menu
- The highlight will remain on the selected text but will disappear once you move the cursor

The general procedure for selecting a format **before you enter the text**:

- Press a shortcut key OR select the format of your choice from the Format Menu
- Type the text
- Reset the format to plain text by selecting **Format/Plain Text** or pressing **CTRL-SPACEBAR**

Note What follows is a list of additional shortcut keys for text enhancement. Further shortcut keys can be found on the third page of the Keyboard/WP section of the HELP Index.

CTRL-B	Bold
CTRL-U	Underline
CTRL-I	Italic
CTRL-SPACEBAR	Plain text

To bold the class titles *Integrated, Word Processing,* and *Spreadsheet*:

1. Place the cursor on the *I* of *Integrated*.
2. Press **F8**.
3. Extend the highlight to the end of the word.
4. Select **Format/Bold** or press **CTRL-B**. The highlight remains on the text; it will be removed as soon as you press an **ARROW** key.
5. Press **DOWN ARROW** to move to the next line to be enhanced.

Bold *Word Processing* and *Spreadsheet.*

See steps 1–4 in the preceding list for specific keystrokes for carrying out this task.

When your cursor is on a character that has been bolded, a capital *B* will appear on the Status Line. On most monitors, the text will also appear bold or in a different color than the rest of the text. On some screens, listing the **Options/Works Settings** command to change the *Screen Mode* to *Graphics* will cause bold, italics, and underlining to be displayed.

To underline the column labels *Workshop, Program Used,* and *Dates*:

1. Place the cursor on the *W* of *Workshop.*
2. Press **F8**.
3. Extend the highlight to the end of the word.
4. Select **Format/Underline** or press **CTRL-U**. The highlight remains on the text; it will be removed as soon as you press an **ARROW** key.
5. Press **RIGHT ARROW** to move to the next line to be enhanced.

Underline *Program Used* and *Dates.*

See steps 1–4 in the preceding list for specific keystrokes for carrying out this task.

When your cursor is on a character that has been underlined, a capital *U* will appear on the Status Line.

To italicize the programs *Works, Word,* and *Excel*:

1. Place the cursor on the *W* of *Works.*
2. Press **F8**.
3. Extend the highlight to the end of the word.
4. Select **Format/Italic** or press **CTRL-I**. The highlight remains on the text; it will be removed as soon as you press an **ARROW** key.
5. Press **DOWN ARROW** to move to the next line to be enhanced.

Italicize *Word* and *Excel.*

See steps 1–4 in the preceeding list for specific keystrokes for carrying out this task.

When your cursor is on a character that has been italicized, a capital *I* will appear on the Status Line.

Note

Not all printers support italics. Some printers do not support italics or only support italics if certain fonts are selected. If your printer copy does not show italics, first be sure that you have correctly selected italics by checking that the Status Line displays an *I* when the cursor is under the italicized letters. Then read your printer documentation to check that italics is supported or to see which font prints italics. If italics is only supported by certain fonts, highlight the entire document, select **Format/Font and Style**, and change the selected font to one that prints italics.

1. Enter the two new lines shown in Figure 5.7 to your table .
2. Use the shortcut keys to bold and italicize the appropriate parts of the Class Listings as shown in Figure 5.7.
   a. Bold the new Workshop names *Database -1* and *Database -2.*
   b. Italicize the Program names *Paradox* and *dBase III+.*
3. Underline the heading *Cost.*
4. Save the letter, using the filename **CLASS.WPS.**
5. Print the letter.

1. *Move the cursor to the beginning of the line following the description of the spreadsheet program. Type the information shown in Figure 5.7 using* ***TAB*** *to move from column to column. Use* ***SHIFT-ENTER*** *at the end of the first line and* ***ENTER*** *at the end of the second line.*
2. *(a) Highlight* Database-1 *and select* ***Format/Bold*** *or press* ***CTRL-B.*** *(b) Use similar procedures to bold and italicize the remaining items.*

=================================

Database - 1	*Paradox*	5/1-5/2	$200.00
Database - 2	*dBase III+*	6/1-6/2	$200.00

=================================

Figure 5.7. Lines to be added to the table

3. *Highlight* Cost *and select* ***Format/Underline*** *or press* ***CTRL-U****.*
4. *Select* ***File/Save*** *and save the file using the existing filename* ***CLASS.WPS****.*
5. *Use the* ***Print/Print*** *command to print the letter.*

Note If the underlined and bold words do not print correctly, check your document to be sure that the letter has been correctly formatted. If problems still occur, select **Print/Select Text Printer** to be sure that the correct printer has been selected.

Applying Multiple Enhancements to Text

So far we have only enhanced text with one characteristic. It is possible to apply more than one enhancement to the same text, however. After selecting one enhancement for a block of highlighted text, the highlight does not disappear. This enables you to simply select another enhancement to the same highlighted text.

Enhance the text *Personal Computer Workshops* with bold and underline.

1. Move the cursor to the *P* of *Personal*.
2. Press **F8**.
3. Extend the highlight to cover the entire phrase *Personal Computer Workshops*.
4. Bold the text by either selecting **Format/Bold** or using the shortcut key **CTRL-B**.
5. Underline the text by either selecting **Format/Underline** or using the shortcut key **CTRL-U**.
6. The text will now be bold and underlined. The highlight still remains on the text; to remove the highlight press an **ARROW** key.

Removing Enhancements from Text

If you have enhanced a block of text and decide you would like the text to appear in plain format, you must highlight the text and select **Format/Plain Text**.

To remove the italics from each of the items in the *Program Used* column:

1. Move the cursor to the *W* of *Works*.
2. Press **F8**.
3. Highlight the entire word.
4. Select **Format/Plain Text**.
5. Use an **ARROW** key to remove the highlight.

Remove the italics from *Word, Excel, Paradox,* and *dBase III+*.

Repeat steps 1–5 in the preceding list.

Changing the Line Spacing

Suppose after looking at your letter, you decide that it would look better if the opening paragraph were double spaced instead of single spaced. The **Format/Double Space** option can be used to change this.

1. Move the cursor anywhere in the first paragraph.
2. Select **Format/Double Space**.

Note To change the format of multiple paragraphs to double spaced, use the **F8** and **ARROW** keys to select the portion of the document to be changed and then select **Format/Double**. As with the tab setting commands, if the line spacing is changed before entering text, the newly entered text will be entered double spaced. Triple or fractional line spacings can be entered using the **Format/Indent and Spacing** command. **TAB** to the Line Spacing Text Box and type a number corresponding to the desired line spacing.

Searching for and Replacing Text

When you only need to replace a few characters in a document, it is easy to delete the unwanted text and replace it with the desired text. However, if you are replacing the same text in several places in one document, it will be easiest to have Works find each occurrence of the text and then replace the unwanted text with new text. To do this you use the **Select/Replace** option.

The **Select/Replace** option will only start searching through the text from the point of the cursor. This means, if the cursor is on page 2 of a document when you initiate **Select/Replace,** page 1 will not be included in the search. To replace the dashes (-) that are in the dates column of the table with commas (,):

1. Move the cursor to the beginning of the document.
2. Select **Select/Replace.** The Dialog Box shown in Figure 5.8 is displayed.
3. In the Search for Text Box, type a dash (-).
4. Press **TAB** to bring the cursor to the Replace with Text Box.
5. Type a comma (,).
6. You can select either the **<Replace>** or the **<Replace All>** button. The **<Replace>** button will allow you to selectively replace the dashes with commas. The **<Replace All>** button changes every occurrence of a dash with a comma. Select **<Replace.>**
7. The cursor moves to the first dash it finds and a prompt is displayed:

   Replace this occurrence?

If you wish to replace this particular dash with a comma, respond **<YES>**. If not, respond **<NO>**, and the next dash will be located. If you started at the beginning of the document, the first dash is found in the phone number. Since you only want to replace dashes in dates, select **<NO>**.

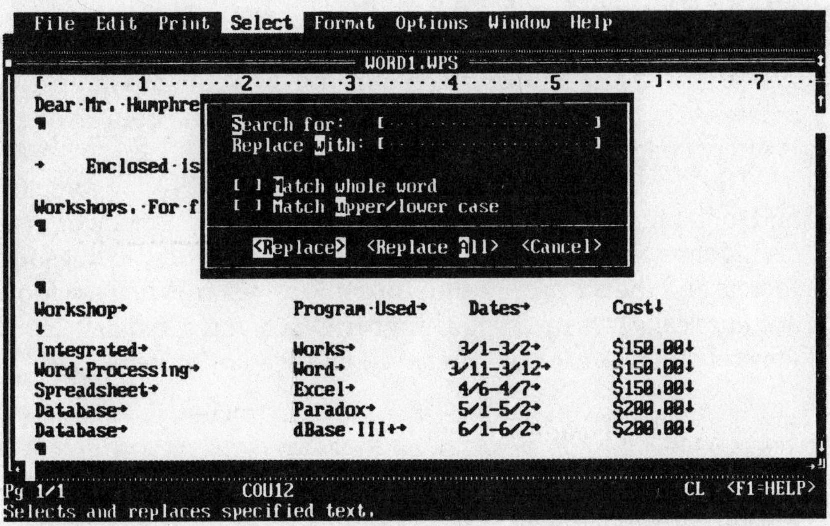

Figure 5.8. Search and Replace Dialog Box

8. Since the next dash will be found in the dates column of your table, select <**YES**>.
9. Continue responding to the prompt until the message *No more occurrences* is displayed. Press **ENTER**.

Starting Text on a New Page

There are times when you want a certain part of your document to start on a new page, even if there is room for more text on the current page. A code called a *page break* can be inserted at any point of your document. The page break will instruct Works to start the following text on a new page.

To start the class listing on a new page:

1. Move the cursor to the blank line above the line that reads *CLASS LIST.*
2. Hold down the **CTRL** key and press **ENTER**. A dotted line signifying the start of a new page is shown on the screen. The Status Line will now reflect that you are on page 2.
3. Move the cursor to the last paragraph mark on the first page.
4. Enter a blank line.
5. Sign the letter by pressing **TAB** six times and typing: **Gerry Hoffberg**

Adding a Header and a Footer

A header is a line of text which will appear at the top of every page, such as a date. A footer is a line of text that appears on the bottom of every page and is often a page number.

The **Print/Headers & Footers** Menu (Figure 5.9) allows you to create header and footer lines on the document. There are two methods of inserting headers and footers. One method allows you to enter multiple lines for headers and footers and the other only allots one line for each. When the footer is created it automatically sets up a page number which you can delete if you choose. The general procedure for entering a one line header/footer is:

- Select **Print/Headers & Footers.**
- Type the text for the header in the Header Text Box
- Type the text for the footer in the Footer Text Box
- Press **ENTER**

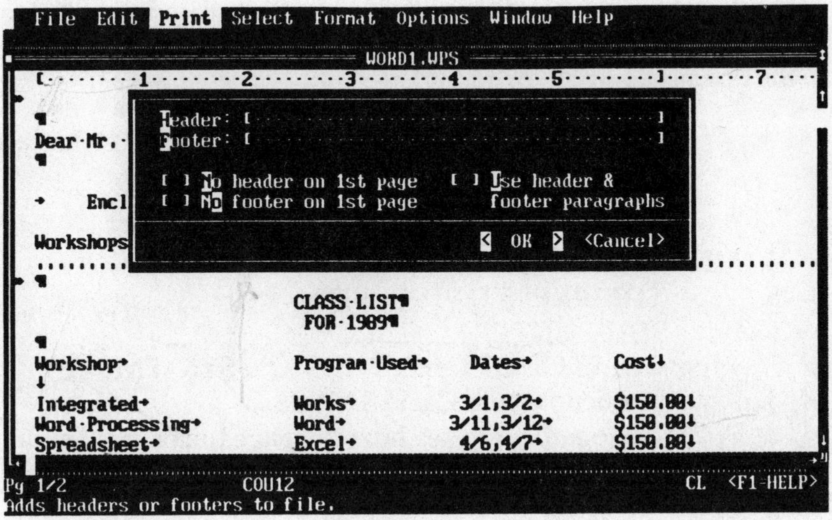

Figure 5.9. Header and Footer Dialog Box

This method will not display the headers and footers on the screen; you can see them if you Preview the document however.

The general procedure for entering multiple line headers/footers is:

- Select **Print/Headers & Footers**
- Select the Use header & footer paragraphs Check Box
- Press **ENTER**
- Two lines will appear at the top of the document. One is preceded by an *H* for Header and the other by an *F* for footer. The footer will already have the text necessary for printing the page number

Move the cursor to the header line and type the text you choose for the first line of your header. Rather than pressing **ENTER** to start the second line, press **SHIFT-ENTER** and then type the text for the second line. Follow the same procedure for the footer.

To add a multiline header and footer to your document:

1. Select **Print/Headers & Footers.** Do not type the text you want as a header or footer in the text box on the Header & Footer Menu.
2. Mark the Use header & footer paragraphs Check Box by tabbing to the box and pressing **SPACEBAR.**
3. Press **ENTER** to select **<OK>**.

On the top two lines of the document a line preceded by a capital *H* (standing for header), and a line preceded by a capital *F* (standing for footer) and the text necessary to print a page number will appear:

H
F *Page - *page**

4. Move the cursor to the header line.
5. Type: **TOMPKINS UNIVERSITY**
6. Press **SHIFT-ENTER.**
7. Type: **COLLEGE OF INFORMATION SYSTEMS**
8. Save the document as **CLASS2.WPS.**
9. Print the document to see how the page break and headers and footers work.

If you want to explore changing the alignment of the header and footer, you can use the Help Menus. To get help, choose **Print/Header & Footer**. Press **F1**, Help. Move your cursor to the **<Page Down>** button and press **ENTER**. On the second page of the Help Menu, there is a table outlining the characters required to change alignments.

This second look at the Word Processor has provided you with some advanced skills to customize the appearance of your documents. Enhancing the appearance of the text encompassed such things as bolding, underlining, and italicizing, as well as changing tab stops and adding headers and footers.

Works is a powerful package that has many advanced features. They are applied using procedures similar to those used in these exercises. Once you become comfortable with the word processing features introduced in this book, browse the menus to see what other features might be useful in your work. To help with this we've included a list of some of the advanced features that you may want to explore and the menu commands used to initiate them. To find out more about how to use these features, move the cursor to the commands mentioned in the instructions and press the **F1** key to access Help. With the aid of the instructions on these screens and the associated tutorials, you should be able to continue mastering the power of Works.

Bookmarks: Works can insert a hidden marker called a bookmark into your document by using the **Edit/Bookmark Name** option. Bookmarks can help you move quickly around your document. For example, if there are several sections in a long document that you may want to find quickly, you can place a bookmark at the beginning of each section. You can use the **Select/Go To** command to display all bookmarks for a document; select the one of your choice and go directly to that section.

Borders: Borders are lines which you can place around a paragraph to add emphasis by using the **Format/Borders** option. You can add lines on the top, bottom, left, and right of any paragraph. The lines can be single, double, or bold lines.

Footnotes: A footnote is text which supplies further information about some particular text on the page. By selecting the **Edit/Footnote** option, a footnote reference mark is placed at the point of the cursor. A portion of the screen will become available for you to enter text for the footnote. Although called footnotes, all of these references will appear at the end of the document, rather than the bottom of each page.

Fonts: The **Format/Font & Style** option can be used to print part or all of the document in any of the different fonts available on your printer.

Indenting a paragraph: An indent is the distance between the margin and the beginning of each line in a paragraph. The indent can be set through the **Format/Indents & Spacing** command.

Changing margins: Through the option **Print/Page Setup & Margins** you can set the top, bottom, left, and right margins.

Inserting special characters: Through the **Edit/Insert Special Characters** option you can have codes such as the current system date and time inserted into your document.

Thesaurus: Works provides you with a thesaurus as well as a spell checker. Place the cursor on the word for which you want to find a synonym and select **Options/Thesaurus**; Works will provide you with a list of synonyms from which to choose.

Preview: Works provides you with a way to see the entire page of a document without having to print the page. Through the command **Print/Preview,** Works displays a full page representation of the page your cursor currently is on.

GO TO: The GO TO command will move the cursor to a selected position. You can move to a bookmark or to a page number by selecting **Select/Go to.**

Exercise

1. Type the cover letter shown in Figure 5.10 using the following formats:
   a. Right justify the date.
   b. Bold the address lines.
   c. Underline *Computer Analyst.*
   d. Double space the paragraph.
2. Insert a page break after the closing of the letter.
3. Enter the list shown in Figure 5.11 with the following formats:
   a. Change the tab settings to two left tabs at positions 2 and 4.
   b. Center the top line.

Today's Date

Ms. Alice Kijak
Computer's Digest
1 Maplemore Ave.
Chappaqua, NY 10606

Dear Ms. Kijak,

I have found several individuals that should fit the requirements for the position of <u>Computer Analyst</u> that you are trying to fill. The resumes of each will be following shortly. My fee will be 10% of the annual salary of anyone you hire that I have referred to you.

Ms. Kate Purdy
Head Recruiter
Purdy Personnel Agency

Figure 5.10. Cover letter

==

Candidates for Position of Computer Analyst

<u>Name</u>	<u>Yrs. of Experience</u>	<u>Earliest Start Date</u>
Jim Carlson	5 1/2 years	ASAP
Elma Dickson	5 3/4 years	2 Weeks from offer
Vicky Rock	6 years	2 Weeks from offer
Danuta Cisek	6 1/2 years	ASAP
Neil Hauptman	7 years	3 Weeks from offer
Steve Shumway	8 years	1 month from offer
Arthur Paletta	8 years	1 month from offer

==

Figure 5.11. Second page of advanced word processing exercise

c. Underline the column headings: *Name*, *Yrs. of Experience*, and *Earliest Start Date*.

d. Search and replace all occurrences of *years* in the list with **yrs.**

e. Add a header with *Purdy Personnel Agency* and a footer with a page number.

4. Save and print the document.

6

Spreadsheets: A Closer Look

In Chapter 3, we explored the basics of spreadsheeting. In this chapter, we discuss more advanced spreadsheet concepts. Specifically, you will learn how to:

- Use advanced functions such as **MIN** and **MAX**, **AVG**, **PMT**, and **NOW**
- Create and modify a chart based on the data in a spreadsheet
- Create and copy formulas using absolute and relative addressing
- Modify existing spreadsheets by inserting columns and rows
- Hide columns so that nonadjacent parts of the spreadsheet can be printed
- Create charts from your spreadsheet data
- Modify charts

The Spreadsheet Tool

Our second look at the spreadsheet tool will focus on expanding your ability to use one of the most powerful features of Works—formulas. You'll learn to create formulas which remain constant when they are copied. You will also practice using some new functions. In addition, we'll introduce the Works charting capabilities which enable you to graph your spreadsheet data.

Relative and Absolute Copying

When you created spreadsheets in Chapter 3, you learned to copy a formula from one cell to other cells. Works automatically adjusted the cell addresses in the formula so that the relationship between the cell containing the formula and the cells making up the formula remained constant. This automatic procedure is referred to as *relative cell adjustment*. Sometimes, however, you do not want the cell addresses to adjust. You can stop a cell address from adjusting when you copy the formula containing it to another cell location by making the reference to the cell address *absolute* when you create the formula. An absolute cell address reference is indicated by dollar signs preceding the row and column names (e.g., *$A$1*).

You are going to revise the budget which you created in Chapter 3, the spreadsheet chapter. Currently, the spreadsheet contains the budget and actual figures for three months and totals for the first quarter. The budget and actual totals for the first quarter are very close, but you want to see if the percentage of the total spent in each category is the same for the budget and actual figures. This can be done by creating new formulas including absolute cell addresses and seeing what happens when you copy these formulas. You will also rearrange the spreadsheet to make room for the new formulas and then graph the results.

First get the worksheet ready for the new formulas.

1. Open **BUDGET1.WKS.** (**Note**: If you have not created this spreadsheet, follow the instructions in Chapter 3, the spreadsheet chapter.)
2. Move the cursor anywhere in column F.

Inserting Columns

To insert a blank column between columns E and F so that you can place the percentages for the first quarter actual figures immediately to the right of the totals:

3. Choose **Select/Column**.

Note

Select/Column is used instead of **F8** and the **ARROW** keys because you must select the entire column and this would be too tedious using **F8** and the **ARROW** keys. (Notice the range selected on the bottom left of Figure 6.1 *F1:F4096*). If only part of a column is selected, the **Insert** command which you will use next, cannot be selected from the **Edit** Menu. If cells from more than one column have been highlighted, **Select/Column** selects the columns containing each of the highlighted cells.

4. Select **Edit/Insert Row/Column**. One column will be inserted moving the data which were in the F column to the G column.

Hint

Some hints for using the **Edit/Insert Row/Column** command are:

- The **Edit/Insert Row/Column** command can be used to insert rows or columns immediately left or above the highlighted row(s)/column(s)
- In the preceding task, the **Edit/Insert Row/Column** command inserted one column because you had only highlighted one column; if you want to insert two rows/columns, you must first select two rows/columns by using **F8**, and so on.

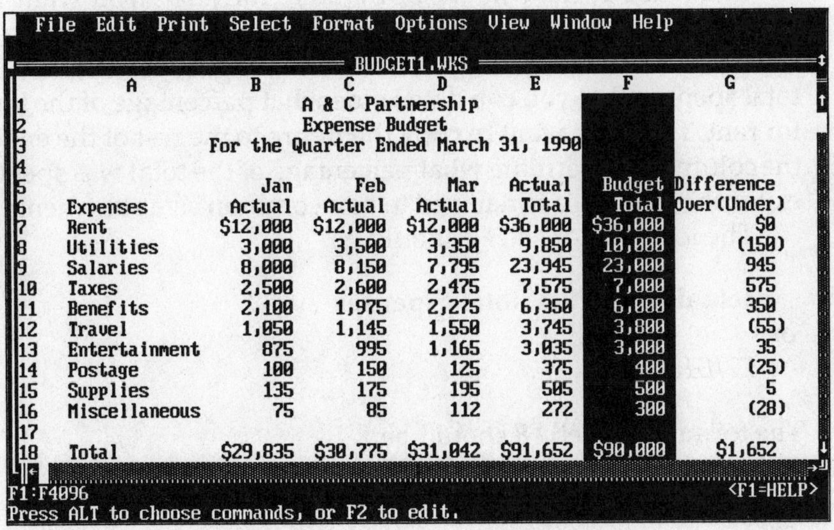

File Edit Print Select Format Options View Window Help

BUDGET1.WKS

	A	B	C	D	E	F	G
1			A & C Partnership				
2			Expense Budget				
3		For the Quarter Ended March 31, 1990					
4							
5		Jan	Feb	Mar	Actual	Budget	Difference
6	Expenses	Actual	Actual	Actual	Total	Total	Over(Under)
7	Rent	$12,000	$12,000	$12,000	$36,000	$36,000	$0
8	Utilities	3,000	3,500	3,350	9,850	10,000	(150)
9	Salaries	8,000	8,150	7,795	23,945	23,000	945
10	Taxes	2,500	2,600	2,475	7,575	7,000	575
11	Benefits	2,100	1,975	2,275	6,350	6,000	350
12	Travel	1,050	1,145	1,550	3,745	3,800	(55)
13	Entertainment	875	995	1,165	3,035	3,000	35
14	Postage	100	150	125	375	400	(25)
15	Supplies	135	175	195	505	500	5
16	Miscellaneous	75	85	112	272	300	(28)
17							
18	Total	$29,835	$30,775	$31,042	$91,652	$90,000	$1,652

F1:F4096 <F1=HELP>

Press ALT to choose commands, or F2 to edit.

Figure 6.1. Selecting a column

Note — **Edit/Insert Row/Column** inserts a row/column the entire width/length of the spreadsheet. This can cause damage if there are data in a part of the spreadsheet which is not visible on the screen and which should **not** have a row/column inserted into it.

Creating Absolute Cell Address References

Before creating the new formulas using absolute cell referencing, examine the formulas already in the spreadsheet.

1. Move the cursor to the cell containing the total January Actual figures (cell *B18*). Look at the formula in the Formula Bar. It should read:

   =SUM(B7:B16) or
   =B7+B8+B9+B10+B11+B12+B13+B14+B15+B16

2. When you created the spreadsheet you entered the formula in cell *B18* and copied it across the row. Move the cursor across row 18 and look at each formula. Each formula adds the cells above it. Therefore, the contents of the formula have been adjusted to reflect the column being added.

Think about the content of the new formulas you want to create. Do NOT enter the formulas on the spreadsheet yet. You want to create a formula in cell *F7* that will divide the actual figure for the rent by the actual total spent so that you can determine what percentage of the total was spent for rent. Then you want to copy the figure to the rest of the expense items in the column to determine what percentage of the total was spent on the other expense items. This is referred to as a common size statement.

The formula for cell *F7* should be:

actual rent/actual total expenses

or

E7/E18

The formula for cell *F8* should be:

actual utilities/actual total expenses

or

E8/E18

Notice that the cell address used in the first part of the formula, the expense category, should be different for each formula, but in each case the cell address of the divisor remains the same—cell *E18*. Therefore, when you create the formula for the rent percentage, you must tell Works that the divisor must remain constant or **absolute**. To do this you will use the **Reference** or **F4** key when creating the formula. The directions that follow will demonstrate how this works.

1. Move the cursor to cell *F7*.
2. Start the formula by typing: =
3. Move the cursor to cell *E7* and then type a / (slash) to indicate division.

The cursor will return to cell *F7*.

4. Move the cursor to cell *E18*. The Formula Bar should read: =*E7/E18*
5. Press the **F4** function key *one* time and watch how the formula changes. It should now read:

   =*E7/$E$18*

The **$** preceding the column and row names indicates that both the column and the row will remain absolute when the formula is copied.

Note **F4** is a toggle key. If it is pressed one time, dollar signs are inserted before the row and column designations (*$E$18*). If it is pressed multiple times, the $ may precede only part of the cell address (*$E18* or *E$18*) or disappear completely. Continued key presses repeat the cycle. Therefore, it is important to check that the dollar sign precedes both the row and column. If it does not, continue pressing **F4** until it does.

Note When the $ precedes only part of the cell address, the formula is part absolute and part relative. When mixed formulas are copied, the relative part adjusts while the absolute part remains the same.

6. Press **ENTER**. Your screen now should resemble Figure 6.2.

Note Cell address references can also be made absolute by typing the **$** before the column and row names.

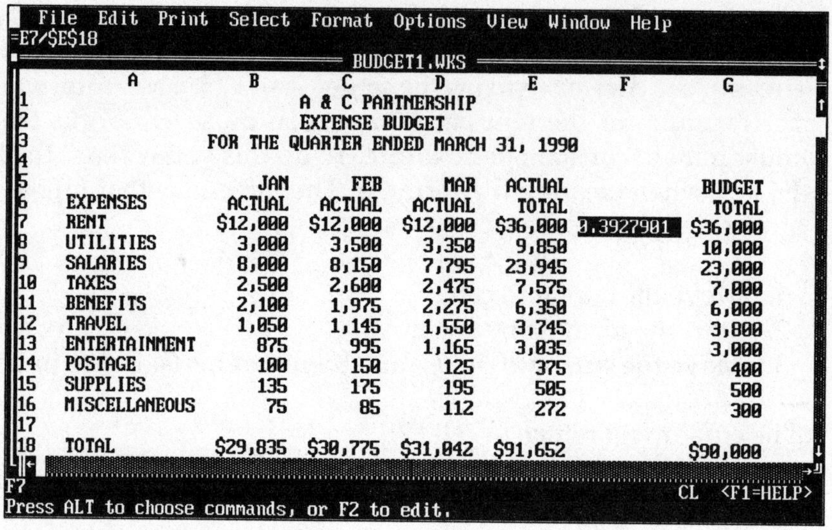

Figure 6.2. Formula using absolute addressing

Now you can use the **Edit/Fill Down** command to copy the formula to the rest of the column:

7. Highlight cells *F7* to *F18* by using the **F8** key.
8. Select **Edit/Fill Down**.
9. Move the cursor to each of the cells into which the formula was copied and watch the Formula Bar. Notice that the first cell address in the formula adjusts while the absolute portion of the formula does not change (Figure 6.3).

You want to create a similar formula for the 1st Quarter Budget figures in column G.

1. Follow the procedure in the preceding list to create a formula to determine the percentage of the budgeted expenditures spent on rent. Create this formula in cell *H7*. Remember you need to insert a column prior to creating the formula.
2. Copy the formula to cells *H8–H18* (Figure 6.4).

---

1. *Place the cursor in the H Column.*
2. *Choose **Select/Column.***
3. *Choose **Edit/Insert.***
4. *Place the cursor in **H7**.*

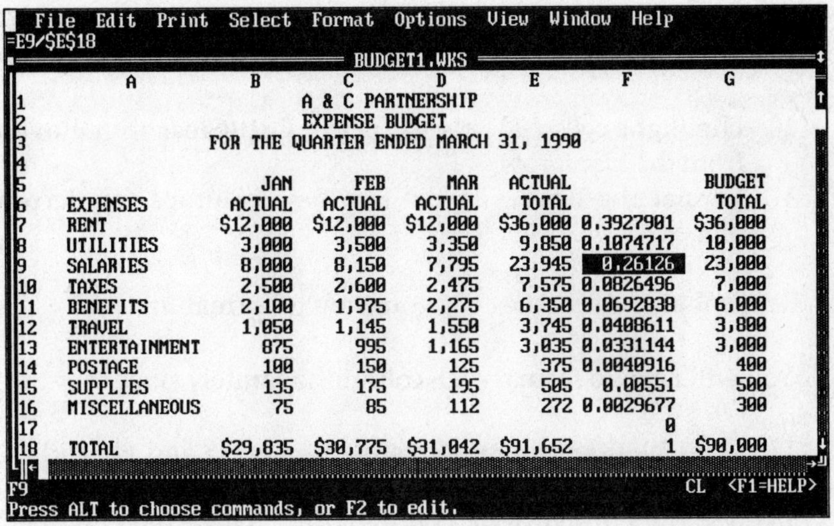

File Edit Print Select Format Options View Window Help
=E9/$E$18
BUDGET1.WKS

	A	B	C	D	E	F	G
1			A & C PARTNERSHIP				
2			EXPENSE BUDGET				
3		FOR THE QUARTER ENDED MARCH 31, 1990					
4							
5		JAN	FEB	MAR	ACTUAL		BUDGET
6	EXPENSES	ACTUAL	ACTUAL	ACTUAL	TOTAL		TOTAL
7	RENT	$12,000	$12,000	$12,000	$36,000	0.3927901	$36,000
8	UTILITIES	3,000	3,500	3,350	9,850	0.1074717	10,000
9	SALARIES	8,000	8,150	7,795	23,945	0.26126	23,000
10	TAXES	2,500	2,600	2,475	7,575	0.0826496	7,000
11	BENEFITS	2,100	1,975	2,275	6,350	0.0692838	6,000
12	TRAVEL	1,050	1,145	1,550	3,745	0.0408611	3,800
13	ENTERTAINMENT	875	995	1,165	3,035	0.0331144	3,000
14	POSTAGE	100	150	125	375	0.0040916	400
15	SUPPLIES	135	175	195	505	0.00551	500
16	MISCELLANEOUS	75	85	112	272	0.0029677	300
17						0	
18	TOTAL	$29,835	$30,775	$31,042	$91,652	1	$90,000

F9 CL <F1=HELP>
Press ALT to choose commands, or F2 to edit.

Figure 6.3. Column with absolute and relative formulas

5. *Type the formula =**G7/G18** but **DO NOT** press **ENTER***
6. *Press **F4** to make **G18, $G$18***
7. *Press **ENTER***
8. *Select **F8** and highlight **H7 to H18***
9. *Choose **Edit/Fill Down***

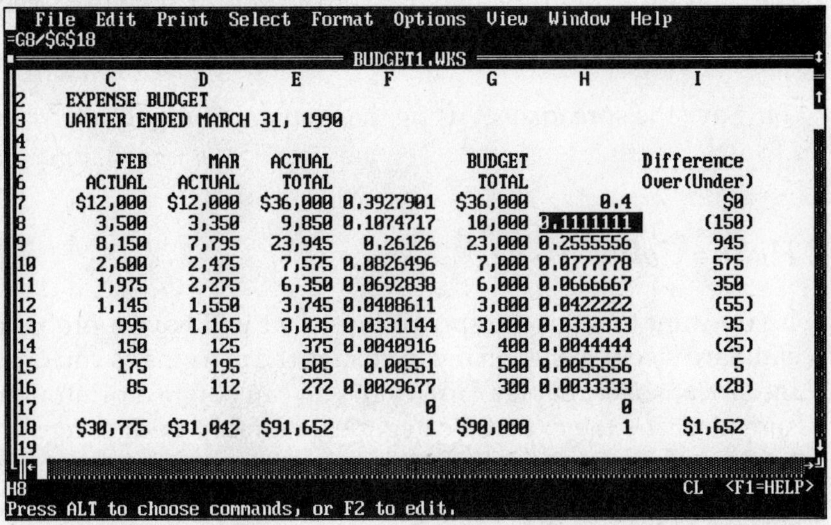

File Edit Print Select Format Options View Window Help
=G8/$G$18
BUDGET1.WKS

	C	D	E	F	G	H	I
2	EXPENSE BUDGET						
3	UARTER ENDED MARCH 31, 1990						
4							
5	FEB	MAR	ACTUAL		BUDGET		Difference
6	ACTUAL	ACTUAL	TOTAL		TOTAL		Over(Under)
7	$12,000	$12,000	$36,000	0.3927901	$36,000	0.4	$0
8	3,500	3,350	9,850	0.1074717	10,000	0.1111111	(150)
9	8,150	7,795	23,945	0.26126	23,000	0.2555556	945
10	2,600	2,475	7,575	0.0826496	7,000	0.0777778	575
11	1,975	2,275	6,350	0.0692838	6,000	0.0666667	350
12	1,145	1,550	3,745	0.0408611	3,800	0.0422222	(55)
13	995	1,165	3,035	0.0331144	3,000	0.0333333	35
14	150	125	375	0.0040916	400	0.0044444	(25)
15	175	195	505	0.00551	500	0.0055556	5
16	85	112	272	0.0029677	300	0.0033333	(28)
17				0		0	
18	$30,775	$31,042	$91,652	1	$90,000	1	$1,652
19							

H8 CL <F1=HELP>
Press ALT to choose commands, or F2 to edit.

Figure 6.4. Common size statement for columns F and H

The only steps that remain are improving the appearance of the spreadsheet and saving and printing it.

10. Highlight cells *F17* to *H17*. Select **Edit/Clear** to remove the formulas from the blank row.
11. **Format** the figures in the two new columns for **Percent, 2** decimal places.

Hint Remember to select the cells you want to format first.

Note You will need to format each column separately since they are not adjacent.

12. Type the title **Budget Percents** in cells *H5* and *H6* and the title **Actual Percents** in cells *F5* and *F6*.
13. Use the **Format/Style** command to change the alignment for **Budget Percents** and **Actual Percents** to **Right** (Figure 6.5).

Note The titles Budget Percents and Actual Percents do not appear to be right justified when compared to the percentages which appear in the same column. In Works when right justification is selected, a space is left on the far right-hand side of the cell which is filled only if the value includes a percent sign or a right parenthesis (which is used to indicate negative numbers in some formats). If the title is more than one space from the right-hand side of the cell, you probably typed a space at the end of the label. Retype the label without pressing the **SPACEBAR** at the end of the text.

14. Save the spreadsheet using the filename **Budget2.**

Hiding Columns

If you want to print the spreadsheet, you will have a problem fitting it on standard size paper even if you change the margins as you did in Chapter 3, the spreadsheet chapter. However, you can obtain a printout of parts of the spreadsheet—the expense categories, monthly budget figures, 1st quarter totals, and percentages by hiding the columns that you do not want to include. The procedure for doing this is similar to that used in Chapter 4, the database chapter. Be sure that you save the current spreadsheet and then complete the following instructions.

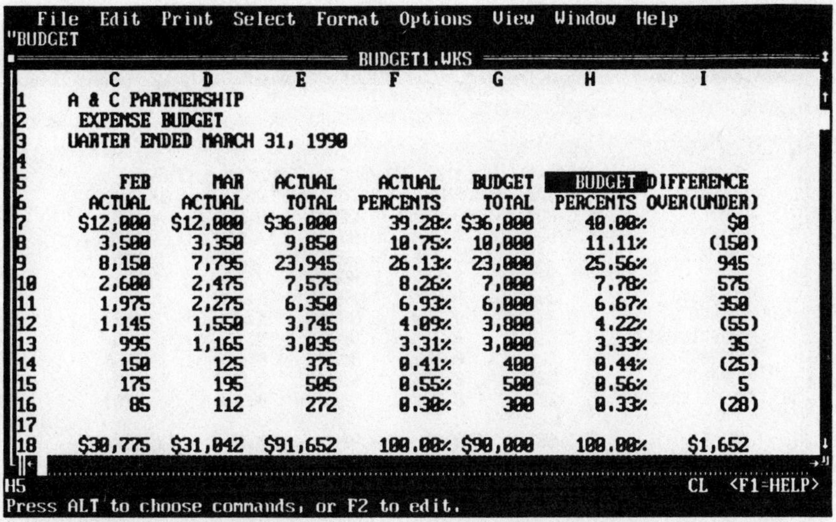

Figure 6.5. Completed spreadsheet with percent columns

1. Highlight one cell each in columns B, C, and D by using **F8** (Figure 6.6).
2. Choose **Format/Column Width**.
3. Type: **0** in the Width Text Box.
4. Press **ENTER**. Columns C, D, and E will no longer be visible on the screen. The cursor will also not be visible since it was in a hidden col-

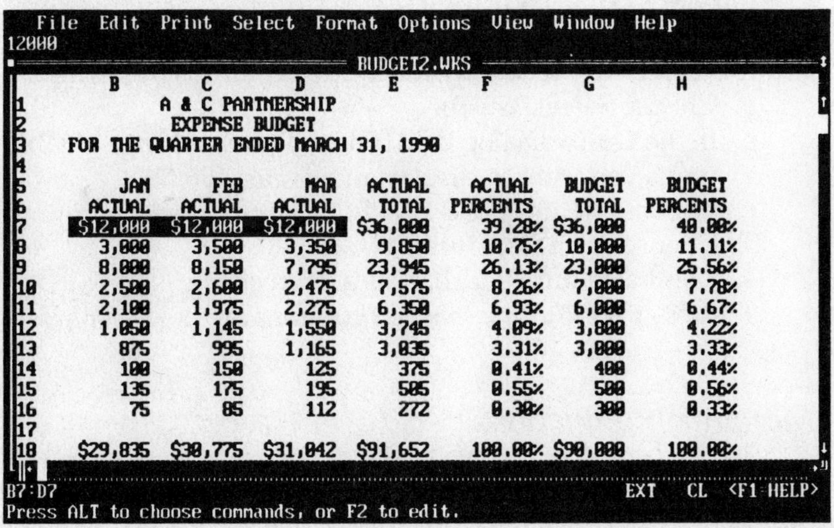

Figure 6.6. Select a cell in the three columns you want to hide

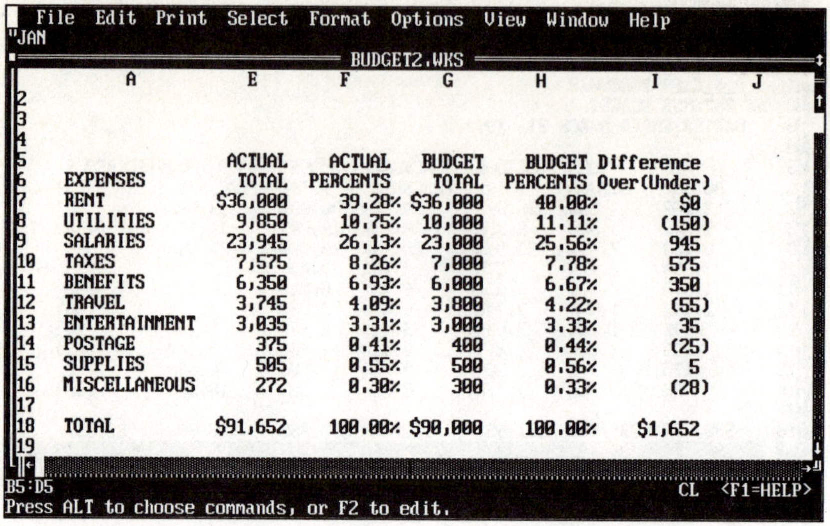
File Edit Print Select Format Options View Window Help
"JAN
BUDGET2.WKS

	A	E	F	G	H	I
2						
3						
4						
5		ACTUAL	ACTUAL	BUDGET	BUDGET	Difference
6	EXPENSES	TOTAL	PERCENTS	TOTAL	PERCENTS	Over(Under)
7	RENT	$36,000	39.28%	$36,000	40.00%	$0
8	UTILITIES	9,850	10.75%	10,000	11.11%	(150)
9	SALARIES	23,945	26.13%	23,000	25.56%	945
10	TAXES	7,575	8.26%	7,000	7.78%	575
11	BENEFITS	6,350	6.93%	6,000	6.67%	350
12	TRAVEL	3,745	4.09%	3,800	4.22%	(55)
13	ENTERTAINMENT	3,035	3.31%	3,000	3.33%	35
14	POSTAGE	375	0.41%	400	0.44%	(25)
15	SUPPLIES	505	0.55%	500	0.56%	5
16	MISCELLANEOUS	272	0.30%	300	0.33%	(28)
17						
18	TOTAL	$91,652	100.00%	$90,000	100.00%	$1,652
19						

B5:D5 CL <F1=HELP>
Press ALT to choose commands, or F2 to edit.

Figure 6.7. Columns B, C, and D are hidden

umn (Figure 6.7). Press the **RIGHT** or **LEFT ARROW** until the cursor is visible.

5. To print the document:
   a. Highlight the cells to be printed, *A3* through *I18*, by using **F8**.
   b. Select **Print/Set Print Area**.
   c. Select **Print/Print**.
6. It is possible to redisplay the hidden columns by doing the following:
   a. Choose **Select /Go To.**
   b. In the **Go To** Dialog Box, type the label or range of labels for the columns you want to display, in this case, *B6:D6*.
   c. Choose OK and press **ENTER.** The columns are now selected.
   d. Choose **Format/Column Width.**
   e. Select a column width; 10 is a good choice.
   f. Press **ENTER**. The selected columns are now displayed.

More About Functions

In Chapter 3, you used the SUM function to total a range of figures. Works provides 57 functions designed to perform statistical, mathematical, financial, logical, date, and special computations which help you to rapidly analyze data. Next, you will learn two more functions: MIN and MAX.

More Functions

In Chapter 3, you created a simple budget and then used formulas to calculate information about the budget. Formulas were used to total expenses for each month and to calculate the quarterly amount and percentage of the total budgeted and actual expenses for each of several categories. Since the Works spreadsheet tool makes calculating so quick, it's easy to manipulate the data to obtain more information. For example, you are going to find the minimum and maximum amounts spent in each category and use them to see what an *austerity* and *high-spender* budget might be like.

Figure 6.8 shows the format of the part of the spreadsheet that contains the new calculations when you have finished the exercise.

Using More of the Spreadsheet

Before finding the minimum and maximum values for each expense category, it is necessary to set up new columns to contain the calculations.

1. Open **BUDGET2.WKS**, if it is not already open.
2. To copy the category titles to a new part of the spreadsheet:
   a. Highlight cells *A6–A18*.

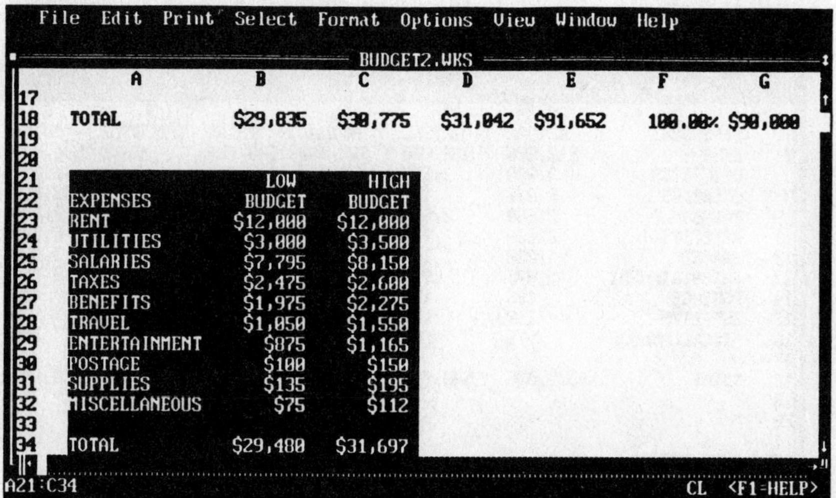

Figure 6.8. Completed spreadsheet using MIN and MAX functions

Note You already know how to select cells by pressing **F8** and then using the **ARROW** keys to **EXTEND** the highlight. An alternative method is to place the cursor in a cell at one end of the range, press **SHIFT** and keep it depressed while using the **ARROW** keys to extend the highlight. The word **EXTEND** does NOT appear on the Message Line when this method is used, but the same result is achieved.

b. Select **Edit/Copy**.
c. Move the cursor to *A22* and press **ENTER**.
d. Move the cursor down the A column until you see that all of the expense categories have been copied to cells *A22* to *A34*.

Your spreadsheet no longer fits vertically on one screen. Therefore, periodically you will need to scroll the screen so that the part of the spreadsheet with the information relevant to the current task will be visible.

3. First you should move the cursor so that rows 6 to 23 are visible on the screen (Figure 6.9).
4. Enter the title **Low Budget** in cells *B21* and *B22* and **High Budget** in cells *C21* and *C22*.

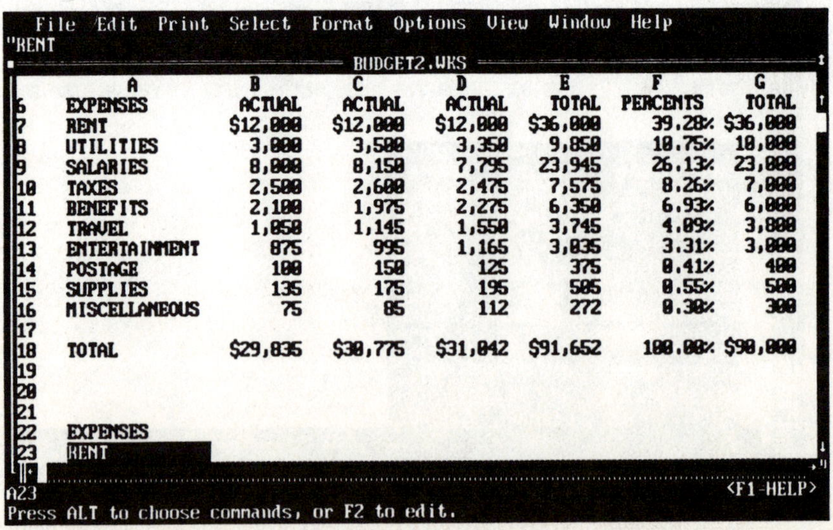

Figure 6.9. Screen display

The MIN, MAX, and SUM Functions and Pointing

In Chapter 3, on the spreadsheet, you entered a function by typing it in the cell. First you had to type = to inform Works that you were entering a formula rather than a label. Then you typed the function, which in Chapter 3 was **SUM**. You typed the range of cells inside parentheses, and you included a colon (:) just like the one that appears in the Message Line whenever a range of cells has been highlighted (i.e., *C9:E9*). The colon is very important in selecting a range, because it anchors the starting point of the highlight in a particular cell. When you enter a function in this spreadsheet, you will type part of it and then use *pointing* to highlight the range on which the function will act. This will enable you to actually see the range and, therefore, it is less likely that you will accidently include the wrong cells.

5. Move the cursor to cell *B23*.
6. Start the function by typing: **=min(**

You want to find the minimum of the Jan., Feb., and Mar. Actual Rent expenditures.

7. Move the cursor to cell *B7*.

The word *POINT* will appear on the Status Line indicating that you are using pointing.

8. Press the : (colon) to anchor the pointer. — Shift + ; Key.

A colon and the current cell, *B7*, will be added to the formula indicating that the selected range so far is cell *B7* .

Once the pointer has been anchored, the cursor key can be moved to highlight a larger range of cells. As discussed in Chapter 3, on the spreadsheet, a range is any rectangular group of cells. The letters *EXT* appear on the Status Line as an indication that Works is waiting for you to extend the highlight and select a range of cells.

9. Use the **RIGHT ARROW** to extend the range to cells *C7* and *D7* (Figure 6.10).
10. Type: **)** to complete the formula entry. press shift +) key.
11. Press **ENTER**. The value 12000 should appear in cell *B23*.

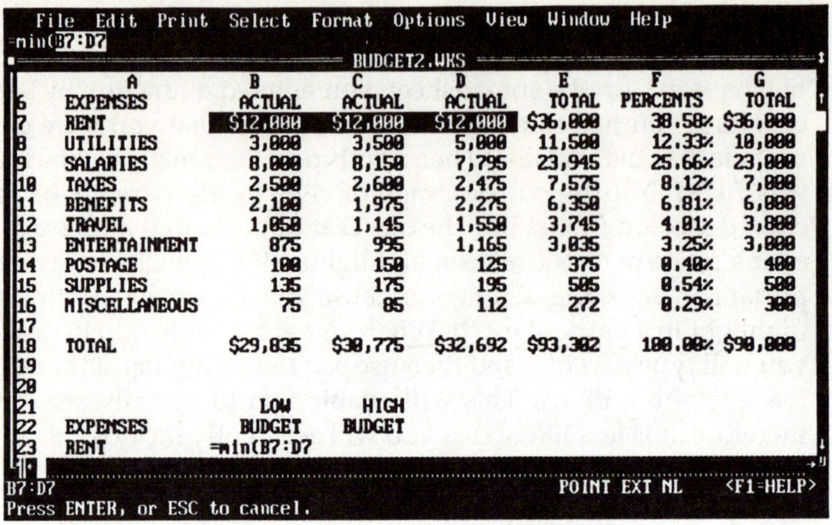

File Edit Print Select Format Options View Window Help
=min(B7:D7

BUDGET2.WKS

	A	B	C	D	E	F	G
6	EXPENSES	ACTUAL	ACTUAL	ACTUAL	TOTAL	PERCENTS	TOTAL
7	RENT	$12,000	$12,000	$12,000	$36,000	38.58%	$36,000
8	UTILITIES	3,000	3,500	5,000	11,500	12.33%	10,000
9	SALARIES	8,000	8,150	7,795	23,945	25.66%	23,000
10	TAXES	2,500	2,600	2,475	7,575	8.12%	7,000
11	BENEFITS	2,100	1,975	2,275	6,350	6.81%	6,000
12	TRAVEL	1,050	1,145	1,550	3,745	4.01%	3,000
13	ENTERTAINMENT	875	995	1,165	3,035	3.25%	3,000
14	POSTAGE	100	150	125	375	0.40%	400
15	SUPPLIES	135	175	195	505	0.54%	500
16	MISCELLANEOUS	75	85	112	272	0.29%	300
17							
18	TOTAL	$29,035	$30,775	$32,692	$93,302	100.00%	$90,000
19							
20							
21		LOW	HIGH				
22	EXPENSES	BUDGET	BUDGET				
23	RENT	=min(B7:D7					

B7:D7 POINT EXT NL <F1=HELP>
Press ENTER, or ESC to cancel.

Figure 6.10. MIN formula for rent

In this case all of the cells in the range contained the same value. If they had not, the lowest value would appear in the cell containing the MIN function. You'll see how this works when you copy the formula to other expense categories.

Beginning in cell C23, use the procedure described above to create a formula for the maximum value contained in the same three cells. The formula should begin: **=MAX(**

- *Move the cursor to cell C23*
- *Type: =MAX(*
- *Point to cell **B7**, press the :, and point the cursor through cell **D7***
- *Close the parentheses,)*
- *Press **ENTER***
- *The high budget result should be $12,000*

To copy the MIN and MAX functions to the remaining expense categories and find the High and Low Budget totals:

12. Highlight the area containing cells *B23* to *C32* (use **F8**).
13. Select **Edit/Fill Down** (Figure 6.11).

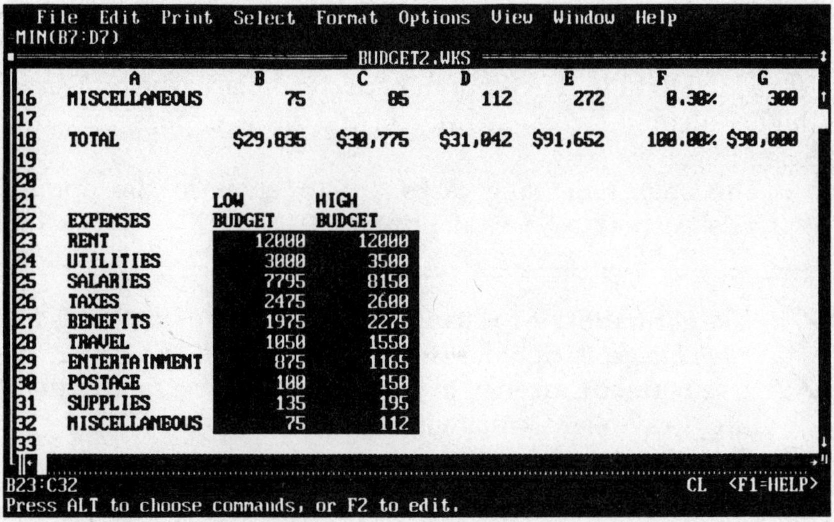

Figure 6.11. MAX and MIN values for the months Jan–Mar

Remember that when part of the screen is highlighted, any command you select will act upon the entire highlighted area. Since two columns were highlighted, the **Edit/Fill Down** command copied the contents of the first cell in each column to the rest of that column. You could have highlighted each column separately, but this is more efficient.

14. Move the cursor into the cells to which you copied the formula. Notice that the formulas have been adjusted.
15. Now, use the **SUM** function and pointing to find the total for the low budget.
    a. Move the cursor to cell *B34*.
    b. Type: **=SUM(**
    c. Move the pointer to cell *B23*.
    d. Type a colon to anchor the pointer.
    e. Use the **DOWN ARROW** to extend the highlight so that it includes the range *B23:B32*.
    f. Type: **)** and press **ENTER**.

Copy the formula from *B34* to *C34*.

- *Use F8 to highlight* ***B34:C34***
- *Choose* ***Edit/Fill Right***

Now you can see how much your monthly budget would be if you always spent the least amount possible. Notice how much lower it is than the lowest actual total in the 3-month period. Similarly the *high-spender* budget is higher than the total in March, the most expensive month for actual spending.

The only remaining tasks are to enhance the appearance of the spreadsheet and to save and print it.

1. Use **Format/Style** to change the alignment of the labels *Low Budget* and *High Budget* to right justified.
2. Use **Format/Currency** to format the expense figures and the total figures to a dollar format with 0 decimals (Figure 6.12).
3. Save the spreadsheet.
4. Print only the new section of the spreadsheet (cells *A21* through *C34*).

1. *Press F8 to highlight* ***B21:C22***
2. *Choose* ***Format/Style/Right.*** *Press* ***ENTER***
3. *Press F8 to highlight* ***B23:C34***

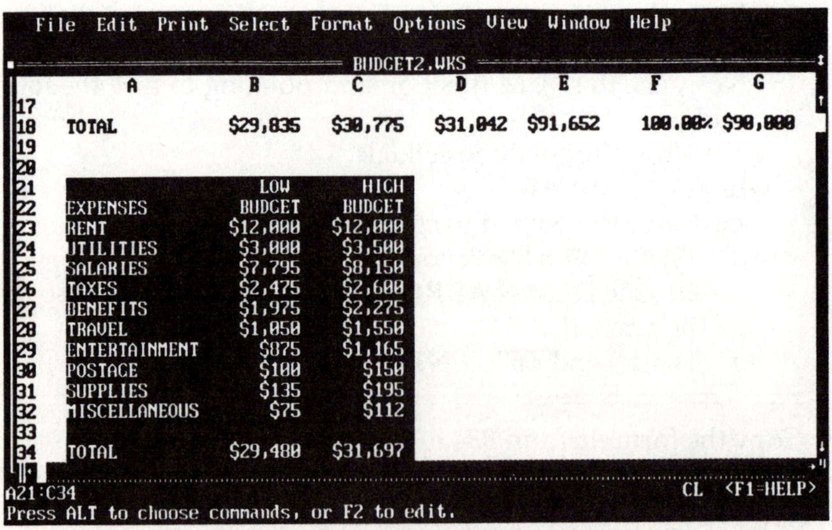

Figure 6.12. Completed maximum and minimum spending budgets

4. *Choose **Format/Currency***
5. *Select **0** decimal places and press **ENTER***
6. *To save the spreadsheet, choose **File/Save***
7. *To print, use **F8** to highlight **A21:C34***
8. *Choose **Print/Set Print Area***
9. *Select **Print/Print;** press **ENTER***

Additional Helpful Works Functions

In addition to the **MAX, MIN,** and **SUM** functions, 54 other functions are available for your use in Works. Although it is unlikely you will use them all, we explore others that might be of use to you while using a spreadsheet.

The **MIN** and **MAX** functions found the high and the low values in a range. **SUM** calculated the total of a range of data. Another useful function is **AVG** which calculates the average of a range of data. An average is calculated by adding up all the entries within a range and dividing by the number of filled cells. Therefore, if there are any blank cells within a range, they are not counted as a filled cell. The formula is written in a spreadsheet in the same format as the **SUM** formula. To use the **AVG** formula in the **BUDGET2.WKS** spreadsheet:

1. Place the heading AVG BUDGET in cells *D21* and *D22*.
2. Move the cursor to *D23*.
3. Start the function by typing: **=avg(**

You want to find the average expenditures for the months of January, February, and March.

4. Move the cursor to *B7*. The word **POINT** will appear on the Status Line indicating that you are using pointing.
5. Press the **:** (colon) to anchor the pointer.
6. Use the **RIGHT ARROW** to extend the range to cells *C7* and *D7*.
7. Type: **)** to complete the formula entry.
8. Press **ENTER**. The value 12000 should appear in cell *D23*. Again, in this case, all the cells contained the value 12000 and therefore the average of the range is 12000.

1. Copy the formula to cells *D24* through *D32*.
2. Use **Edit/Copy** to copy the formula from C34 to *D34*.
3. Format the average column in **Currency** notation with **0** decimal places.
4. Right justify the heading **AVG BUDGET.**

1. *To copy the formula to cells* ***D24*** *through* ***D32:***

- *Place cursor in* ***D23***
- *Press* ***F8*** *to* ***EXTEND*** *the range through* ***D32***
- *Choose* ***Edit/Fill Down***

2. *To copy the sum:*

- *Place the cursor in cell* ***C34***
- *Choose* ***Edit/Copy***
- *Move the cursor to cell* ***D34*** *and press* ***ENTER***

3. *To format the column:*

- *Place the cursor in cell* ***D23***
- *Press* ***F8*** *to* ***ENTEND*** *the range through* ***D34***
- *Choose* ***Format/Currency/0;*** *press* ***ENTER***

4. *To right justify the heading:*

- *Place cursor in* ***D21***
- *Press* ***F8*** *to* ***EXTEND*** *the range through* ***D22***
- *Choose* ***Format/Style/Right.*** *Press* ***ENTER***

Now you can see how much an average monthly budget would be, as well as a high and a low budget (Figure 6.13).

9. Save the spreadsheet as **BUDGET2.**

Two Other Useful Functions

The two functions described here are not useful in the **BUDGET2** spreadsheet, but will be useful at other times. These functions are the **PMT**

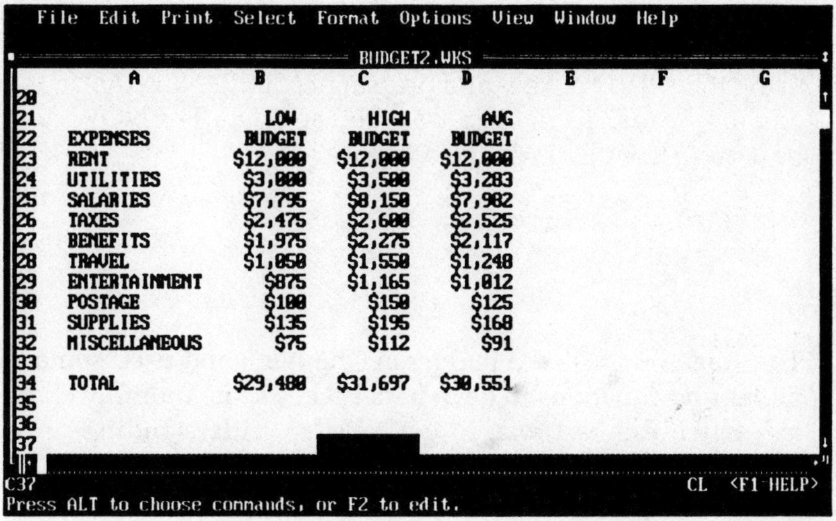

Figure 6.13. Completed **MAX**, **MIN**, and **AVG** budgets

and **NOW** functions. The **PMT** function will calculate periodic loan payments given the amount borrowed, the interest rate, and the period of the loan. Works assumes that payments occur at the end of periods of equal length. The **NOW** function gives the date and time number for the current date and time. It is updated at every recalculation. The integer portion of **NOW( )** is the date number and the decimal fraction is the time number. The **NOW** function can be used to display the actual date and time on a spreadsheet.

We present a quick example of how to use these two functions. In any blank cell within the spreadsheet, you want to calculate the monthly loan payments if you were to purchase a car. You need to borrow $12,000 at a rate of 10% for 3 years. The monthly loan payment would be calculated as follows:

=PMT(12000,10%/12,36)
$387.21

The format of the function is **=PMT(Principal,Rate,Term)**. Remember if you want to calculate monthly payments, the Rate and Term **must** be stated on a monthly basis.

The **NOW** function is useful for placing date and time stamps on your spreadsheet. To use this function, choose a blank cell. In this cell, type **=NOW( )** and press **ENTER**. You will notice that a number appears in the cell. To make this number appear as a date, format it for date notation. To do this, choose **Format/Time-Date.** Select a format you would like to appear by using the **ARROW** keys and pressing **ENTER**. Now the date should appear on the spreadsheet in the format you selected. The **NOW** function will also be used in Chapter 7, on the database.

Charting

Thus far, you created a budget in Chapter 3 and used some additional formulas and functions to get a better feel for the monthly changes in spending. Often the best way to get a better understanding of the patterns in spreadsheet data is by creating a picture—or chart—of the data. Works makes this task easy by creating charts for you. Once the chart is created, you can easily enhance or edit it. More importantly, since the chart is attached to the spreadsheet, changes made to the spreadsheet are instantly reflected in the chart. Some computer setups do not have the ability to display graphics. If the computer you are using cannot display graphics, skip this section on Charting.

You're ready to start creating charts. In this section you will display your first chart. If the chart does not appear on your screen, check to be sure that you selected the correct monitor while installing your program.

Charting Monthly Expenditures

Before you create the chart you should review some basic terminology. *Chart* is another word for graph. In charts, bars, lines, pies, and points on a grid are used to show the relationships within or among sets of data. You will create the bar chart shown in Figure 6.14. This chart has horizontal and vertical axes. The horizontal axis, or *X-axis*, in most bar charts, shows the category classifications of the data being charted. Our X-axis categories are the expense categories—rent, utilities, salaries, and taxes. The vertical axis, or *Y-axis*, is used to measure each of the items being charted. Notice that the chart consists of four clusters of bars, one for each expense category noted on the X-axis. Each cluster of bars contains three bars—one representing each month, January, February, and March. A *legend* at the bottom of the chart indicates which bar represents each series of data. The data for each month are called *Y-series*. Therefore, the values from January form the first

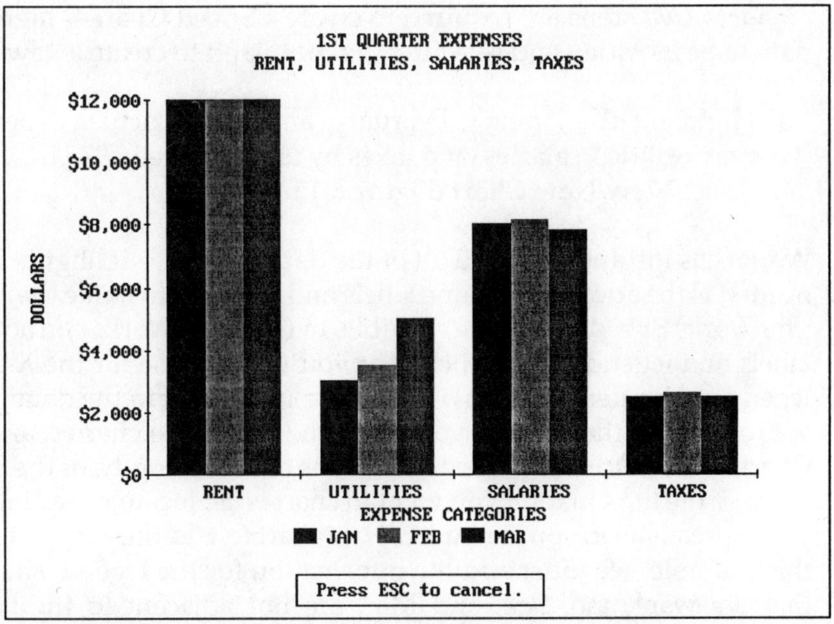

Figure 6.14. Completed Bar Chart

Y-series, February values form the second Y-series, and March values form the third Y-series.

Now let's create the chart. If you are still at the DOS prompt,

1. Load Works.
2. Open **BUDGET2.WKS** which was used earlier in the chapter.

If you did not create **BUDGET2.WKS,** use the instructions in the beginning of Chapter 3 to create it.

Creating a Speed Chart

In Works you may create a chart from scratch by specifying the content of each X- and Y-axis series, or you may highlight a range of your spreadsheet and let Works create a *Speed Chart* from the data in the highlighted range. Depending on the type of data in the selected range, the Speed Chart will contain only the graphed data, or the data plus the X-axis labels and a legend. You will use the Speed Chart to enter the data only on your chart.

Only two steps are required to create a Speed Chart— highlighting the data to be included and selecting the command to create a new chart.

3. Highlight the January, February, and March actual expenditures for rent, utilities, salaries, and taxes by using **F8** (cells *B7:D10)*.
4. Select **View/New Chart** (Figure 6.15).

Works has instantly charted all of the data that you highlighted. All that is needed is the addition of some labels and a legend to make the chart clearer. The Works Speed Chart is so flexible, in fact, that Works can add the X-axis labels and legend. If the labels that you want to use for the X-axis and the legend are located in the row and column adjacent to the data you charted, you can select them when you select the data to be charted and the Speed Chart will include this information. One of the strengths of the Speed Chart is that if the information you want to chart is *not* located in a single range on your spreadsheet, you can modify the chart to add the extra information. In this example, we must add the information for the legend, since the labels that we want, Jan, Feb, and Mar, are not adjacent to the values being graphed. We examine more closely the chart that Works created before you add a legend and labels to make it clearer.

5. Press **ESC** to return to the Chart Screen.

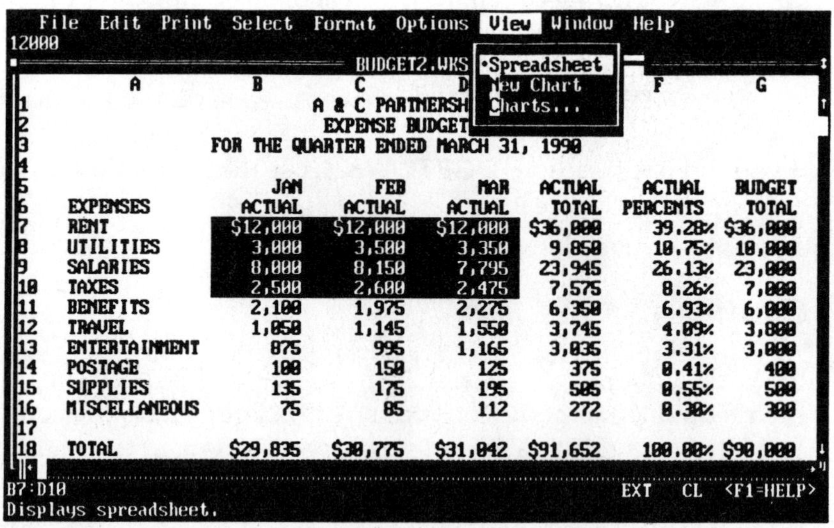

Figure 6.15. Creating a CHART

The Chart Screen should appear. The Work Area of the screen remains the same, but the Menu Bar now contains the commands used to create and use charts. The word *CHART* now appears on the Status Line.

Using Figure 6.15 and the information on your screen you can compare values and see how the information was charted. For example, the first bar on the left is 12,000. This corresponds to the rent expenditure for January. The next two bars correspond to the February and March expenditures for rent. Therefore, you can see that the first cluster contains the values from the first highlighted row—rent, and each highlighted column contributed one bar to the cluster. This indicates that you want to use the row labels (the expense categories) as X-axis categories and the columns as Y-axis categories. We explore how to include this information on our graph.

1. Highlight the four expense category labels in cells *A7:A10*, by using the **F8** key.
2. Select **Data/X-Series.**
3. Select **View/Chart1** or press the shortcut key, **SHIFT-F10,** to view your chart (Figure 6.16).

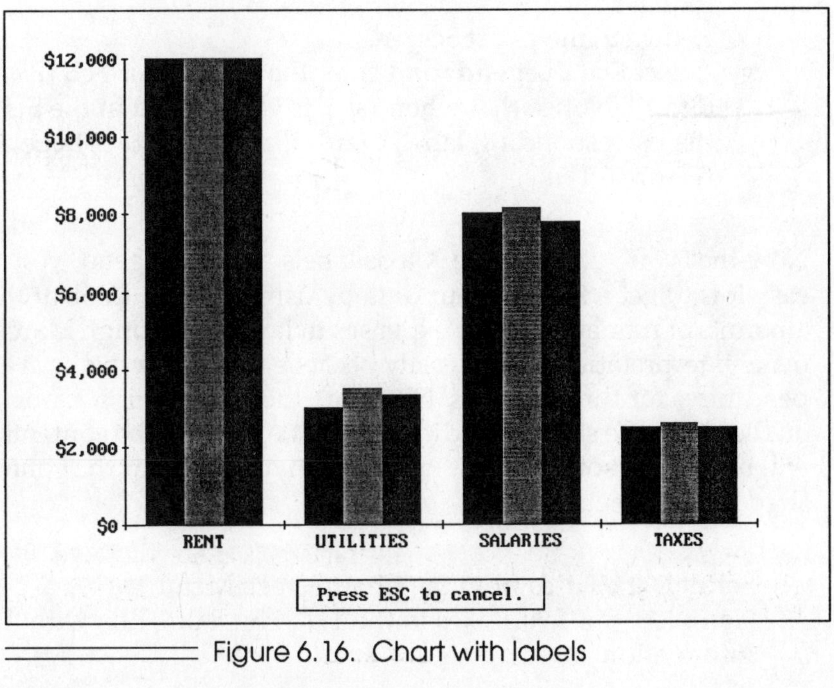

Figure 6.16. Chart with labels

Note If you accidently press just **F10** when you attempt to use the shortcut key combination **SHIFT-F10,** you will exit the Chart Screen and return to the original spreadsheet screen. If you want to get back to the Chart Screen, select **View/Chart 1.**

The highlighted labels have been added to the chart.

Note On some low resolution screens, some of the letters in the longer labels may not be visible. They are still in memory and will be included if the chart is printed out. If you cannot see all of the letters in the labels and your chart currently is displayed in color, select **Options/Format for B&W.** The monochrome screen may have a higher resolution, enabling it to display more of the letters.

4. To create a legend for the chart:
   a. Select **Data/Legends.**
   b. Be sure the **1st Y** listing in the **Series** List Box is highlighted.
   c. Press **Alt-L** or **TAB** to the **Legend** Text Box; type: **Jan**
   d. **TAB** to **<Done>**; press **ENTER** or press **Alt-D** to create the legend.
   e. View the chart. Notice that the legend for *Jan* has now been added to the chart.
   f. Return to the Chart Screen.
   g. Select **Data/Legends** and enter the legends for **Feb** *(2nd Y)* and **Mar** *(3rd Y)*. Notice that when *1st Y* is highlighted in the Series List Box, the corresponding label, **"Jan** appears in the **Legend** Text Box (Figure 6.17).

Now that you've added the X-axis labels and the legend, you can see how easy it is to get a feel for your data by using a chart. Look at the consistent amounts of money spent on expenses in January through March. You could make interpretations fairly easily because you knew this was a chart of expenditures for three months. However, this information is not yet included on the chart. We suggest adding a few titles so that the contents of the chart will be clear to someone not knowing anything about the content of the related spreadsheet.

1. Select **Data/Titles** from the Chart Screen Menu.
2. Complete the Text Boxes in the TITLES Dialog Box with the following information:

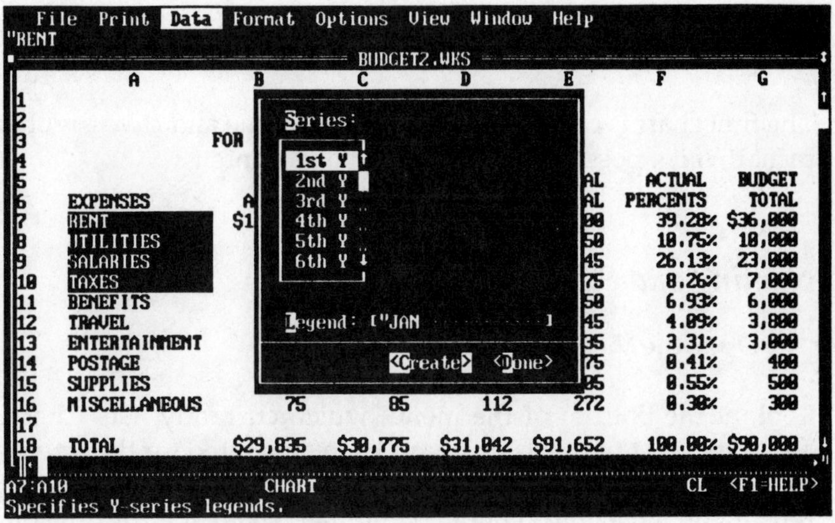

Figure 6.17. Data legends

Chart Title: **1st Quarter Expenses**
Subtitle: **Rent, Utilities, Salaries, Taxes**
X-Axis: **Expense Categories**
Y-axis: **Dollars**

Note If you fill a Text Box, the text scrolls to the left allowing you to type additional text. Each title may contain as many as 37 characters (Figure 6.18).

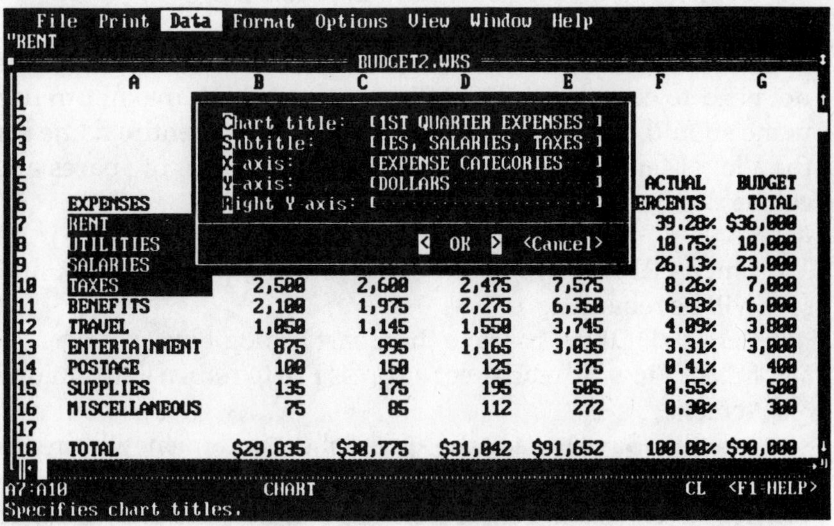

Figure 6.18. Data Titles Dialog Box

3. Press **ENTER.**
4. View your graph.

The first chart is complete. Next we will name and save the chart and try to print it, if it's possible to do so with your printer.

Naming and Saving a Chart

1. Open the View Menu.

Look at the bottom of the menu, which currently lists **Chart1.** The View Menu lists all the charts that have been generated for the active spreadsheet (up to a maximum of eight) and lets you change the one that is active or current. If you have only generated one chart so far, it is the only one listed. The mark next to it indicates that it is the current chart.

If you saved your spreadsheet now, the chart you created would be saved as **chart1**. However, you may give it a different name which will make it easier to identify on the View Menu. This name will not appear on the chart itself.

2. Select **View/Charts.**
3. Use **ALT-N** or **TAB** to the Name Text Box.
4. Type the name for your chart: **Expense Bar**

Note

Since the chart name is only used for identification on Works menus, it does not need to conform to DOS filename rules. For maximum usefulness, the name should be 15 characters or less so that the entire name can appear on the View Menu. Any characters or combinations of spaces and characters can be used.

5. Since **<RENAME>** is the active button, press **ENTER** and your chart will be renamed.
6. Select **<DONE>** to leave the Chart Dialog Box.
7. Select **View/Spreadsheet** or press **F10** to return to the main spreadsheet screen.
8. Use **File/Save** to save the spreadsheet and the newly created chart.

When you say that the chart is saved, you don't actually mean that the chart that appears on the screen is saved. What is actually saved are ranges of data which form the X- and Y-series, along with any titles, legends or enhancements that you might have added. This is actually more useful than saving the chart because as data in your spreadsheet changes, the chart automatically changes as well. We explain how this works.

9. Open the Chart Menu by selecting **View.** Notice that a new section consisting of the name of our new chart, **Expense Bar,** has been added to the View Menu on this screen. A mark preceding the chart name indicates it is the current chart. The **Charts** Option is the same as the one you just used from the CHART Screen, and can be used to rename, delete, or copy a chart. The other options are used to view the current chart, create a **New** chart or return to the Spreadsheet.
10. Select **1 Expense Bar.** Take another look at the chart so that you can see how it changes when you change the data it includes.
11. Press **ESC.**

Suppose that you just received a late bill from one of your vendors that was to be accrued in the month of March.

12. Choose **View/Spreadsheet.**
13. Change the *Mar Actual* expenditure on utilities to: **5000**
14. Use **View/1 EXPENSE BAR** or **SHIFT-F10** to view your chart again (Figure 6.19). The bar showing the March Utilities expenditure has been changed to reflect the changed spreadsheet entry.

Printing a Chart

Try to print the graph.

1. Select **View/1 Expense Bar** to return to the Chart Screen for the current graph, **Expense Bar.**
2. Select **Print/Printer Setup.**

The PRINTER SETUP Dialog Box is similar to the SELECT TEXT PRINTER Dialog Boxes that you used when printing documents, spreadsheets, and databases, except that the printer options are different. Choose the type of printer you have. See the section on installing Works in Chapter 1 and checking your printer in Chapter 2 for information on the **Page Feed** List Box and **Connect to:** List Box settings. If you are using the

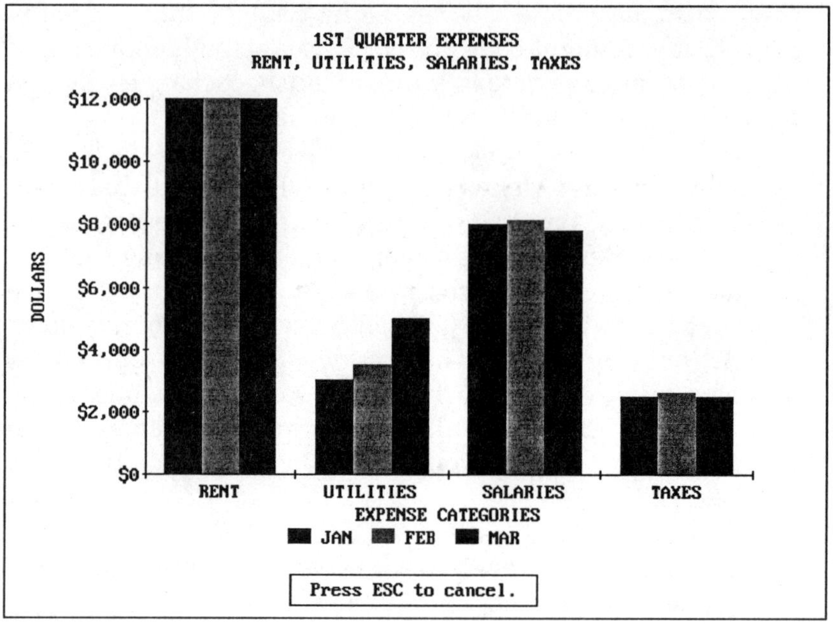

Figure 6.19. Bar Chart with new expenses for March

same printer to print graphs as you used to print text, these settings should be the same as in the SELECT TEXT PRINTER Dialog Box.

3. Select **Print/Print.**

Your chart will be printed horizontally on the paper as this is one of the default **Print Layout** settings.

If you have worked through both Chapter 3 and this spreadsheet chapter, you have seen most of the spreadsheet features that Works offers. Functions can be explored in more detail, and reports can be enhanced, but you should be able to build on your skills with the help of the Works Help Screens and lessons. Also, charting can go beyond the complexity demonstrated here. Chart types can be mixed, grid lines can be added, and charts can be inserted into the word processing portion of Works. Again, you should be able to use the Works Manual and Help Screens to build these skills.

Although freezing titles and protecting data in the spreadsheet is also not explored in either Chapter 3 or in this spreadsheet chapter, both can be used once the spreadsheet is created. Freezing titles permits you to keep row and column titles within a window as you scroll through other parts of the spreadsheet. Protecting data safeguards cells against accidental or unauthorized change. This is very important if other people will be using your spreadsheet. Both commands can be accessed through the **Options** Menu.

Also not covered in either Chapter 3 or in this spreadsheet chapter, but covered in Chapter 4, the database chapter, is sorting of data. Text, dates, or values can be sorted in the spreadsheet according to the contents of the cell selected. It is always a good idea to save the spreadsheet prior to sorting. Therefore, if you sort the data incorrectly, you can simply retrieve the saved file. Data sorting can be accessed through **Select/Sort Rows.**

An option in Works that can make moving around the spreadsheet easier is naming ranges. If you have a large spreadsheet, it becomes clear that cursor movement becomes very cumbersome. However, by assigning names to different pieces of the spreadsheet, you can move to a specific area by pressing two keys. This is called *naming ranges.* To name a range, choose **Edit/Range Name**. Work then prompts you for a name and lists the names already used. To go to an area of the spreadsheet named, press **F5** (Go To) and eiter type in the name of the range you want to go to, or use the **Arrow** to point to the name. Press **ENTER**. Named ranges can also be used in formulas when referring to a cell or a group of cells.

Similarly, if you know you are looking for specific information in a spreadsheet, you can search for this information in the same manner you searched for it in the database. For example, if you want to find the amount of money budgeted for *Entertainment*, choose **Select/Search**. Works then asks the name for which you are searching. Type: **Entertainment**. Press **ENTER**. Works will search through the spreadsheet for the information requested. This is useful if you are looking for a specific term or a specific piece of data.

Finally, a capability of Works that can be used in the word processing, spreadsheet, or database is *Macros*. A *Macro* is a series of saved keystrokes. Macros are used to save time when creating data files. For example, if you save your file regularly, the keystrokes to do that are: **File/Save As/*filename*** and **ENTER**. If you were to write a macro to execute these keystrokes, you would only have to "play the macro," and your file would be saved. To explore in further detail the concepts of macros, refer to Appendix E in your Microsoft Works Reference Manual or Procedures/Macros in the Help Index.

The exercise that follows can be used to practice the skills learned in both Chapter 3 and this spreadsheet chapter. Then you can explore the advanced spreadsheet capabilities.

Exercise

Here you will prepare a Travel and Expense Budget for one week. Your results should resemble Figure 6.20. After preparing the report, calculate statistics about the report using the *Works* functions, and then graph the results. Below is a step-by-step list of what has to be done to complete the spreadsheet. If you are unable to complete any of these steps, a solution guide can be found in Appendix A.

1. Type a heading for your Travel and Expense Report in cell *C2*.
2. Type the categories of expenses down the A column starting in *A4*, and the days of the week across row 4 starting in *B4*.
3. Type in the expenses for the week in cells *B6* through *G13*.
4. Change the width of Column A to 15, and columns B through G to 7.
5. Place a formula in *I6* to total row 6. Copy that formula down the I column.
6. Place a formula in *B15* to total column B. Copy that formula across row 15.
7. Format all the data in Comma notation with two decimal places.
8. Copy the Titles, Breakfast through Miscellaneous, to cells *A19* through *A23*.
9. Place the headings High, Low, and Average in cells *B18* through *D18*.

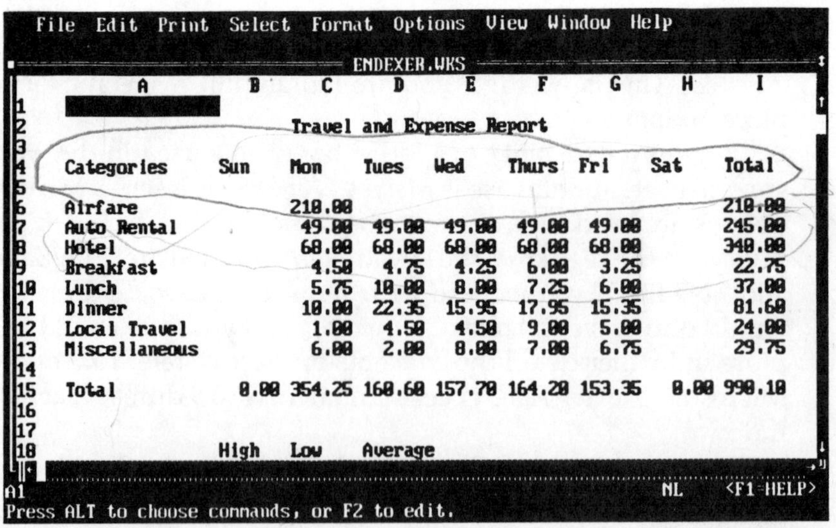

Figure 6.20. Completed travel and expense budget

10. Using the Works functions, calculate the high, low, and average expenditures for each of the categories for the week.
11. Format the results in comma notation with 2 decimal places.
12. Create a chart of the high, low, and average expenditures. Be sure to place on the chart:
    a. Titles
    b. Labels on the X and Y axes
    c. A legend to note which is the high, low, and average
13. Print the spreadsheet and the graph.
14. Save the file as **ENDEXER**.

7

A Second Look at the Database Manager

An Introduction to the Database Manager, Chapter 4, focused on the basic procedures for creating, saving, and printing databases. The steps used to search for specific information, sort the database, and print only selected portions of the database were also explored. Here we extend your ability to perform these basic tasks. Now that you know how to create a database, you can learn how to modify one that has already been created or how to add labels to make the database structure clearer for someone else who wants to use your database. Methods of finding records that meet more complex criteria than possible using the **Select/Search** command, and of obtaining better control of how data can be printed will also be covered. Finally, we show how some of the commands covered in Chapter 3, on the spreadsheet, such as the ability to format numeric values, can be used in exactly the same way with the database. Specifically, in this chapter you will learn how to:

- Add descriptive labels in FORM View
- Modify the structure of the database by adding fields to the database
- Modify the appearance of the database by moving fields and adding labels in FORM View
- Enter data in LIST View

- Use the operators in the query formulas
- Create a simple query based on one field
- Create a query to find records that meet conditions in more than one field or multiple conditions in one field
- Create a database report

Another Look at Creating a Database

1. Use the **File/Create New File** command to create a new database file.

Create a database containing the following fields:

Field Name	Width
First Name	10
Last Name	10
Departure	10
Return	10

For now just enter the fields at the left margin leaving a blank line between field names.

Figure 7.1 shows the database design. This is a review of skills introduced in Chapter 4, An Introduction to the Database Manager. Check that all your field names end with a colon (:). If not, move back to the field name and retype it with the colon. If you have trouble, review the sections in Chapter 4 on creating a database.

Modifying the Database Design

Moving Fields in FORM View

The four fields, First Name, Last Name, Departure, and Return, are currently aligned vertically on the screen. Suppose you want to change their arrangement so that First Name and Last Name are on the same line and De-

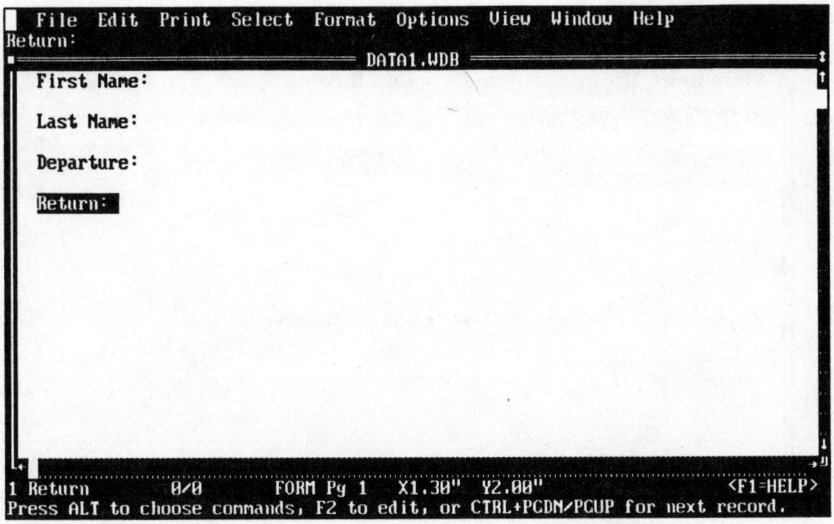

Figure 7.1. The Database design

parture and Return are together on another line. It would also be helpful to add labels, or comments, so that the Departure and Return fields can be filled in consistently.

2. Use the **ARROW** keys to move the cursor to the Last Name field.
3. Select **Edit/Move Field**.

The size of the highlight increases to include the field name and space for the field contents, and the Message Line displays instructions for completing the move.

4. Use the **ARROW** keys to move the cursor about halfway across the screen on the line containing the First Name field and press **ENTER**.
5. Repeat the preceding three steps to move the Return field to the same line as the Departure field. When completed your screen should resemble Figure 7.2.

Adding Labels in FORM View

Data entered into a field should always be entered in the same format so that they can be sorted more easily. Therefore, let's add some information explaining how to enter the departure and return dates.

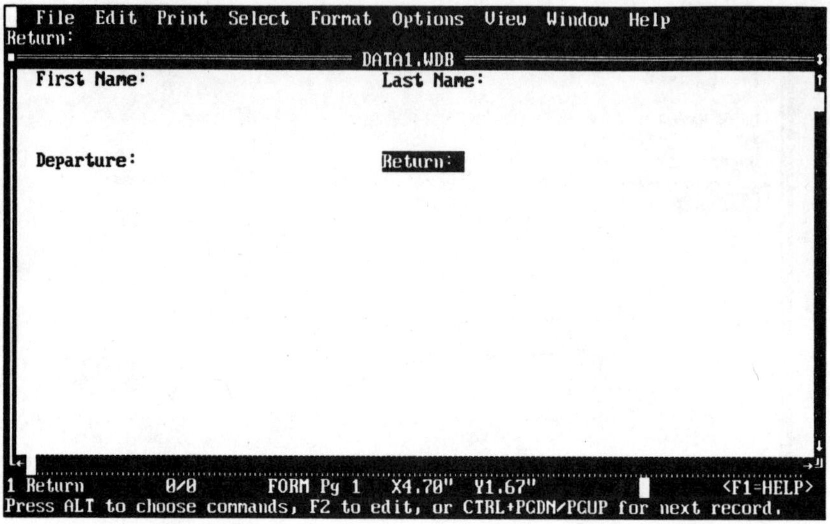

Figure 7.2. Reorganized database FORM

Information added to the FORM Screen which is not a field name is called a *label.* Works assumes that any characters which are not followed by a colon are labels.

6. Move the cursor to the line below the Departure and Return fields. Type the information for the label:

   (Enter dates as numerals, in the form: mm/dd/yy)

   and press **ENTER.**

Adding a Field in FORM View

Finally, add a new field. Fields can be added anywhere on the FORM Screen.

1. Enter the field **Destination** on the blank line between the name and date fields. Select a field width that would be appropriate for the names of cities. (Remember that field names must be followed by a colon.)
2. On the line beneath the new field, enter the following label explaining the data that will be contained in the Destination field:

(Enter destination as a city name.)

Inserting Blank Lines in FORM View

3. To improve readability, insert a blank line between the label describing the Destination field and the Departure and Return fields:
   a. Move the cursor to the Departure field.
   b. Select **Edit/Insert Line**. The form should now resemble Figure 7.3.
4. Check the form. If you don't like the placement of any of the fields, use **Edit/Move** to move them. If you want more or less blank lines between fields, use the **Edit/Delete Line** or **Edit/Insert Line** commands. If you have made any typing errors, move the cursor to the field name or label containing the error and retype the information.
5. Save the database. Use the filename **TRIPS**.

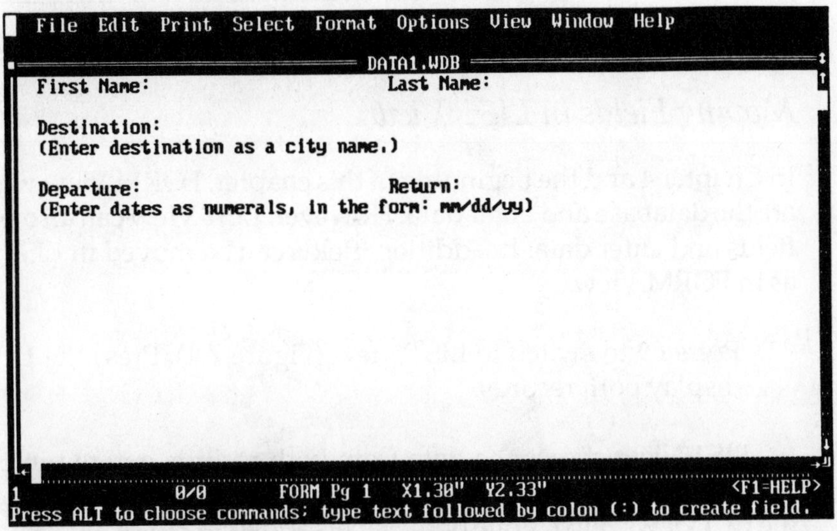

Figure 7.3. Modified FORM View

Enter data for the first two records. Remember to use **TAB** to move from field to field. Use **TAB** or **CTRL-PGDN** to move from the first to the second record.

First Name:	**Nathan**
Last Name:	**Swift**
Destination:	**Rome**
Departure:	**2/2/90**
Return:	**2/16/90**

First Name:	**Chris**
Last Name:	**Epple**
Destination:	**Mexico City**
Departure:	**12/17/89**
Return:	**12/30/89**

If pressing the **TAB** *skips a field, check to be sure the field ends with a colon. If not, go back to the field name and retype it with a colon. This is a review of information introduced in Chapter 4. Therefore, if you have problems entering data, refer to the section on Entering Data in Chapter 4.*

Moving Fields in LIST View

In Chapter 4 and the beginning of this chapter, FORM View was used to create the database and enter data. However, LIST View can also be used to add fields and enter data. In addition, fields can be moved in LIST View as well as in FORM View.

1. Press **F9** to switch to LIST View (Figure 7.4). Press the **UP ARROW** to display both records.

LIST View shows the data from both records entered in column form. There are several other differences in the way information is presented in the two views. First, none of the labels added in FORM View appear in LIST View. Second, the order of the fields is the order in which they were entered in FORM View, not the order in which they appeared on the FORM screen. Since the Destination field was the last field entered, it is the right-most field in LIST View. However, fields can be moved in LIST View just as they can be moved in FORM View.

2. To move the Destination field before the Departure Field:
   a. Move the cursor to any entry in the Destination field.

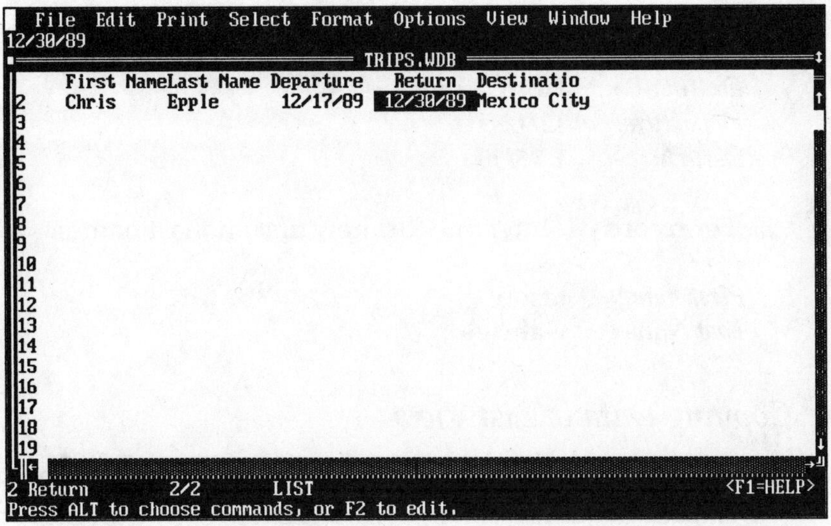

Figure 7.4. LIST View

b. Use **Select/Field** to highlight the entire field.

c. Select **Edit/Move**. You will be prompted to:

*Select new location and press **ENTER**. Press **ESC** to cancel.*

d. Move the cursor to any record in the Departure field and press **ENTER.** The Destination field will be inserted to the left of the Departure field.

Entering Data in LIST View

Entering data in LIST View is similar to entering data on the spreadsheet. It can be easier than in FORM View if you have repetitive data. For example, suppose you wanted to enter two people who were taking the same trip.

1. First, use the **Format/Field Width** command to increase the width of the Destination field so that the two cities that you have already entered and the field name are completely visible on the screen.
2. Enter the data for the third record on the line below the last current record. Just as in the spreadsheet, after typing the information in the Formula Bar, you may enter it on the database by pressing **ENTER** or an **ARROW** key.

First Name: **Jessica**
Last Name: **Gaines**
Destination: **Hong Kong**
Departure: **12/1/89**
Return: **1/15/90**

3. For record #4, enter only the new first and last names.

First name: **Jason**
Last Name: **Gabriel**

Copying Data in List View

4. The rest of the information is the same as in record #3. Therefore, you can use the **Edit/Fill Down** command to copy the data. Follow along:
   a. Move the cursor to **Hong Kong**.
   b. Press **F8** to begin highlighting. *EXT* should appear on the Status Bar.
   c. Use the **ARROW** keys to extend the highlight to the Departure and Return fields in record #3 and to the three empty fields in record #4 (Figure 7.5).
   d. Select **Edit/Fill Down.** The Destination, Departure, and Return fields should now be the same in record #3 and record #4.
5. Save the database again using the **File/Save** command.

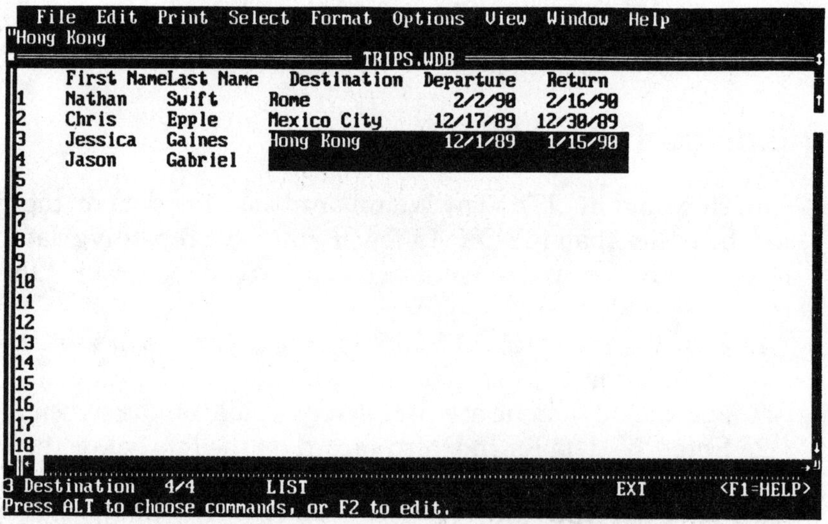

Figure 7.5. Preparing to Edit/Fill Down

Adding a Field in LIST View

Although most people use FORM View to design their databases, they can also be designed or modified in LIST View. Suppose you want to add a field to **TRIPS.WDB** to keep track of how long the trip takes. To add a field to the end of the database:

1. Move the cursor to the right of the Return field.
2. Select **Edit/Field Name**. The Field Name Dialog Box will be displayed (Figure 7.6).
3. Type the new field name: **Duration** and press **ENTER**.

Entering Formulas in Database Fields

So far the data entered in the database fields has been limited to text and numeric values. Formulas and functions can also be entered in the same manner as they are in the spreadsheets. We describe the process briefly. However, if you have not already used formulas in the spreadsheet, refer to the sections on Entering Formulas and Functions in Chapters 3 and 6. To enter a formula for the duration of the trip:

4. Move the cursor to the Duration field for record #1.

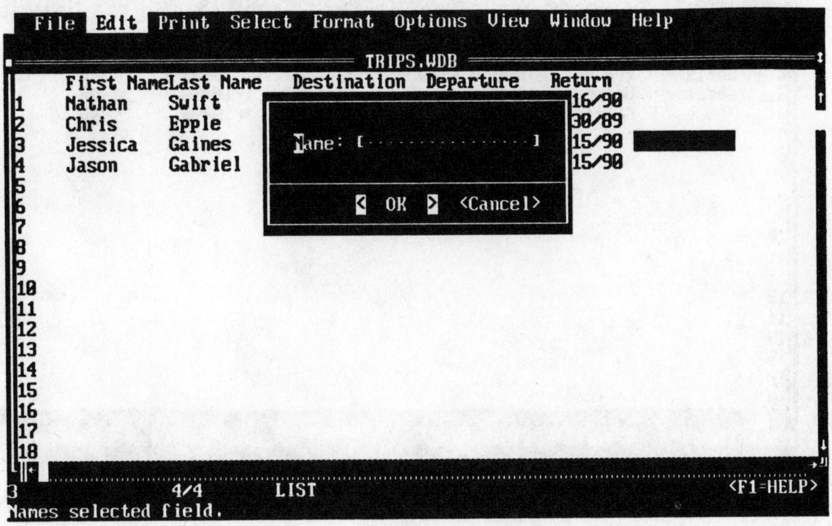

Figure 7.6. Field Name Dialog Box

5. Type an = sign to indicate that you are entering a formula.
6. Use the **LEFT ARROW** to move to the Return field.

Just as in the spreadsheet, the Formula Bar records the development of the formula. The only difference is that the field name of the cell that you moved the cursor to is entered into the formula instead of the cell address.

7. Type: - to indicate that something is going to be subtracted from the value in the Return field.
8. Move the cursor to the Departure field.
9. Press **ENTER**.

Did the results surprise you? When you pressed **ENTER**, the duration was calculated for all four records (Figure 7.7). Unlike the spreadsheet, where every cell in a column can have a different formula, when you use a formula in a database field, that formula applies to all entries in the field. Therefore, as soon as you enter the formula in one cell, Works copies the formula to all of the empty cells in that field.

10. Save the database again.

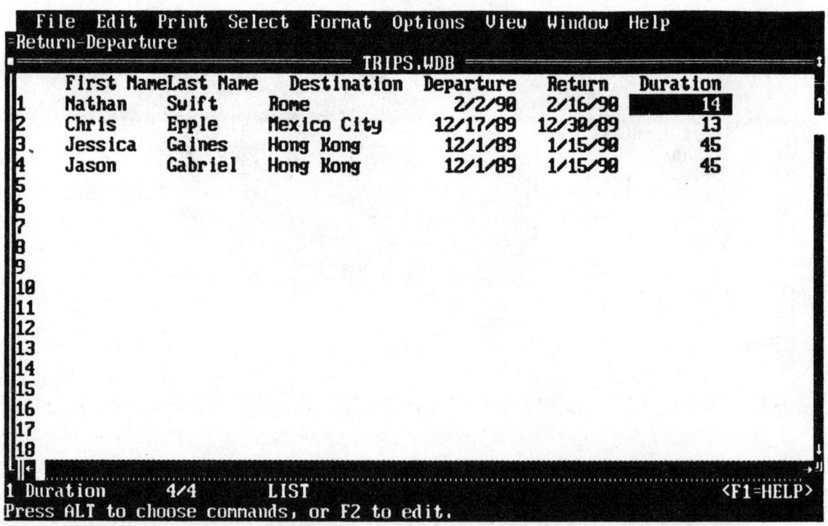

Figure 7.7. Entering a formula in the Duration field

It is also possible to include more complex formulas and functions in fields. The following example uses the NOW( ) function to calculate the number of days from the current date until the departure date. If you worked through Chapter 6, you may remember that the NOW() function inserts the current system date. Assuming that your computer has a built-in clock or that you enter the correct date each time you turn the computer on, this date is updated daily.

11. Move the cursor to the right of the last field.
12. Name the field: **Countdown.**
13. Enter the formula: **=departure-now( )** as the value for the first record in the Countdown field. To enter the formula, you may either type it as shown or:
    a. With your cursor still in the Countdown field, type: =
    b. Move the cursor to the Departure field.
    c. Type: **-now( )**
    d. Press **ENTER.**

Formatting Values

When entering the date equal to the NOW( ) function, Works includes hours and minutes. Therefore, when it subtracts the departure date, the resulting number is a decimal. Since you're probably interested in the number of days remaining, it would be preferable to format this as a whole number. Values can be formatted in the database in the exact same way as the spreadsheet, except that all values in the same field must have the same format. Therefore, to format the Countdown field so that no decimals will be displayed:

1. Move the cursor to any entry in the Countdown field, unless it's already there.
2. Select **Format/Fixed.**
3. When prompted for the number of decimals, type: **0** and press **ENTER.** The database should resemble Figure 7.8, but the exact values will be different since NOW( ) indicates the current date. If the departure date has already passed, your values will be negative.
4. Save the database again.

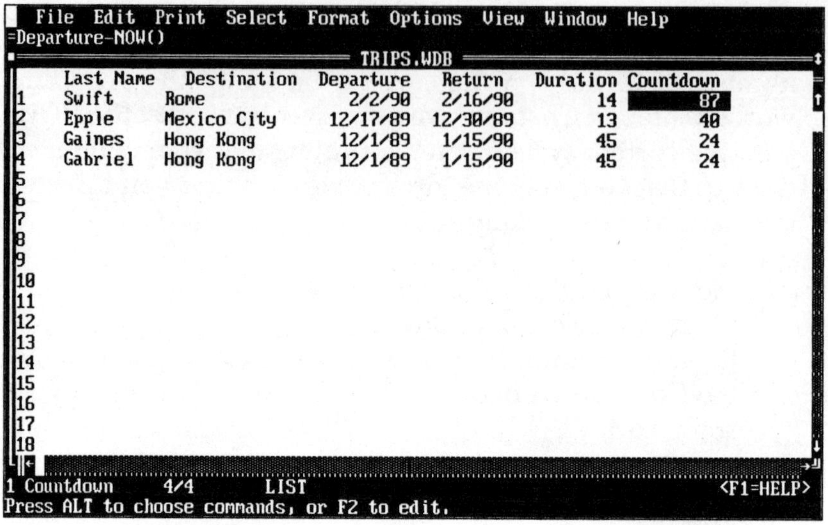

Figure 7.8. Countdown field with fixed format

1. Insert a field for the price of the trip between the Destination and Departure fields. You may use either the FORM or LIST screens. When entering a field in the middle of the list, you must first use the **Edit/Insert Record/Field** command to insert a blank space for the new field.
2. Make up some data for the price field and enter it.

1. *To insert the field:*
   a. *Move the cursor to the Departure field.*
   b. *Select **Edit/Insert Record/Field**.*
   c. *When the Dialog Box appears change the selected option to Field and press **ENTER**.*
   d. *Select **Edit/Field Name**.*
   e. *Enter a name of your choice and press **ENTER**.*
2. *Type data of your choice in the field. Since you are entering data in only one field, pressing the **DOWN ARROW** at the end of each entry would be the fastest way to enter the data and move to the next entry.*
3. *Save the database again.*

Database Queries

One of the most important aspects of a database is the ease with which you can locate records which meet specific criteria. Chapter 4, the introductory database chapter, used the **Select/Search** command to find information that was contained in one field. An advantage of **Select/Search** is that information searched for can be found regardless of the field in which it is contained. However, **Select/Search** cannot be used to find records containing information in more than one field or to find a range of data.

When the information that you need to find is located in more than one field (e.g., all of the people who live in Connecticut and who owe more than $400) or falls within a range of values (e.g., all of the estimates that are less than $500), you must create a query using QUERY View.

It is possible to use queries to find records meeting very simple or very complex criteria. For example, assuming you had a Personnel file containing the necessary information, you could create queries to find the records of everyone:

- Earning less than $40,000 a year, or
- With a title of Manager in the Sales Department, or
- Earning between $30,000 and $50,000 a year, working in the Sales or Advertising departments, and hired after April 15, 1986.

We'll start by looking at fairly simple queries. In Chapter 4, we created a database containing information on a group of clients. Let's use that database here and create queries to find records meeting specific criteria. The real power of the query command may not be apparent in the exercises that you will perform. Since your database is small, you could quickly scan the data and find most of the information you will obtain through the queries. To get a better feel for the importance of the query commands imagine that the database has expanded to thousands of records!

1. If there are any open files, use the **File/Close** command to close them.
2. Use the **File/Open Existing File** command to open **CLIENTS.WDB**. If you did not create it, follow the directions in Chapter 4. If you want to limit the amount of typing, you only need to include the Last Name, City, State, Zip, and Estimate fields.

Commands from two different menus are used when querying the database. The **View/Query** command is used to create each new query.

Once created, a query can be applied using the **Select/Apply Query Command**. Since queries select a group of records from the database, once a query has been applied, the **Select/Switch Hidden Records** and the **Select/Show All Records** commands can be used to change the selected records.

Defining a Query

To define a query:

1. Switch to **LIST** View if that is not already on the screen.
2. Select **View/Query**.

The QUERY View Screen will appear (Figure 7.9). Works marks the screen by including the word *QUERY* on the Status Line. It contains each of the field names followed by a colon. The criteria on which a query is based are entered on the QUERY Screen.

Each criterion is typed next to the field name to which it will be applied. The criterion contains an *operator* followed by the text or numbers to which the entries in each record are going to be compared. The operator defines the relationship between the records you want to find and the

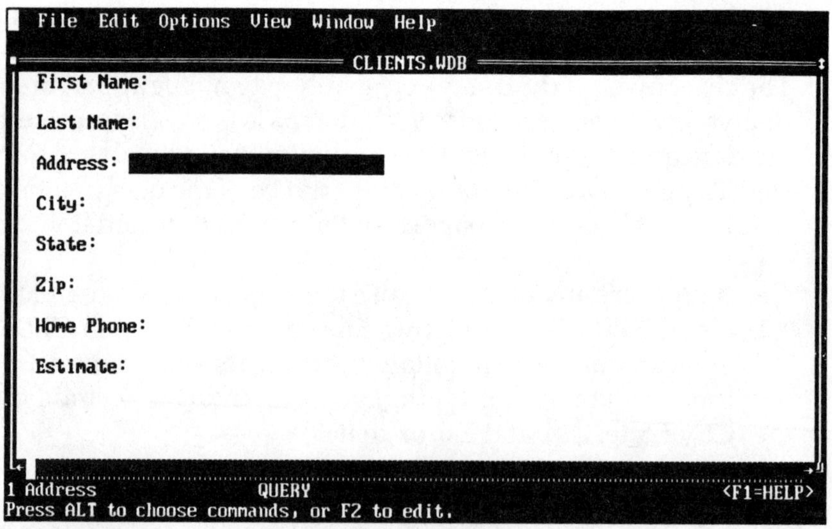

Figure 7.9. QUERY View

text or numbers you specify. For example, you may want records containing the exact same information, values that are greater or less than what is specified, or only those records which do not contain certain information. Some of the operators used to define queries may be familiar to you because they are mathematical symbols. In fact, Works calls them criteria formulas. For example, to find those records in which the information is the same as or equal to the specified text or numbers, type = (equal sign). The basic Works operators used in queries and examples of their use are listed in Table 7.1.

Let's try entering some criteria.

3. To find everyone whose estimate was greater than 1200:
   a. Use **TAB** to move the cursor to the Estimate field.
   b. Type: **>1200**

Table 7.1. Operators Used in Queries

Operator	Name	Example	Records Found
=	Equals	=50 ="NY"	50 ny (or) NY (or) Ny, etc.
<	Less Than	<50 < "N" <'1/1/80'	Values less than 50 Data alphabetically before N Dates prior to 1980
>	Greater Than	>50 >"Nathan" >'12/31/80'	Values greater than 50 Data alphabetically after Nathan Dates after the year 1980
<=	Less Than or Equal to	<=50	50, and values less than 50
>=	Greater Than or Equal to	>=50 >="n"	50, and values greater than 50 Any entry beginning with an N through Z
<>	Not Equal to	<>50 <>"ny"	Any value except 50 Any entry except ny (NY,nY,Ny)

c. Press **ENTER**. The query criterion now appears in the highlight box next to *Estimate:* and can be applied to the database (Figure 7.10).

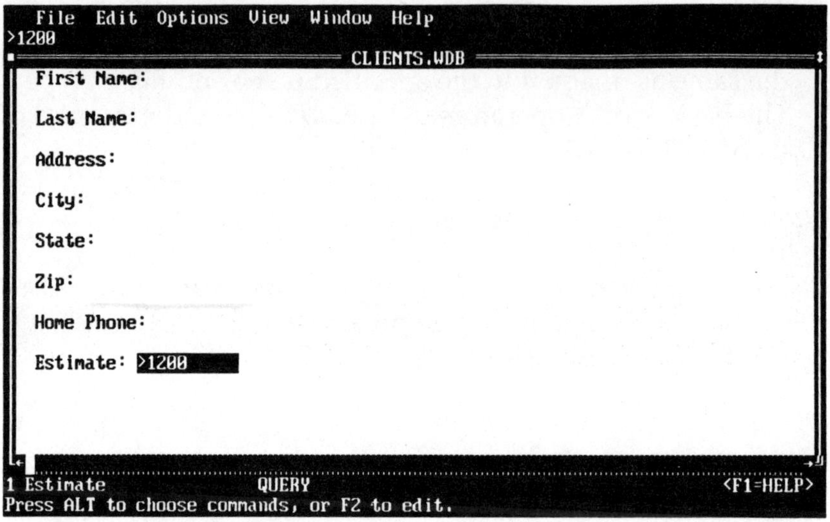

Figure 7.10. Query criterion

d. Press **F10** to exit the QUERY Screen and apply the query.

Since you entered QUERY View from LIST View all of the records for which the Estimate field is greater than **1200** have been extracted and appear on the screen (Figure 7.11). The original record numbers are retained; only records #1, #2, #3, #8, #9, and #10 appear because these are the only clients for whom the estimate was greater than 1200. The number 6/10 should appear on the Status Line because only six of the ten records in the database have been selected.

The cursor remains where it was before QUERY View was entered, and only those fields previously visible are still visible.

e. If the Estimate field is not visible on the screen, use the **RIGHT ARROW**, or **CTRL-PGDN** keys to display the Estimate field and check that the correct records are displayed.

If you are in FORM View before entering QUERY View, Works will display the FORM View of the first record that meets the criteria. Additional records can be viewed by using **CTRL-PGDN**.

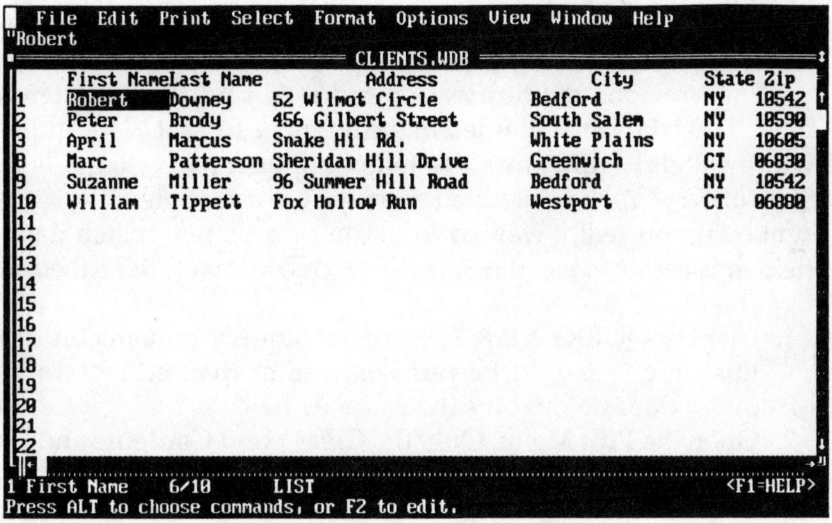

Figure 7.11. Results of a query

To select a group of records meeting different criteria, it is necessary to return to QUERY View. This time let's view all the records with estimates greater than or equal to 1200.

1. Select **View/Query**.

The previous query *Estimate: 1200* is still on the QUERY Screen.

2. Use **TAB** to move the cursor to the Estimate field.
3. Since the new query is similar to the previous one, the quickest approach is to edit the previous query. Press **F2,** the same key you used to edit other entries in the database and spreadsheet tools.
4. Use the **RIGHT ARROW** to move the cursor under the *1* and type: = The edited query should say >=*1200*.
5. Press **ENTER.**
6. Press **F10** to apply the query.

Note It is also possible to use the **View** command to apply the query. Since you initiated the query from LIST View, you must select **View/List; View/Form** is only active if you entered QUERY View from FORM View.

The screen should show the seven records with estimates greater than or equal to 1200 (records: #1, #2, #3, #5, #8, #9, #10).

The previous queries were performed on a field containing numeric data. If text data are included in the field, the format of the query expression will be slightly different. The following query for clients who live in the State of New York is included as an easy illustration of the difference in the syntax. If you really wanted to locate records that match data in only one field, it is easier to use the **Select/Search** command described in Chapter 4.

1. Display QUERY View.The previous query remains on the screen, but this time it should be removed rather than edited since the current query does not involve the Estimate field.
2. Open the **Edit** Menu. Only the **Clear Field Contents** and **Delete Query** options are available for use.

Edit/Clear Field Contents	Used to clear the query in the field containing the cursor only
Edit/Delete Query	Used to clear all of the query formulas on the screen

3. Select **Delete Query**.
4. Move the cursor to the State field and type: **="ny"**

When the criterion contains text, the text should be enclosed in quotation marks.

Just as with the **Select/Search** command, the Works queries are not case specific—text can be entered in either uppercase or lowercase letters or a mixture.

Note

If some parts of the simple queries that we are now creating are omitted, the query will still work. However, if the same characters are omitted in slightly different or in more complex queries, Works either looks for different records than you intended or displays an error message. It is, therefore, recommended that you habitually use the full syntax, as presented in this book, for all queries.

5. Press **ENTER** and then **F10**. Seven of the records contain **NY** in the State field and are selected.

6. Move the cursor, if necessary, so that the Estimate field is displayed. Estimates greater than and less than 1200 are displayed. This illustrates a difference between the **Select/Search** and **Query** commands. When you initiate a search, only those records that are not currently hidden are searched. However, a **Query** displays all records meeting the criteria whether they are displayed or hidden at the time the query is initiated.

Greater than and less than queries also can be applied to text. Works finds the entries which are alphabetically before or after the stated criterion.

7. Use the procedures above to find all of the records with a Last Name field **>"M"**. Remember to delete the existing query before entering the new one.
8. When the query is applied and LIST View reappears on the screen, move the cursor so that the Last Name field is visible (Figure 7.12).

Did the results surprise you? Works found all of the records with Last Name entries beginning with **M** or a letter occurring later in the alphabet. Works interprets the expression >"M" as any entry that would be alphabetized after the letter M followed by a blank space. Therefore, Marcus, McDonald, and Miller meet the criterion >"M".

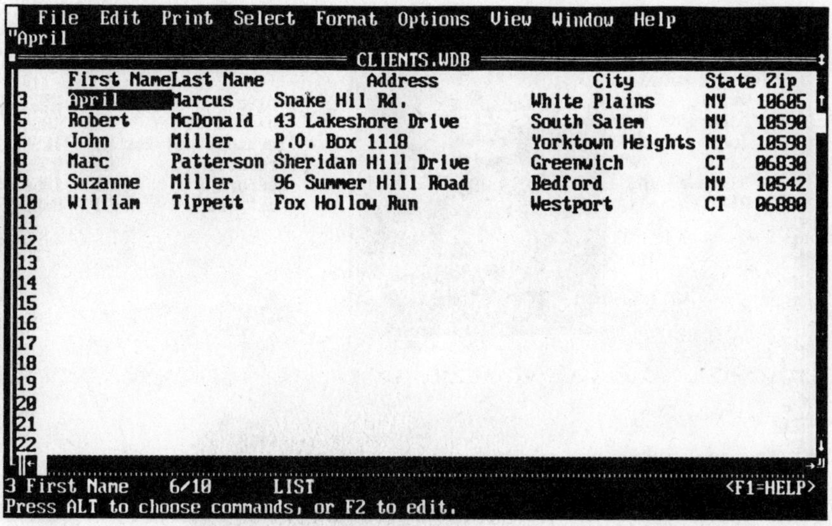

Figure 7.12. Results of the query: *Last Name: >"M"*

The Select Menu and Queries

Once queries have been created using **View/Query**, they can be repeated or the hidden records switched using some of the **Select** Menu commands.

1. Open the **Select** Menu (Figure 7.13).

The first four commands in the bottom section, **Apply Query, Hide Record, Show All Records,** and **Switch Hidden Records,** change the records which are visible on the screen.

2. Select **Switch Hidden Records** to hide the records currently visible and display the records which were hidden because they did not meet the last query criteria.
3. Redisplay all the records by selecting **Select/Show All Records.**

All ten records in the database should reappear on the screen.

Suppose that after you have redisplayed all the records you remembered that you needed to do something else with the records extracted by the last query.

4. Select **Select/Apply Query.**

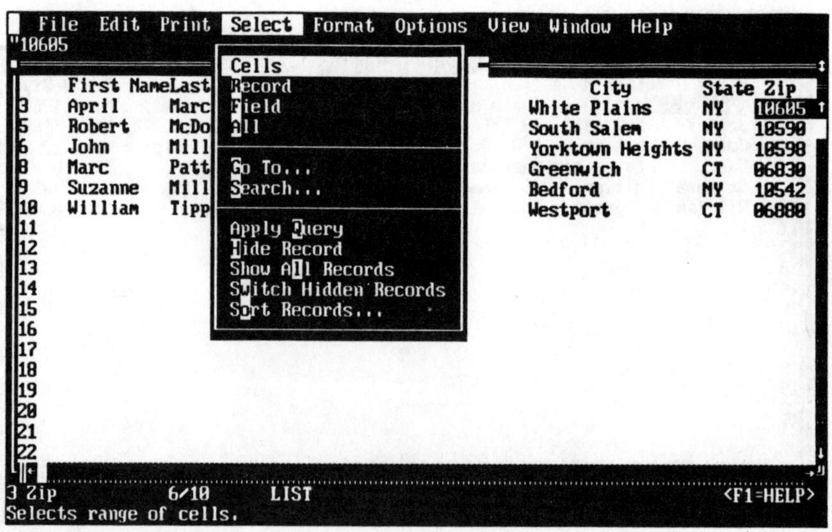

Figure 7.13. Select Menu

The records meeting the last criterion established, *Last Name:* **>"M"**, are extracted once again.

Since the QUERY Screen retains the last created query until it is deleted, that query can be repeated directly from the LIST View or FORM View Screens by using the **Select/Apply Query** command. Also, if you save the database after defining a query, that query is saved and may be used the next time that you retrieve the file.

You've just seen the basic format for simple queries. The <,<= , and <> operators may be applied in the same way as the =, >, and >= operators that were used in the examples. These basic queries can be combined in several different ways to find records meeting more than one condition.

Queries Using Criteria in More Than One Field

Suppose you want to find all of the clients living in New York with an estimate greater than 1200.

1. Select **View/Query**.
2. Delete the criterion already on the QUERY Screen.
3. Enter **="ny"** in the State field. Remember, the text used in queries may be typed in either uppercase or lowercase letters.
4. Enter **>1200** in the Estimate field (Figure 7.14).

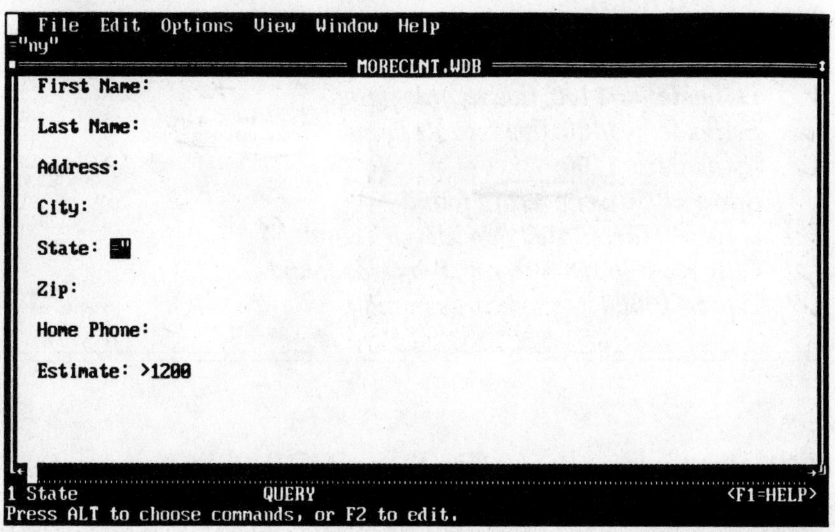

Figure 7.14. State field is too narrow to display the query

Note The amount of space allowed for the query criteria in each field is equal to the field width in FORM View. In Figure 7.14, only two spaces were allotted to the field width so the entire query does not appear on the Work Area. To see the query you must either move the cursor to the field and look in the Formula Bar (as in Figure 7.14) or use the **Format/Field Width** command in FORM View to increase the field width and then return to QUERY View.

5. Press **F10** to apply the query.

The records of the four clients living in New York with an estimate greater than 1200 are displayed.

Find and print the records in the **CLIENTS.WDB** that meet the following criteria:

1. All clients who live the city of Bedford.
2. All clients whose estimate was less than or equal to 1400.
3. All clients whose estimate was more than 1400.
4. All clients whose estimate was more than 1400 and who live in Connecticut.
5. All clients for whom the city entry is Hartsdale. (What happens when you press **F10** to apply this query?)
6. All clients for whom the city entry is not South Salem.
7. All clients with a zip code higher than 10600. (Remember that zip code is a text field).

---

1. *City:* **="Bedford"**; *two records found*
2. *Estimate:* **<=1400**; *five records found*
3. *Estimate:* **> 1400**; *five records found*
4. *Estimate:* **> 1400**;
   State: **="Ct"**; *one record found*
5. *City:* **="Hartsdale"**; *No Match Found*
6. *City:* **< >"South Salem"**; *8 records found*
7. *Zip:* **>"10600"**; *two records found*

Queries Using the AND (&) and OR (|) Operators

In the previous section you found the records that met the criteria set in two different fields. Sometimes, you want to find records that meet a criteria in one field *or* in another field (e.g., everyone who makes more than $40,000 or was hired before 1/1/80), meet one of several criteria in one field (e.g., live in ny or ct), or fall within a certain range (e.g., have a salary of between $30,000 and $40,000). In order to find these groups of records, you must use the AND or the OR operators to connect individual criterion.

The syntax used with the OR and AND operators is the same. Table 7.2 shows some examples of the syntax.

Note An extra equal sign is added if a query begins with an "equal to" relationship.

Note In this book, the OR operator will appear as a solid vertical line (|), but on your computer keys, there will be a break in the line. The OR operator is often found on the same key as the backslash (\) key.

Troubleshooting Your Queries

What follows is a list of some questions to ask yourself if your query does not work or selects different records than you intended. The longer (and more complex) your query is, the more likely it is that you will omit an operator, quotation mark, etc.

List of troubleshooting queries: Check out the problems listed below if you receive the ERROR message, *Invalid reference or wrong operand type.*

Table 7.2. The AND and OR Operators

Operator	Name	Example	Records Found
|	Or	==50|=60 =="n"|="m"	The values 50 and 60 The entries n and m
&	And	>50&<75 >='1/1/80'&<='12/31/80'	Values between 50 and 75 All dates in 1980

Note If you receive the above error message, press ENTER to clear the message from the screen. Check the Status Line at the bottom of the screen to see if you are in Edit Mode. If you are not, press the F2 key so that you can edit your query.

1. If the query contains text, did you remember to put quotation marks (") before and after the text?

   Incorrect entry: <>ny
   Correct entry: <>"ny"

2. If the query contains a date, did you remember to enclose the date in single quotes (')?

   Incorrect entry: >=1/1/80
   Correct entry: >='1/1/80'

3. If the query is searching for a number which has been entered as text (such as a zip code) did you remember to enclose it in quotes?

   Incorrect entry (for zip): =12345
   Correct entry (for zip): ="12345"

4. If the query is complex, did you put in too many (too few) operators?

   Incorrect entry: ="Jerry" | ="Gerry"
   Correct entry: =="Jerry" | ="Gerry"

Often you receive no ERROR message, but your query does not select the correct records because the query you entered does not have the meaning that you think it does, or because the criteria from previous queries are still included on the QUERY Screen.

5. Did you use **Edit/Delete** to delete the criteria from previous queries?
6. Did you enter the criteria in the correct field(s)?
7. Did the format you used in the query match the format that you used in the database?

   ="new york" will not match state entries that were entered using the two letter state abbreviations

8. Did you close the quotation marks around a text entry?

   =="ny | =ct will match the characters ny | =ct
   =="ny" | ="ct" will match the characters ny or the characters ct

9. Did you remember the extra equal sign before a complex query using the equality operator?

   Incorrect entry: =3 | =4
   Correct entry: ==3 | =4

10. Did you use the AND operator when you should have used the OR operator, or vice versa. For example:

    <>"ny" | <>"ct" finds all of the records in your database
    <>"ny"&<>"ct" finds all of the records where the data is anything except ny or ct

---

Use Table 7.2 to help you with the following queries. Remember to delete previous queries from QUERY View before entering the new criteria.

1. Find everyone living in the City of **White Plains** OR **Bedford**.
2. Edit the previous query to delete the initial =. What happens when you press **ENTER**?
3. Find everyone with an Estimate of less than 1000 OR more than 3000.
4. Find everyone with an Estimate between 1000 and 3000. There are two ways that you could do this.
5. Find everyone who does not live in Greenwich or Westport.

Note || Think about whether this query should use the AND or the OR operator.

---

1. *You should find 4 records.*
2. *You should find 0 records; you will get an error message.*
3. *You should find 5 records.*
4. *You should find 5 records.*
5. *You should find 8 records.*

If you did not find the indicated number of records, look at the preceding list of troubleshooting queries to see if you can find your error. The correct queries are also listed here. The format must be exact, so it may be necessary to look very carefully at the queries to find your error. Of course, errors will also exist if you made data-entry errors.

1. *City*: =="White Plains" | ="Bedford"
2. *City*: ="White Plains" | ="Bedford"; will produce error message, *Reference not valid or wrong operand type.*
3. *Estimate*: **<1000 | > 3000**
4. *Estimate*: **>1000&<3000**
5. *City*: **< >"Greenwich"&< >"Westport"**

Creating Reports from Your Database

You've just learned how to find records in the database that meet specific criteria. One of the other main uses of databases is to generate reports. It is possible to use Works to create customized reports containing not only your data, but summary statistics, explanatory text, calculations, and formatting. Works automatically creates the shell of the report. Then you can use the menus to customize it for your needs. As many as eight report formats can be saved with your file and can be used repeatedly as data changes or for reporting on different parts of your database.

First let Works display the general report format. Then edit the report to have it better meet your needs.

To get ready:

1. If any files other than **CLIENTS.WDB** are open, close them.
2. Open **CLIENTS.WDB** if it is not already open.
3. Switch to LIST View.
4. If only some records are displayed, select **Select/Show All Records**.

Creating a Report

Now you should be ready to create and view a report on the CLIENTS database.

1. Select **View/New Report.**

The first page of the report will be displayed on the screen. At this point it looks very much like a printout of LIST View, except that each column is headed by the field name (Figure 7.15). The page number on the Status Line can be used to keep track of where you are in the report.

2. As indicated on the Message Line, continue pressing **ENTER** until you see the entire report.

When each page of the report has been displayed, the Report Definition screen will be displayed. This screen may seem confusing but is related to the report you just saw. Works creates a tabular report. Each column on the REPORT Screen relates to one field, or column, in your database. Each row contains explanatory text, data from your database, or summary statistics or formulas based on your data. The left-most column on the screen indicates the type of row. The rest of the screen shows the contents for each column in the row.

The following rows are always included when you view a new report:

- Two blank *Intr Report*, or Introductory Report, rows. Any information included on these rows will appear at the beginning of your report. Works assumes that you will enter titles here.
- An *Intr Page,* or Introductory Page, row containing the names of the database fields followed by a blank *Intr Page* row. Information in Intr

```
First NameLast Name Address

Robert    Downey    52 Wilmot Circle
Peter     Brody     456 Gilbert Street
April     Marcus    Snake Hil Rd.
Jerome    Adams     15 Martine Ave., Apt. 3M
Robert    McDonald  43 Lakeshore Drive
John      Miller    P.O. Box 1118
Susan     Lippman   Whipporwill Drive
Marc      Patterson Sheridan Hill Drive
Suzanne   Miller    96 Summer Hill Road
William   Tippett   Fox Hollow Run

Page 1                   REPORT
Press ENTER to continue, ESC to cancel.
```

Figure 7.15. Viewing a report

Page rows appears at the beginning of each page of the report. Works assumes that you will head each column with the field name followed by a blank line. The field names can be replaced with other column headings of your choice.

- A *Record* row, which prints one entry for each record covered by the report. Since this information is different for each record, this row always includes a formula. The current formula tells Works to print the data for each field.
- Two blank *Summ Report*, or Summary Report, rows. You may include summary statistics, such as counts, averages, or totals for the information included in the report on these lines.

Printing the Report

Before customizing the report, print it so that you can keep track of how it changes during the editing process.

1. Select **Print/Print** and press **ENTER** to print the report.

Exactly how much is printed on each page depends on your printer, but for most printers only the first three columns of this report will appear on the first page. Works prints as many columns as will fit on the first page and then prints the remaining columns on following pages.

Editing a Report

Now that you've seen the report Works produces, we discuss how to customize it. The report that you're going to create will provide a listing of the clients by state, with information indicating how many clients are in each state and the total estimates for each state. To do this you need to:

- Enter a title for the report
- Divide the records into groups
- Enter summary statistics

Most of these tasks can be accomplished quite easily.

Entering a Title

All information entered on the screen must be entered in a column. Unlike a word processing document, you can't tell Works to center the title in the *Intr Report* line. If the title is wider than the field, that's alright; as long as there is not information to the right of the title, the text can overflow into the next field.

1. Move the cursor to column B of the first *Intr Report* row (Figure 7.16).
2. Type the report title: **Client Estimates by State** and press **ENTER**.

Dividing the Report into Groups

Many reports divide the records into groups so that summary statistics can be calculated for subgroups within the database in addition to the entire database. It is also common to want records within each group listed in some kind of order, such as alphabetically by last name. Both of these can be accomplished by using the **Select/Sort Records** command.

1. Select **Select/Sort Records**.

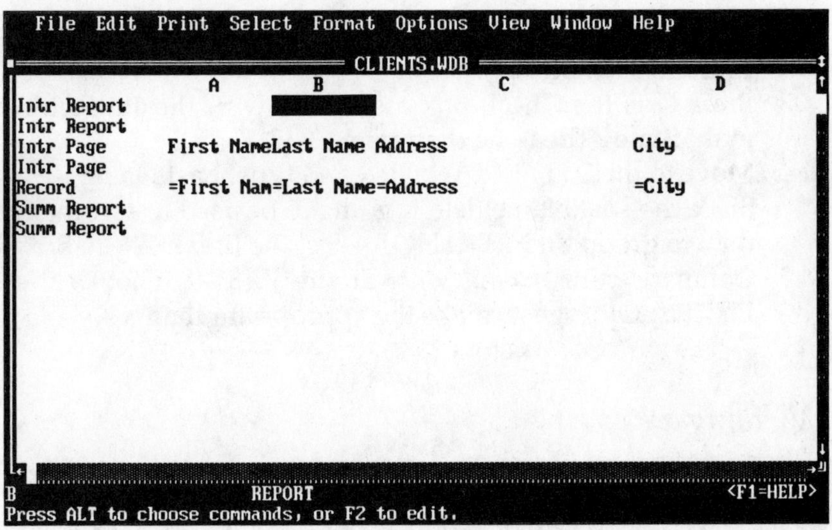

Figure 7.16. Modifying a report definition

The Dialog Box that is displayed (Figure 7.17), is similar to the one displayed when records are sorted within the database except that a Break Check Box and 1st Letter Check Box have been added. The *Break Check Box* allows you to separate a report into groups. If no Break Check Box is selected, the database is sorted on the fields entered in the Dialog Box, but the database will not be divided into groups.

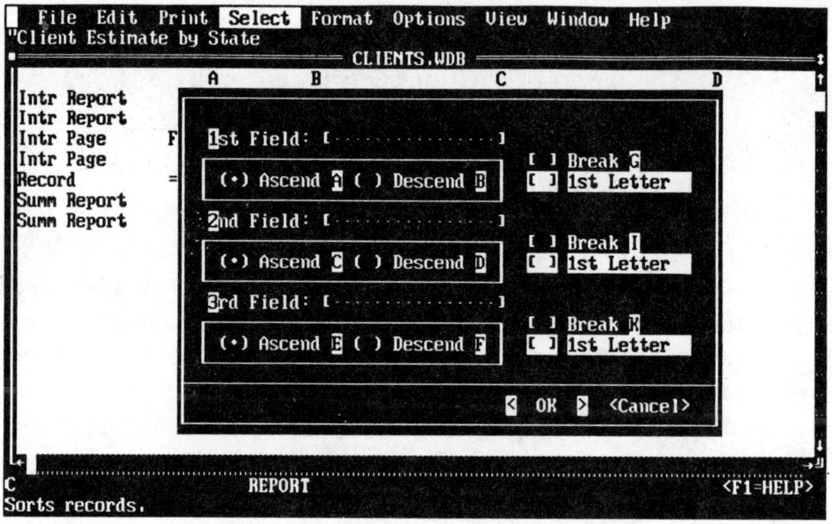

Figure 7.17. Sort Record Dialog Box

2. Since the report is to be grouped on the basis of state, type **State** into the 1st Field Text Box.
3. *Break* G is the Check Box associated with the 1st Field. Therefore, to make State a Break field, press **ALT-G**.
4. Move to the 2nd Field Text Box and type: **Last Name**
   Since the Last Name field is going to be used to sort the records, rather than to group them, DO NOT select the Break Check Box.
5. Compare your screen with Figure 7.18. If it looks the same, press **ENTER**. Otherwise, make the appropriate changes.

Viewing a Report

There are several ways to view the report.

1. To obtain a general overview of what the report will look like:

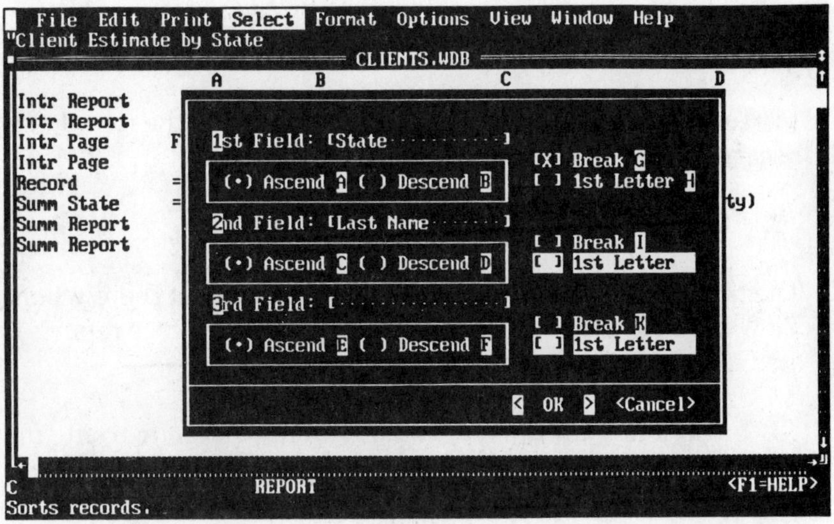

Figure 7.18. Completed Sort Records Dialog Box

a. Select **Print/Preview**.
b. Press **ENTER** when the Preview Dialog Box is displayed.

This displays the report as it would appear when printed (Figure 7.19). Even though you can't read the data, it's clear that the report has been divided into two groups and that there are some numbers at the end of each group.

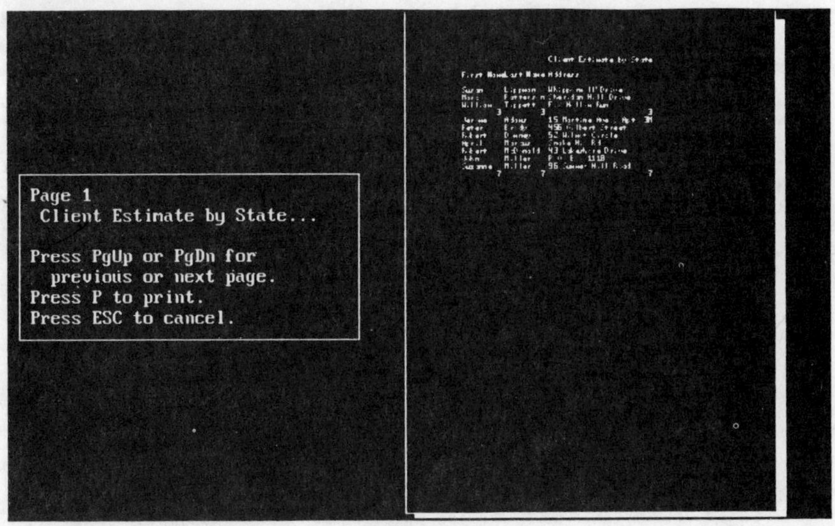

Figure 7.19. Previewing a report

c. Press **PGDN** to view the rest of the report.
d. Press **ESC** to return to the REPORT Screen.

To actually be able to read the information in the report, it is necessary to use the **View** command again.

2. Open the **View** Menu.

The Menu should contain two lines that were not there when you used the View Menu (Figure 7.20) to create a new report. Once reports have been created, they are listed on the report screen.

3. Select **1** to view the report that you have been working on.

The first screen shows that the records have been divided into two groups and are in alphabetical order by last name within each group. The number 3 appears at the end of each field in the first section, and 7 after each field in the second section. These numbers represent a count of the number of records in each group.

4. Press **ENTER** until the second page of the report appears. Now you can tell that the first group were all from the State of CT and the second

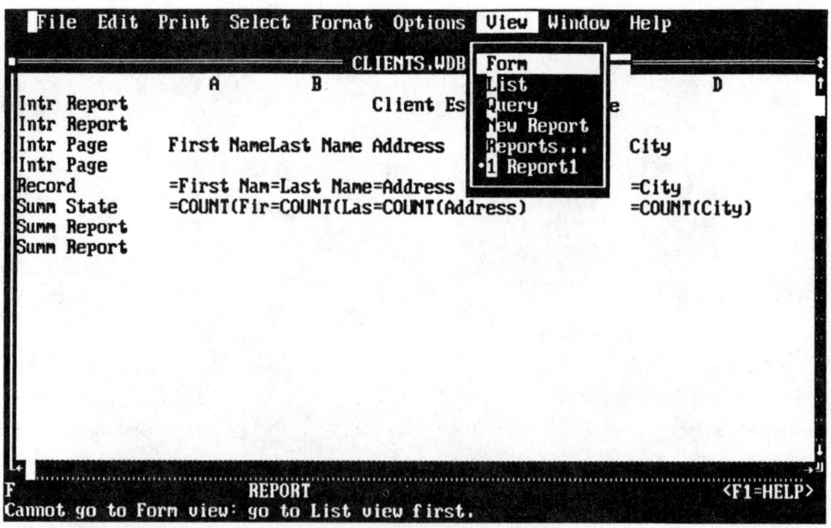

Figure 7.20. View Menu

group from NY. For the Estimate field, the summary statistic is the sum of the estimates for each state.

5. Press **ENTER** until you return to the REPORT Screen. A new row, *Summ State*, has been added. It contains a formula entering a COUNT statistic for each text field, and the SUM statistic for Estimate, which is the only numeric field. (Press the **RIGHT ARROW** to display the Estimate field.)

When a Break field is added to a report, a summary field containing COUNT or SUM statistics is automatically added to the REPORT Screen.

Deleting Information from a Cell

When Works adds summary information, it adds it to every column. It is not necessary to have a count of each field if that number is always the same. Therefore, let's leave the count in column A and delete it in the rest of the *Summ State* row:

1. Move the cursor to Column B in the *Summ State* row.
2. Select all of the columns that contain the information that you want to erase:
   a. Press **F8** to begin highlighting.
   b. Use the **RIGHT ARROW** to move the cursor to Column G.
3. Select **Edit/Clear**.
4. Select **View/1** again. Each group now has one COUNT statistic in column A and the SUM statistic in the Estimate Field column.
5. Press **ESC** or **ENTER** until you return to the REPORT Screen.

Entering Information in a Summary Report Row

When you created groups, summary statistics were automatically entered for each of the groups. However, the *Summ Report* rows remain blank. If you want summary statistics in these rows, you must enter them yourself. There are two ways to enter information in a report row. You may type the information or the formula that you want. However, if you are entering a formula you may also use the menus to enter the information.Therefore, to enter the same formulas that are in the *Summ State* row:

1. Leave the first Summ Report row blank so that there will be a blank line between the summary statistics for NY and the final summary statistics.
2. Move the cursor to column A.
3. Select **Edit/Insert Field Summary**.

Works displays a Dialog Box listing the fields in the database and the available summary statistics (Figure 7.21).

4. Highlight the First Name field.
5. **TAB** to the Statistic Option Box and select Count or press **ALT-C**.
6. Press **ENTER**.

A statistic counting the number of entries in the First Name Field is entered in column A.

7. Move the cursor to the Estimate column and use **Edit/Insert Field Summary** to insert the SUM statistic for the Estimate field.

Note If the Estimate field is not visible in the Field List Box, use the **DOWN ARROW** to scroll through the list until it is visible.

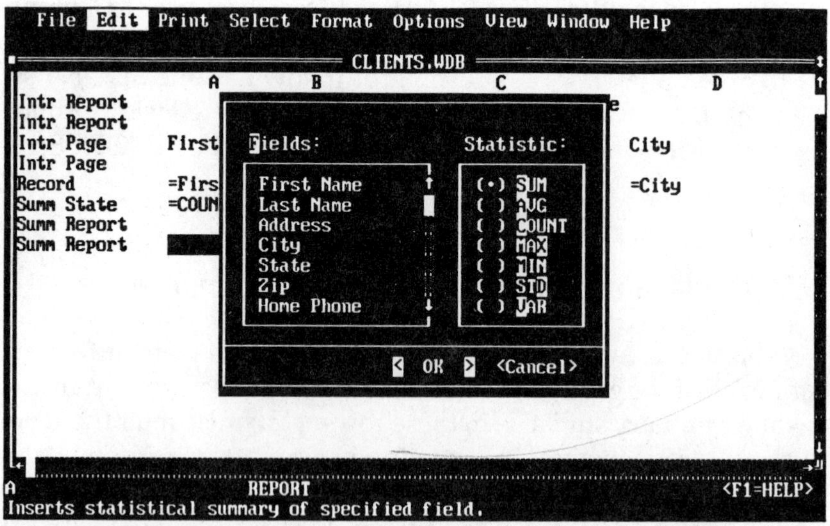

Figure 7.21. Summary Statistics Dialog Box

8. To insert labels:
   a. Move the cursor to column B of the *Summ State* row.
   b. Type: **Clients** and press **ENTER**.
   c. Move the cursor to column D of the *Summ State* row.
   d. Type: **Total Estimate for State:** and press **ENTER**.
   e. Move the cursor to column B of the *Summ Report* row containing the summary statistics.
   f. Type: **Clients** and press **ENTER**.
   g. Move the cursor to column D of the *Summ Report* row.
   h. Type: **Total Estimate:** and press **ENTER**.
9. View the report, pressing **ENTER** until you have seen the entire report. Remember that the screen only displays part of a line at a time, so don't worry if the information on the screen is unclear.
10. Print the report.

This report is almost complete, but it contains more information than is needed. Therefore, suppose that the Address, Zip, and Home Phone fields are not needed.

Deleting Columns from a Report

11. Move the cursor anywhere in the column headed Address.
12. Select **Edit/Delete Row/Column**.
13. When the Row/Column Dialog Box is displayed, select column and press **ENTER**.

The field containing the address has been deleted. The Estimate field is now in column G.

The same procedure can be used to delete the Zip and Home Phone fields. However, since the two fields are adjacent to each other, you can save time by highlighting a row in both fields and then simultaneously deleting both:

14. Move the cursor to a cell in the Zip field.
15. Press **F8** and then use the **RIGHT ARROW** to highlight an entry in the Home Phone field.
16. Use the **Edit/Delete Row/Column** command and select Column from the Dialog Box to delete both columns.
17. Print the modified report.

Naming and Saving a Report

Now you have a printed report containing exactly the information that you want. However, if any of the records in the database change or if you add new clients, this printed report will no longer be valid. If you had to go through all the steps we just completed to generate this particular report definition again each time the database changed, it would be very time consuming. Fortunately, Works will save a report definition as part of the database file. If the database is updated, the report will also automatically be updated to reflect the new information. Before saving the report, it is useful to give it a more meaningful name than Report1.

1. Select **View/Reports**.

The Reports Dialog Box should appear. It is very similar to the Charts Dialog Box used in the spreadsheets. This command can be used to rename, delete, or copy report definitions.

2. Be sure the current report is highlighted in the **Reports** List Box.
3. Use **Alt-N** or **TAB** to the **Name** Text Box.
4. Type a name for your report: **State Estimates**

Note The naming rules for reports are the same as for charts. Any characters or combinations of spaces and characters can be used. In order to have the entire name appear on the **Chart** Menu, use 15 characters or less.

5. If the Dialog Box resembles Figure 7.22, check that the Rename button is highlighted and press **ENTER**.

The new name will appear in the Reports List Box.

6. Select the <*Done*> Command Button to leave the Report Dialog Box.
7. Select **File/Save** to save the file again. All current reports will be saved with the database.

Note You can generate up to eight different reports for each database. When you save the database file, all eight reports will automatically be saved with it.

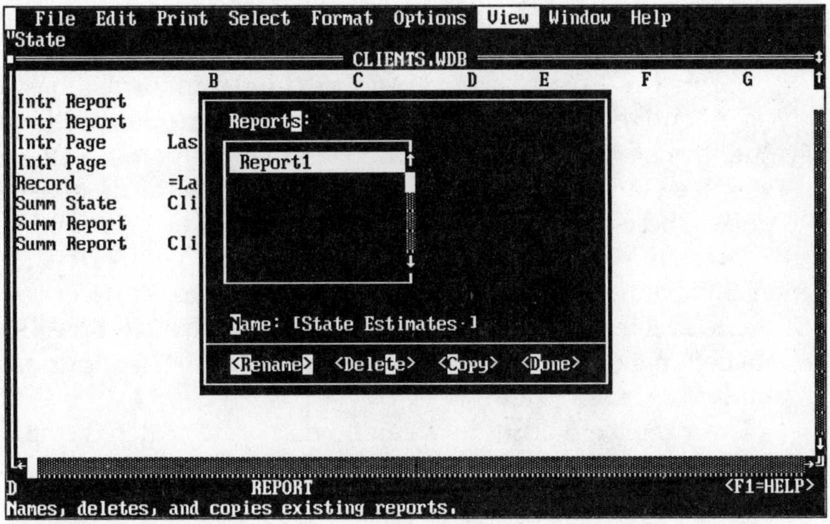

Figure 7.22. Reports Dialog Box

Returning to LIST View

When you use the **Select/Sort Records** command to create a report, the database is sorted in the same order used in the report. This is often not the order that you want. Therefore, before concluding the discussion on reports, let's see how to change the database order back to what it was originally.

1. Select **View/List** to return to LIST View.

Note Just as when you used QUERY View, if you entered REPORT View from FORM View, you cannot switch directly to LIST View. Instead, you must first select **View/Form** and then use **F9** to switch to LIST View.

2. Select **Select/Sort Records**. When the Sort Dialog Box appears, the first field in the database, First Name, is listed in the 1st Field Text Box.
3. Press **ENTER**. The database should be sorted back to its original order.
4. Save the database again to save it in its original order.

If you've worked through Chapters 4 and 7 on the database, you've seen most of the database features that Works offers. Queries can be made more complex and reports further customized, but you should be able to build on your skills with the Works Help Screens and lessons. Similarly, the complexity of the formulas and functions included in databases can go beyond those demonstrated here. Chapters 3 and 6, the spreadsheet chapters, can help you further explore this area.

Formatting is an area only briefly explored in the database chapters, but used extensively in the word processing and spreadsheet chapters. Both the value formats used in spreadsheets and the Alignment and Enhancement Styles used in word processing can be applied to the database and database reports. These commands can be accessed from the **Format** Menu.

Two commands from the **Options** Menu may also merit your further attention. Sometimes, you want to protect your database form or some of the data from accidental destruction. This can be done by using the **Options/Protect Data** commands in either FORM or LIST View or the **Options/Protect Form** command in FORM View.

The Exercise that follows can be used to practice the skills covered in this chapter. Then, the database is yours to explore.

Exercise

Here you will add a field to the CLIENTS database to indicate whether or not the contract has been signed. Then you will produce a report indicating the value of the Estimates for clients with and without signed contracts. Finally, you will print the same report for only those clients who live in New York.

1. Add a field to the database called **Contract**. The data in this field will be either **Y** indicating that a contract has been signed or **N** for no contract.
2. Enter the following data:

Record No.	Data
1	**y**
2	**y**
3	**y**
4	**n**
5	**n**
6	**y**
7	**y**
8	**n**
9	**y**
10	**n**

3. Create a New Report.
4. Delete the Address, City, State, and Zip fields.
5. Add an appropriate title for the report.
6. Modify the report so that:
   a. The Contract field is a Break Field, and the data with the same contract entry are in alphabetical order, first by last name, and, for people with the same last name, by first name.
   b. In the *Summ Contract* row, delete the COUNT statistic for everything except the first field. BE CAREFUL not to delete the =*SUM(ESTIM*, which adds the estimates for each group.
   c. In the bottom *Summ Report* now add a COUNT statistic for the First Name field and a SUM statistic for the Estimate field.
   d. Add appropriate labels for the summary statistics.
7. Print the report.
8. Name the report.
9. Return to LIST View.
10. Sort the records back to the order that they were before you created the report.
11. Select only the records of people who live in New York.
12. Print the report again.
13. Save the database so that the new report will be saved with it.

8

Integrating Works

When you purchased Works, someone may have mentioned to you that you were buying an integrated software package, which at that time, may have meant little or nothing to you. Now, however, that you have seen the word processor, spreadsheet, and database, it is time to think about that concept again.

The first advantage of an integrated software package is that the menus and procedures for the separate components that it includes are quite similar, and in some cases, identical. As you have seen, the Works File commands are identical in the word processor, spreadsheet, and database. In each of them the File Menu contains the commands **Create New File, Open Existing File, Save, Save As, Close, DOS File Management, Run Other Programs, Convert**, and **Exit**.

Many of the other menus in the three tools are similar, and all of them operate in the same way. You select a menu heading and press **ENTER** to pull down a menu of commands and options. Once you make a selection, the procedures are often quite similar, and so too are the Dialog Boxes that are used. This consistent menu and interface structure contributes to increased speed both in using the individual applications and in mastering their concepts.

Another advantage of an integrated software package is the way in which the files created with the separate tools may be used together (integrated). Usually, when you purchase software, the procedures for using your word processor files together with your database and your spreadsheet files is quite complicated. Sometimes it leaves people very frustrated. With an integrated software package, it is simple and comfortable to use files that have been created with the separate tools together, for in reality, the tools are different aspects of the same program.

You will find that the word processor is often the base of operations for integrating information from the various tools. It is frequently useful to include part of a database, spreadsheet, or chart (graph created from spreadsheet data) in a document that you are creating using the word processor. In addition, the word processor can be used to create form letters or mailing labels using information from the database.

In this chapter, you will begin to get a sense of the power that is really yours because you have purchased an integrated software package. You will learn how to:

- Use the Window Menu to move between several active files
- Copy information from a database to a word processor document
- Create form letters
- Print mailing labels
- Move, size, and arrange open files on the screen

Opening More Than One File at a Time

There are several steps to the process of using files in an integrated fashion. The first step, and the one that always begins the discussion, is for you to open or create the files that you wish to use. Let's begin this process.

1. Create a **New Word Processor** file, that functions as a **DESTINATION** file during this project.
2. Open an existing database file on your data disk which you created in the database chapter of this book, **CLIENTS.WDB**.

This file, which functions as our **SOURCE** file, contains all the names, addresses, and phone numbers of the painting contractor's clients. The file **CLIENTS.WDB** should appear on your screen. Don't worry if the order of the records in your file is different than that in Figure 8.1. The order will depend on which of the exercises in Chapters 4 and 7 you completed.

Using the Window Command to Switch Between Files

Now that you have opened two files, how do you use them?

1. Select **Window**. The menu lists the two open files (Figure 8.1).

Note Your menu may list a word processing document as **WORD2.WPS** or **WORDx.WPS** (where *x* is some number from 1 to 8) if you have been working with the word processor since you started Works. We will refer to the file as **WORD1.WPS** throughout this section.

2. Select the new word processing file by moving the cursor down to **WORD1.WPS** and pressing **ENTER**, or by typing the highlighted number **1** preceding the filename. The word processor file is displayed.
3. Select Window again. Notice that the two open files still are listed in the bottom box in the menu.
4. Select **CLIENTS.WDB**, and you will instantly be back into your database file!

Copying from the Database to the Word Processor

Now that you have practiced moving between files, let's see how to use information from the database in a letter.

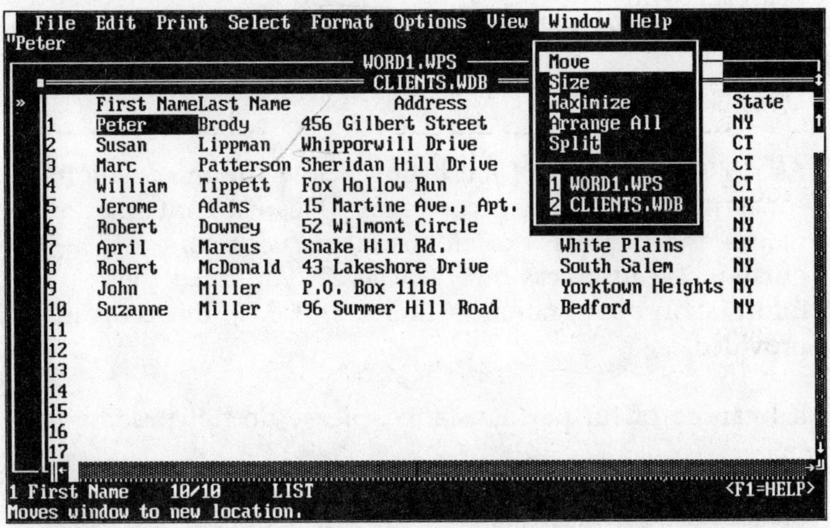

Figure 8.1. Window Menu

Specifically, you need to create a letter to your banker. You have applied for a loan, and the loan officer wants some additional information on your paint contracting business. The information you need is a list of all outstanding estimates greater than $1,000. Therefore, you need to create a letter, find the data in the database, and then copy the information from the database to the letter. To do this, follow these instructions:

1. Move back to the word processing document by using Window.
2. Enter the text in Figure 8.2.
3. End the second paragraph by pressing **ENTER** twice.

Now you are ready to get information that you want to insert in the letter. After displaying the database, sort it so all of the contracts over $1,000 are listed together in alphabetical order. Then copy the names and addresses to our letter. To do this, follow these instructions:

1. Select **Window/CLIENTS.WDB** to display the **CLIENTS** database.
2. Select **Select/Sort Records.**

George Starr, Vice President
Home State Bank
222 Broadway
New York, NY 10019

Dear George:

As per your request, I am listing below the information concerning outstanding contracts. This list contains the names and addresses of all customers with contracts outstanding in excess of $1,000.00. If you need the information about contacts under $1,000.00, this too can be provided.

If I can be of further assistance, please do not hesitate to call.

Figure 8.2. Letter prior to insertion of spreadsheet data

3. Type: **Estimate** in the **1st Field** Text Box.
4. Press **ALT-2** or **TAB** to the **2nd Field** Text Box.
5. Type: **Last Name**
   You want the records to be sorted (Figure 8.3), first by the amount of the estimate, and then by last name.
6. Press **ENTER.**
7. Choose **View/Query.**
8. Move your cursor to the Estimate field, and type: **>1000**. Press **ENTER.** Press **F10** to execute the query and return to LIST View.
9. Move the cursor to the left corner of the first record displayed.
10. Press **F8** and use the **ARROW** keys to highlight the First Name, Last Name, Address, City, and State fields for the records displayed. This will highlight the data we want brought into the word processing document. All clients with estimates greater than $1,000 will appear in order by estimate and then by last name. .

1. Select **Edit/Copy.**
2. We wish to copy this information to our Destination file. Using **Window,** select the word processing document that contains the letter to your bank.
3. Press **ENTER** to place the information in the letter at the current cursor position.

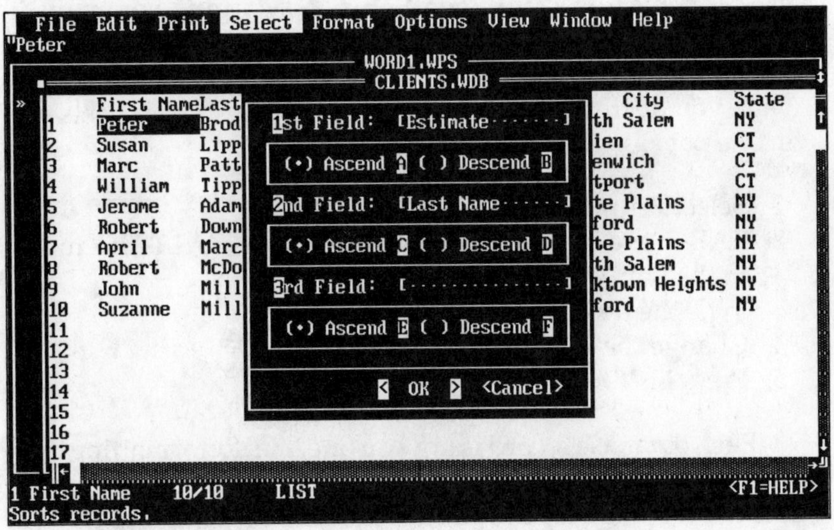

Figure 8.3. Database sort criteria

Reformatting Copied Information

You might be wondering why the information is separated by tabs. In databases and spreadsheets data are stored in rows and columns. When this information is copied to the word processor, Works inserts a tab between each column.

The present problem is that the information that we wish to have is on the screen, but it is not displayed in quite the style that we would have chosen. It is simple to reformat this text. Directions for editing the information follow.

1. If the tab symbols are not displayed on your screen, select **Options/Show All Characters** to display them.
2. Press **DEL** to delete the initial tab for each record.
3. Move the cursor to the end of the last line.
4. Press **ENTER** to leave a blank line and type a closing to the letter.

The data from the database still don't appear quite the way they should. However, it is fairly easy to correct these problems. The first problem is the one most commonly encountered when data are integrated into a Word Processor Document. The width of the database section copied is wider than the line length. Therefore, the addresses word wrap to the next line. If you read down the first column, you will notice that the states are mingled with the names. Since the difference in width is small, we can correct this problem by using the **Print/Page Setup & Margins** command to change the width of the margins (and thereby increase the length of each line of text). You have already used this technique in Chapter 3, the spreadsheet chapter, when you decreased the margins so that the spreadsheets could be printed on one page.

1. Select **Print/Page Setup & Margins.**
2. **TAB** to the **Left Margin** Text Box or press **ALT-E** to move the highlight to the Left Margin Text Box.
3. Type the new Left Margin size: **.5"**
4. Change the **Right Margin** Text Box to: **.5"**
5. Press **ENTER.**

Each database record is now on one line. Reformatting copied data is not always this easy. It sometimes requires a significant amount of editing if the data are too wide for the page. If the data brought into the word processing file are very large, it might be easier to transfer the data in multiple segments.

6. Save the letter using the filename **BANKLTR.WPS**.
7. Print the letter.

Managing the Files

If you have just completed the first exercise, you should close the files that you have been using before creating or opening the files for this exercise. Works will permit you to have eight files open at one time. Usually this is more than sufficient for the work that you wish to do. However, if you are spending a great deal of time using the program, it is conceivable that you might have eight files open and still want to open another one.

If you have eight files open, and you attempt to open another file or create a new one, the **ERROR** Dialog Box will appear on your screen. Works will inform you that there are too many files open. At that time, you will have to use **File/Close** to close one or more of your files.

We will use **File/Close** at this time to close the files you were using.

1. Select **File/Close**.

Works will close the current file. If you have not saved your changes, a Dialog Box will appear, asking if you want to save the changes. **TAB** to the **<No>** button and press **ENTER**, or use **ALT-N** to close the file without saving the changes.

2. Continue selecting **File/Close** until all files are closed.

Creating Form Letters

The word processor and database files can be used together to create personalized letters or other documents. This *merging* of the data from database files with documents created in a word processor is the procedure used to generate the personalized mass mailings that we often receive and is thus often called a *mail merge.*

The general steps used to create a letter which will include information from a database are:

- Open (or create) a database file containing the information that will be merged into each individualized document

- Create the word processor document; whenever variable information is to be included, use the **Edit/Insert Field** command to insert a place holder for the variable information
- Select the records to be merged with the document
- From the word processor document, use the **Print/Print Form Letters** command to print the documents with the variable information from the database file

Let's implement these steps using the **CLIENTS.WDB** database that you created in Chapter 4.

1. Close any open files.
2. Open the database file **CLIENTS.WDB** on your data disk.
3. Select **File/Create New File/New Word Processor** to create a new word processor file.
4. Type the current date at the left-hand margin.
5. Press **ENTER** six times.
6. To enter a field name:
   a. Select **Edit/Insert Field**. The names of all of the open databases will be shown in the Databases List Box (Figure 8.4).
   b. Highlight **CLIENTS.WDB**. The fields in the selected database will be shown in the **Fields** List Box.

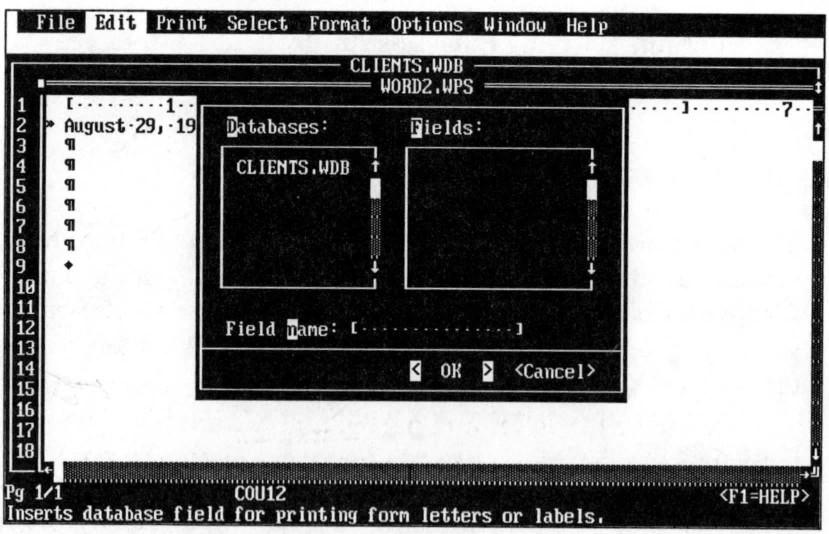

Figure 8.4. All open databases

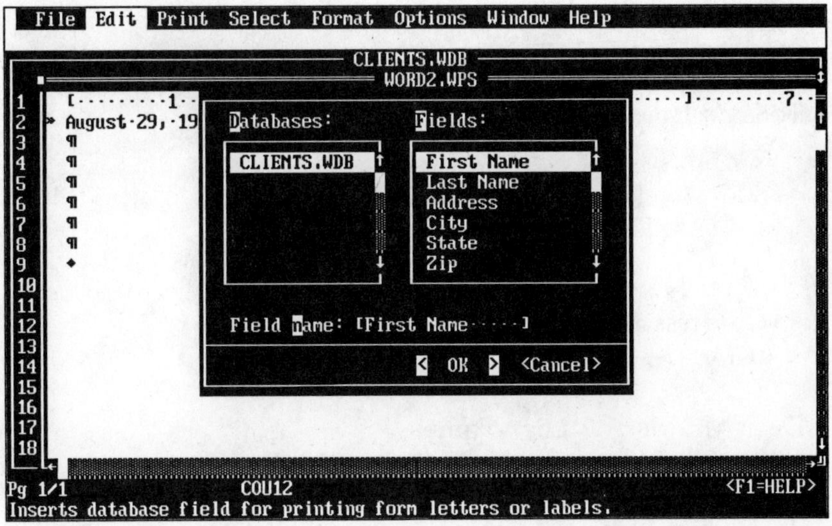

Figure 8.5. Selecting a field name from the database

c. Highlight: **First Name** (Figure 8.5).

d. Press **ENTER**. <<First Name>>, the field name enclosed in double brackets, will be entered in the document.

7. Press the **SPACEBAR** once and then repeat the steps above to insert the field name <<Last Name>>.
8. Type the remainder of the letter as shown in Figure 8.6.

Note

<<Last Name>>, **<<Address>>**, **<<City>>**, **<<State>>**, **<<Zip>>**, and **<<Estimate>>** are included below to indicate where you should use **Edit/Insert Field** to place the field names. Be sure to type the comma and space between **<<City>>** and **<<State>>**.

Selecting Database Records to Merge

If the **Print/Print Form Letters** command is used to print this letter now, one letter will be printed for each record in the **CLIENTS.WDB** file. Sometimes you want to print a letter for only some of the records in the database. Therefore, you may define a query to select only some records.

Let's print letters for a partial list of clients by using the **View/Query** command to select those clients whose last names begin with the letters A through G.

Today's Date

<<First Name>> <<Last Name >>
<<Address>>
<<City>>, <<State>> <<Zip>>

Dear Mr./Ms. <<Last Name>>:

This is a written confirmation of the estimate we discussed during my visit to your home. The total fee for supplies and labor will be: $<<Estimate>>.

If you have any questions, please call me at 564-5464.

Sincerely yours,

Peter Milkey

Figure 8.6. Form letter containing inserted fields

1. Select **Window/CLIENTS.WDB.**
2. Change to LIST View if that is not currently on the screen.
3. Select **View/Query**.
4. Move the cursor to the Last Name field. Type: **<"H"** and press **ENTER**.
5. Press **F10** or select **View/List** to execute the query and return to LIST View. The records of those clients shown in Figure 8.7 should be displayed.

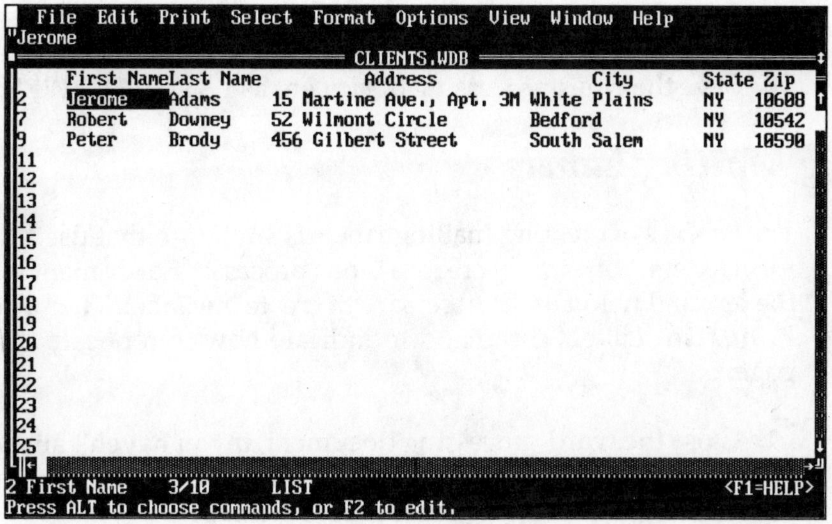

Figure 8.7. Clients with names starting with A through G

Merged Document

To print the document:

1. Return to the word processing document.
2. Select **Print/Print Form Letters**.
3. A list of all open databases will be displayed. Highlight the name of the database that contains the information to be merged, **CLIENTS.WDB** and press **ENTER**.
4. The Print Dialog Box should appear. Press **ENTER** to accept the default values.The following message may be displayed if you are using a laser printer:

   Your printer cannot print at edge of page.
   If text is cut off, adjust margins and label size and print again.

   This is just a warning to you about changing your margins if the text is too wide for a page. Press **ENTER**.
5. A copy of your letter will be printed for each one of the records that is currently displayed in the selected database. As the letters are being printed, the number of the current record whose data is being merged

will appear on the middle of the Status Line. Works will word wrap the text correctly as the variable information is inserted.

6. Save the word processing document as **ESTIMATE.WPS.**

Printing Mailing Labels

The process of creating mailing labels is similar to that used when printing form letters. You simply create a word processing document which contains the text and field names necessary to create one label. Then you will use the **Print/Print Labels** command to indicate how to replicate the label on the page.

1. Close the word processing document, if you haven't already.
2. If you haven't already done so,
   a. Open the database file **CLIENTS.WDB**.
   b. Select only the clients whose last names start with the letters A through G (see the section Selecting Database Records to Merge in this chapter).
3. Create a new word processing document.
4. Enter the field names for the mailing label shown in Figure 8.8 by using the **Edit/Insert Field** command.

```
===================================

<<First Name>> <<Last Name>>
<<Address>>
<<City>>, <<State>>  <<Zip>>
===================================
```

Figure 8.8. Field names on the mailing label

5. Save the document as **MAIL.**
6. Select **Print/Print Labels.**
7. Highlight the **CLIENTS.WDB** database.

We will leave the *Vertical* and *Horizontal* Label Spacing as it is, since this is a standard spacing. If you are using labels, measure the distance from the top of one label to the top of the next to determine the Vertical Line Spacing. If there is more than one label across a page, measure the distance from the left margin of one label to the left margin of the next label to determine the Horizontal Line Spacing.

8. If you are using mailing labels, and your measurements are different than the default values, change the values for the Vertical and Horizontal Line Spacing. If not, leave the default values.
9. Tab to the Number of Labels Across Page Text Box and change the value to **2.**
10. Press **ALT-T** to select the **<Test>** button. The test option is supplied so that you can print the first row of labels and see if the margins are set correctly.
11. The Page Setup & Margins Dialog Box will be displayed.

Most of you will probably print the "labels" on a piece of paper. However, we will make the type of adjustment that you would typically make if you were printing the information on standard sheets of labels made for computers.

12. Unless you are using a laser printer, change the *Top*, *Bottom*, *Left*, and *Right* Margins to **0**. If you are using a laser printer, you may need to consult your user's manual for the correct setting, but try a small number such as **.1**.
13. Press **ENTER** to set the new margins.
14. The Print Menu will be displayed. Press **ENTER**. The following message may be displayed if you are using a laser printer:

    Your printer cannot print at edge of page.
    If text is cut off, adjust margins and label size and print again.

    This is just a warning to you about changing your margins if the text is too wide for a page. Press **ENTER**.

15. Works will print the test row of labels, and display the message:

    Print all labels or reprint test labels?

16. If the margins are not correct, press **ESC** to cancel the Dialog Box and repeat steps 6 to 14 to change the margins.
17. If you are satisfied with the appearance of the labels, adjust the paper so that it is at the beginning of a new sheet of paper (or sheet of labels). This time select **<Print>** to print the entire set of labels.
18. Save the document as **MAIL.WPS** and close all the files.

Moving, Sizing, and Arranging Windows

Release 2 of Works has introduced several commands on the Window Menu which provide greater flexibility in displaying multiple files. To see how these operate:

1. Use the **File/Open Existing File** command to open any four Works files. At least two of the files should be databases or spreadsheets.

Figure 8.9 shows the screen after four files have been opened. Works keeps the Title Bar and the left margin of each previously opened file visible. This clearly indicates the open files, but also limits the size of the Work Area for the later files. In Figure 8.9, **BUDGET2.WKS**, which was the last opened file, displays only 15 rows, while **BUDGET1.WKS**, the first opened file, displays 18 rows. The screen for **BUDGET2.WKS** is also narrower, so fewer columns are displayed than if the entire screen is available.

2. Select **Window/2** to make the second file that you opened the active file. The Title Bars for the third and fourth opened files are no longer visible.
3. Select **Window/4**. The Title Bars for the first, second, and fourth opened files are visible. The fourth file remains the same size it was

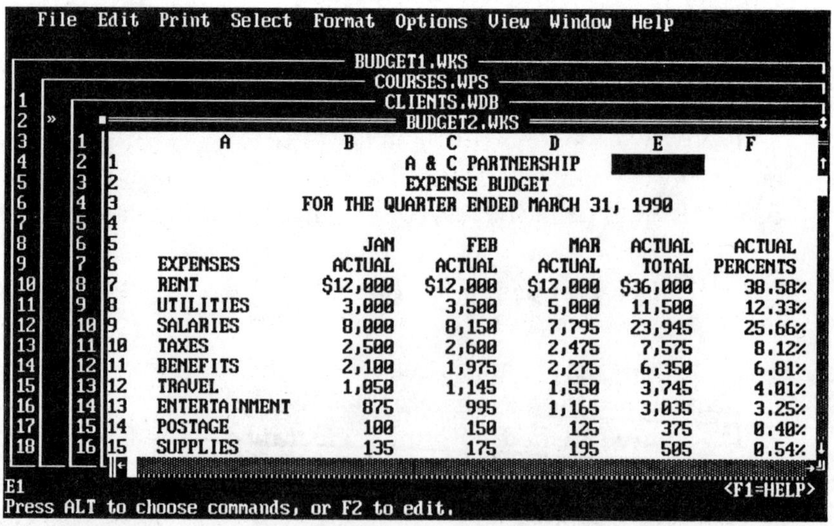

Figure 8.9. Screen after four files have been opened

when you opened it so more of the second file is visible than before (Figure 8.10).

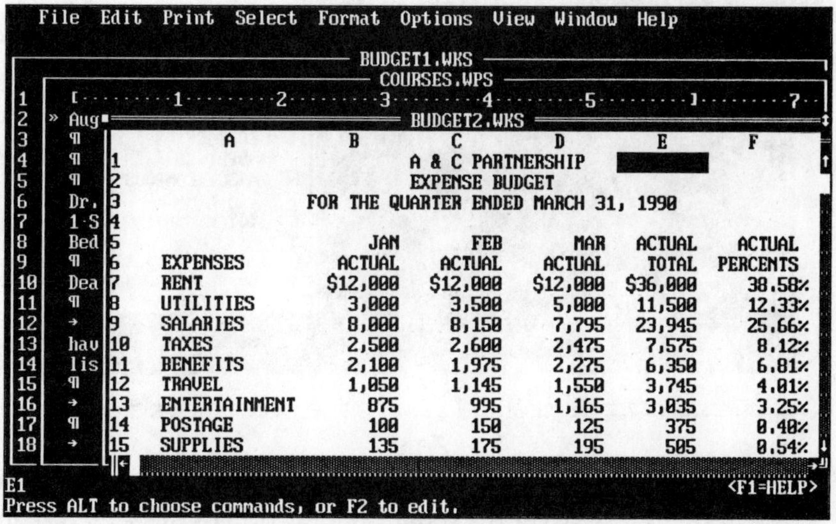

Figure 8.10. Screen with three of four opened files displayed

There is a way to make the current file use the entire screen.

4. Select **Window/Maximize**. The current file is now the only one visible.
5. Press **CTRL-F6** to cycle through the open files. **CTRL-F6** and **SHIFT-CTRL-F6** are shortcuts for selecting files using the Window Menu.
6. Open the Window Menu. *Maximize* is preceded by a mark indicating that it has been activated. Select **Maximize** again to toggle off the Maximize feature.
7. Use **CTRL-F6** or **Window/4** to display the fourth file that you opened.
8. Select **Window/Move**. Use the **ARROWS** to move the window anywhere you want on the screen.
9. Now select **Window/Size**. Use the **ARROWS** to change the size of the window. If you decrease the size, part of the underlying file is visible. The **Window/Move** and **Window/Size** commands can be used to display parts of several files at one time. For example, to obtain the screen display in Figure 8.11, **CLIENTS.WDB** was first moved to the upper left-hand corner of the screen and sized so it covered approximately half

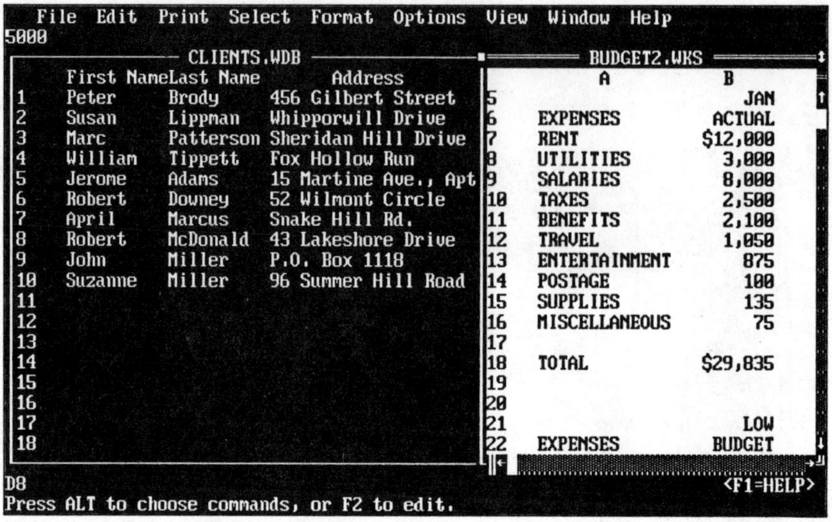

Figure 8.11. Files have been moved and sized

the screen. **BUDGET2.WKS** was then moved next to **CLIENTS.WDB** and sized to cover the remaining portion of the screen. The ability to see parts of more than one file can be useful if you want to refer to information from one file while working on a different file.

10. Select **Window/Arrange All**. Works automatically arranges all open files on the screen. You can then resize or move them to get an arrangement that is useful for you.

This chapter introduced some of the concepts used in integrating the different parts of Works. As you have seen, we are able to move quickly back and forth between our word processor and database files. The same concepts apply also with the spreadsheet files as you will see in the Exercise at the end of this chapter. The **Window** commands also allow multiple files to be displayed simultaneously, making it even easier to refer to more than one file at a time. While there are some more sophisticated techniques available when using the integrated aspect of Works the ones you have learned in this chapter should provide you with a feeling for the power of Works!

Exercise

Now you will integrate a spreadsheet and a word processing file. You will quickly see that the process of integrating these two is very similar to integrating the database and the word processor.

First, be sure that the files that you wish to work with are open.

1. Our SOURCE file is **BUDGET1.WKS**. Open that file.
2. The DESTINATION file is a new word processing file. Create that file now.
3. Begin in the word processor and type a short note to precede the data from the spreadsheet (Figure 8.12).
4. Type the following:

==

Mr. Lee Acres
234 Main Street
Bronxville, New York 10708

Dear Lee:

I enjoyed our conversation last evening at the club. As I promised you, below is our financial results for the first quarter 1990. As you can see, our projected and actual results for the first quarter are right on the money.

As a potential investor, I welcome any comment or questions that you might have. You can feel free to call me at (914)422-4378 during business hours.

==

Figure 8.12. Letter prior to insertion of spreadsheet data

5. Be sure that you press **ENTER** twice at the end of the letter so that the cursor is positioned correctly for the spreadsheet data.
6. Save the letter as **Lee**.
7. Select the spreadsheet as the active window.
8. Use **F8** to **EXTEND** all data from *A1:F18*.
9. Copy the spreadsheet data to the Lee letter.
10. If the tab symbols are not displayed on you screen, select **Options/Show all Characters**. Reformat the data if it is not correctly aligned.
11. Place the following conclusion on your letter.

a. Type: **Sincerely,**
b. Insert four blank lines.
c. Type: **Joanna Peterson**

12. Save your finished letter under the same name.
13. Print your letter.
14. Close all files.

9

A Brief Look at Communications

The fourth Works tool is the Communications manager. With one additional piece of hardware and a telephone line, it enables you to connect your computer to a remote computer and have the two exchange data. This opens a world of information for immediate use or within the word processing, spreadsheet, and database tools. In this chapter you will learn:

- The hardware necessary for communications
- Basic terminology used in communications
- How to use Works to set up your computer to communicate with an on-line information service
- How to use Works to automatically dial telephone numbers from the word processing, spreadsheet, or database tools

An Introduction to Communications

As you may have guessed by the limited nature of these objectives and the placement of this material at the end of the book, treatment of the Communications tool is different than that of the other Works components. That's because the Communications tool has some important differences from the three tools already examined. The word processor, database, and spreadsheet can all be used by themselves on a single computer to accomplish a task. The Communications tool is used to connect your computer with another computer. This requires separate hardware that some users of Works do not have. In addition, those of you who do have the necessary hardware wish to communicate with different computers or information-sharing systems. Therefore, the instructions in this chapter are more general than in the other chapters. This chapter is of value even if you do not have the hardware necessary to use the Communications tool; this discussion will give you an idea of some of the concepts involved. If you do have access to communications hardware, the instructions supplied by the communication source will provide the specific information needed to supplement this chapter.

What Is Communications Software?

The Communications tool is used to set up a connection between your computer and another computer in order that information can be exchanged. It requires using a piece of hardware, known as a modem, and the telephone system to actually transmit information between the communicating computers. The process of communicating across large distances using telephones, teletypes, radios, or televisions is referred to as *telecommunications*.

In order for two computers to communicate, they must have access to both specialized hardware and software. The types of information that you can access and the tasks that you can accomplish with a modem, a telephone, and a communications program such as the Works Communications tool are varied and growing daily. For example, you can leave or receive messages or exchange information or even noncopyrighted software (known as shareware or freeware) using one of the many Bulletin Board Systems sponsored by clubs, organizations, or groups of computer users. Dial-in computer information services (also called on-line information services) provide access to information such as stock quotes, airline schedules, book reviews, and the latest news or weather—generally for a fee. You may even initiate bank transactions, conduct bibliographic searches, shop, send mail, or play games. Software, electronic mail, or data can also be exchanged with any other compatibly equipped computer. It is also possible to use your PC to receive and send data and commands to a larger computer at your school or office.

The Hardware: A Modem

If you want to use the telephone system to communicate with another computer, you must use a *modem*. Modems are necessary because computers and telephones represent information differently. Telephones use an *analog signal,* which is a continuous, smoothly varying signal well suited to the transmission of voices. Computers use a *digital signal,* which represents information by discrete on/off signals. The modem (short for MOdulator/DEModulator) converts the signal from digital to analog so that it can be transmitted via the telephone, and then the modem on the receiving end converts the analog signal back to a digital signal. During communications each computer spends some time sending and some time receiving information so each modem spends some time converting from digital to analog and some time converting from analog to digital.

There are different types of modems. Acoustic modems use an acoustic coupler as a receptacle for an ordinary telephone handset. Once the handset is placed in the coupler, the coupler converts the computer signals so that they can be carried on the telephone system. Extraneous environmental sounds can interfere with data transmission when acoustic modems are used.

The newer modems, which are more commonly used, are either installed in your computer or alongside it and are actually plugged into standard telephone jacks. These modems tend to be more reliable and often have extra capabilities such as dialing for you, redialing busy numbers, and automatically receiving calls. Works can take advantage of these advanced features only if you are using a Hayes or Hayes-compatible modem. If you have an acoustic or non-Hayes-compatible modem you can still use it with Works, but without automatic dialing and some of the other time-saving features.

After purchasing a modem, you must install it in or next to your computer. If it is necessary for you to install a modem, consult the installation instructions provided with your modem.

It is also possible to directly wire two computers and use the Works Communications tool to enable the computers to communicate. This is a less frequently used application and will not be covered here.

Communications Example: Communicating with an On-line Information Service

This example illustrates the steps you should use to access an on-line information service. The instructions will not enable you to actually carry out this activity because telephone numbers, account numbers, and similar information necessary to actually make the connection will not be supplied here. If you have access to an on-line information service or bulletin board, you should be able to follow the general steps to establish communication.

The Communications Screen

The first step you take to access on-line information, just as you do when using any of the other tools, is to tell Works which tool you are using. Select **File/Create New File/New Communications.**

The general appearance of the communications screen (Figure 9.1) should be quite familiar. The Menu Bar contains the familiar **File, Edit, Select, Options, Window,** and **Help** Menus, as well as two new menus: **Connect** and **Transfer**. The essential menus in communications are **Options,**

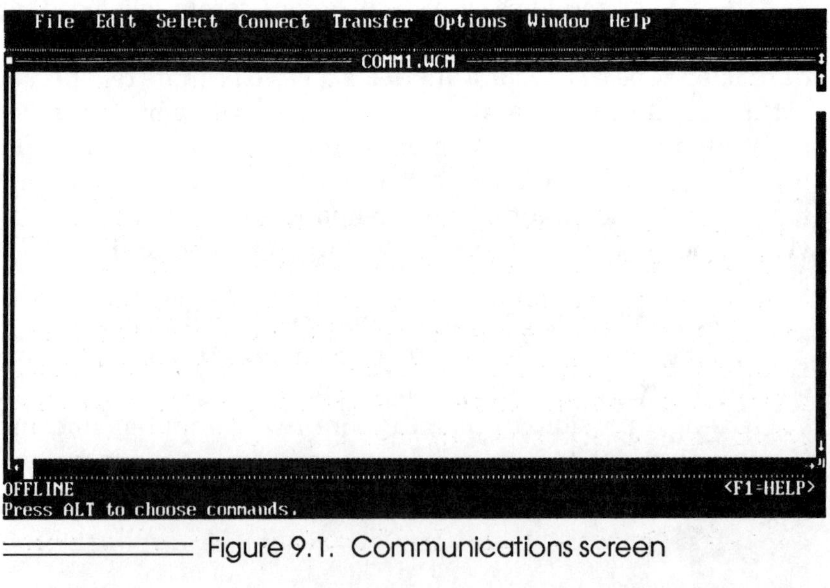

Figure 9.1. Communications screen

Connect, and **Transfer**. The **Options** Menu is used to tell your computer how to communicate with a specific partner. The **Connect** Menu is used to actually make the connection with the other computer. The **Transfer** Menu is used only if you wish to save the information you receive to a file or send information from a file rather than by typing it in at the keyboard. The **Transfer** Menu will not be described here.

The Work Area is currently blank and, while it does contain the cursor, it will not allow any typing until a connection to another computer has been made. If you try to type, you will get an error message in a Dialog Box that says *Must be Connected*. To remove the error message, press **ENTER** to select *OK*. In the Communications tool the Work Area is used only to record the information being communicated between the two computers. Prior to the connection, you may use the tool only to make menu selections that specify how the communications will take place.

The Status Line currently indicates that you are *OFFLINE*. This means that your computer is not currently communicating with another computer. Once you attempt to connect to another computer, the Status Line will indicate the time elapsed since you began the connection. The Title Bar contains the current default filename: **COMM1.WCM.** Unlike the files that we created in the other tools, the communications file will not contain the information that is displayed in the Work Area. Instead, .WCM files contain the set-up information used to establish contact with each information service or computer with which you communicate. This means that once you set up Works to communicate with a particular on-line information service, you can just open the existing .WCM file and skip the setup procedure described below.

Setting Up Works for Communication

Next, it is necessary to give Works information about the telephone number that you are calling and how you are making the call, about the way in which the information will be communicated between the two computers, and about the way the information will be displayed on your monitor. This information is entered using three of the **Options** commands: **Terminal, Communication,** and **Phone**. The following paragraphs outline the settings available for each of these commands.

First let's fill in the **Phone** settings.

1. Select **Options/Phone.**The Phone Dialog Box will appear (Figure 9.2).

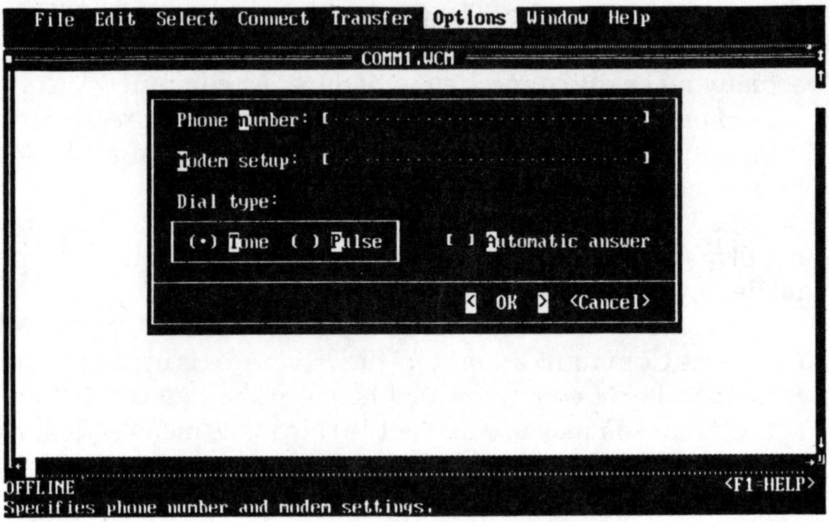

Figure 9.2. Phone Dialog Box

2. Select **Phone Number**. Enter the telephone number of the information service. Type all of the numbers that you would need to dial if you were going to dial the number yourself. The number can be entered as a string of digits or with parentheses and dashes as typically used when designating telephone numbers. Also, a comma in the number will cause a brief pause, such as that encountered on a business telephone following dialing a 9 to establish an outside connection. Some examples of phone numbers are:

   1(914)123-4567 (if you are calling a long distance number)
   19141234567
   1-914-123-4567
   123-4567 (if you are calling a local number)
   9,123-4567 (if you are using a business phone that requires dialing 9 to access an outside line; the comma causes Works to pause to allow connection to another line)

3. The **Modem Setup** Text Box can be used to send special commands to the modem that it will use when dialing. For example, you can tell the modem to change volume or to allow a certain number of rings before assuming that a connection cannot be made. The specific commands available depend on your modem, so consult the modem's manual. It is not necessary to enter any information in this box.

4. If you have touch-tone service leave the **Dial Type** Option Box as it appears. If your phone only accepts pulse (rotary) dialing, select **Pulse**.
5. If you are initiating a call, you are finished with this menu. Press **ENTER** to accept the current settings.

Note The **Automatic Answer** Check Box is only used if you want to use your PC to accept a call from another computer.

Setting up the computer so that it can dial the number of the information service is finished. Remember, you can use the Phone Dialog Box only to dial the information service number if you have a modem that uses Hayes commands.

Now, look at the settings that control how the information is actually transmitted. The speed and manner in which the data are transmitted are determined by a number of variables. The **Options/Communication** command is used to specify these variables for the current connection. Each of these settings will briefly be described. Don't worry if you don't understand what the settings really do. The important fact is that the settings you use **must correspond** to the settings being used by the receiving modem. When you subscribe to an information service they will tell you the settings that you need. In many cases these will be the same as the Works default settings. If they differ, all you have to do is use your knowledge of how to use Works Dialog Boxes to change the incorrect settings to those supplied by the information service.

First we discuss the one piece of information that is related to your computer alone rather than to how the information will be exchanged between computers, the **Port** Option:

1. Select **Options/Communication.**The Communication Dialog Box will appear (Figure 9.3).
2. In Chapter 1 when the installation procedure was discussed, one piece of information that you needed to tell Works was the port, or slot, at the back of the computer to which the printer was connected. Similarly, you now need to tell Works the port to which the modem is connected. The modem can use only serial ports, which are named COM1 or COM2. Typically your modem will use COM1. If something else, such as a serial printer, is connected to COM1 and your modem is connected to COM2, press **ALT-M** to select COM2.

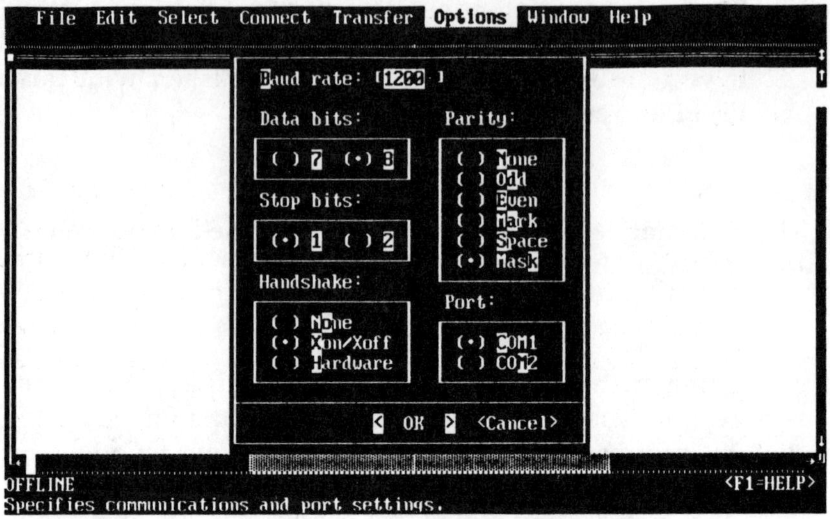

Figure 9.3. Communication Dialog Box

Note If in doubt, leave the port as **COM1.** If this choice is incorrect, the message *Wrong COM port selected* will be displayed when you try to connect, and you can then select **Options/Communication** and change to COM2.

3. The *baud rate* refers to the speed at which data are being transmitted. The baud rate can be set anywhere between 50 and 9600. However, the baud rates for most communications using modems are 300, 1200, or 2400.

Some information services give you a choice of baud rates, such as between 300 and 1200. You may need to experiment to see which is the more cost-effective option. Data are transmitted faster at 1200 baud than at 300 baud so the connect time (the time for which you are charged) and the amount of time that you need to spend waiting for information to appear on your screen are shorter. However, many services charge less for a 300 baud connection than for one at 1200 baud.

The faster response time afforded by a 1200 baud rate can be important when using an information service, since most of the communication involves the service's transmission of responses to your short queries for information. On the other hand, if you have a poor phone connection, a 300 baud rate should cause less loss of data. Also, if much of the time spent in a particular situation involves your entering data at the keyboard, or if you want to read the information as it appears on the screen, a 300 baud rate might be more appropriate.

If you want to transmit at a rate other than 1200 baud, select **Baud Rate** and type the desired rate.

4. *Data bits* refers to the number of bits which make up a character. A bit is an electrical impulse which is the smallest unit of computer information. Works can transmit characters composed of 7 or 8 bits, although 8 bits is more typically used. If you need to transmit data as 7 bits, select **ALT-7**.
5. *Stop bits* are the bits used to indicate the end of each character. Most information services use one stop bit. If the service you are using requires two, select **ALT-2.**
6. *Parity* is a means of checking for errors. In Works if data bits is set at **8,** the parity setting must be the default setting of **Mask,** or else **None. Mask** allows communication regardless of the other computer's setting. If data bits is set at **7,** your service is probably using a parity check. Select the option in the **Parity** List Box that matches the parity type specified by your information service.
7. *Handshake* refers to the way in which the two computers know when the other is sending/receiving data and when it is involved in other tasks that might interfere with the transmission of data. The specific signals most often sent by on-line information services to indicate pauses and resumptions in data transmission conform to the rules of the **Xon/Xoff** convention. A **hardware** handshake involves computers attached via a cable rather than a modem, so it would not be used in this example.If you know that the other computer uses no handshaking, select **None** from the **Handshake** Option Box.
8. When you have selected the port to which your modem is connected, and set all of the other options so that they match the specifications provided by your information service, press **ENTER.**

The final group of settings refers to the way in which your monitor and keyboard will display and send information.

1. Select **Options/Terminal.** The Terminal Dialog Box will be displayed (Figure 9.4).

Terminal is a term that originally referred to the video display and keyboard used to communicate with a large multiuser computer before the development of personal computers. The Terminal Dialog Box is used to define

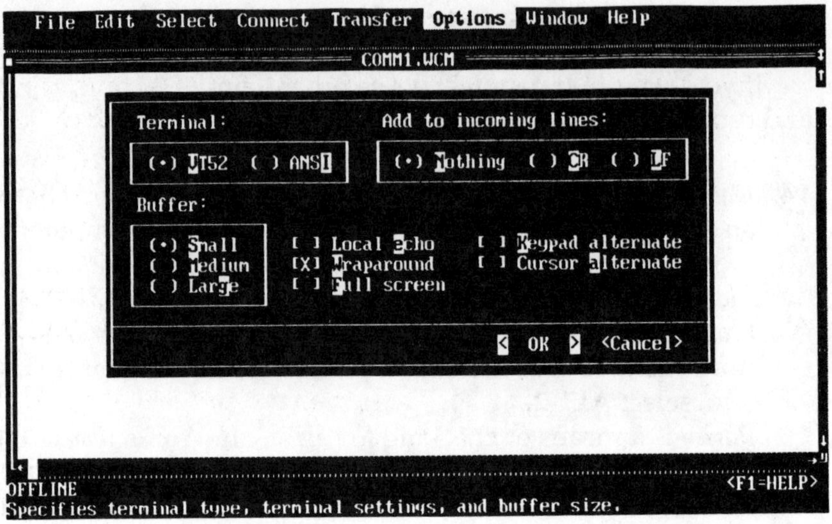

Figure 9.4. Terminal Dialog Box

the way your computer monitor displays and responds to information even if your computer is communicating with another personal computer. In addition, when a PC is used to communicate with a mainframe, the PC often needs to act like, or *emulate*, a specific type of terminal, and this Dialog Box is used to indicate the required terminal emulation.

2. **VT52** and **ANSI** refer to different terminal types; for most information services, VT52 is the correct setting although, frequently, no terminal emulation is required.

Buffer is the term for a block of computer memory that can hold information while you (or the computer) are working with it. The size of the buffer that will hold the data received by Works can be selected. The available sizes are **Small** for up to 100 lines, **Medium** for up to 300 lines, and **Large** for a maximum of 750 lines of information. Normally, **Small** is sufficient for exchanges of short comments or information that is not lengthy. **Medium**, or even **Large**, would be a better choice when receiving a larger block of data such as a very long news story or a database downloaded from a mainframe computer.

3. **Buffer** should be left as **Small** unless you know you will be receiving a large amount of data.

Typically the data transmitted by the information service will appear on your monitor in the same way that information that you type appears. If it doesn't, you probably need to change the **Add to Incoming Lines** Option Box or the **Local Echo, Wraparound,** or **Full Screen** Check Boxes. The following explanation of these options is designed to give you an idea of how to correct potential problems. In most cases, however, the default settings will be fine for use with an information service.

4. Problems with line spacing can usually be resolved by changing the option selected in the **Add to Incoming Lines** Option Box. If the cursor seems to move to the right side of the screen and then get stuck or if the lines break in the middle of the screen, select **ALT-C** to add a carriage return. If the data keep rewriting the same line on the screen, select **ALT-L** so that a line feed will be added and the cursor will move down one line. If incoming data are consistently double spaced, try selecting **ALT-C** or **ALT-N.**
5. The **Wraparound** Check Box will typically be checked so that incoming information that is too wide to fit on the screen will wrap to the next line. If Wraparound is not marked with an **X,** select **ALT-W.**
6. The **Local Echo** Check Box does not usually need to be checked when using an information service. However, in some other applications, you may not be able to see what you are typing and transmitting to the other computer. If this is the case, select **ALT-E** to turn **Local Echo** on so that your transmission will be "echoed" back on your monitor. On the other hand, if you begin typing and notice that each letter is displayed twice (e.g., ttwwiiccee) and **Local Echo** is checked, select **ALT-E** to turn **Local Echo** off.
7. Finally, if you want to see 25 lines at a time (instead of the 22 normally visible), select **ALT-F** to turn the **Full Screen** Check Box on. This will remove the Status, Menu, and Message Lines from the screen as soon as you try to connect to the other computer.
8. The **Keypad Alternate** and **Cursor Alternate** modes do not apply when using your PC to connect to an information system, so they should be left unchecked.
9. When the settings are selected, press **ENTER.**

The final step is to save the settings so that you will not need to reenter them the next time the same information service is used.

1. Select **File/Save.**

2. When the Save As Dialog Box appears, give the file a name that will reflect the information service for which the settings are to be used. Remember to type only the one to eight character filename, allowing Works to add the **.WCM** extension.

Making a Connection

Once you have specified the settings, you are ready to begin communicating.

1. Select **Connect/Connect**. Several changes will occur on the screen (Figure 9.5). The left-hand side of the Status Line will change from *OFFLINE* to a digital indication of the hours, minutes, and seconds elapsed since **Connect** was selected. The right-hand side notes that the Help key has been changed to **ALT-F1**. Only during this connect time is the Help key switched; when you disconnect, it reverts to **F1**. The Work area will display the modem setup command, if you entered one, and the modem's response to the command. (No modem setup command was used in the setup shown in Figure 9.5.) It then displays the command to the modem which tells it to dial the telephone number. Next, a message indicating the status of the attempt to connect with the information system will be displayed. The message *CONNECT*, sometimes followed by other infor-

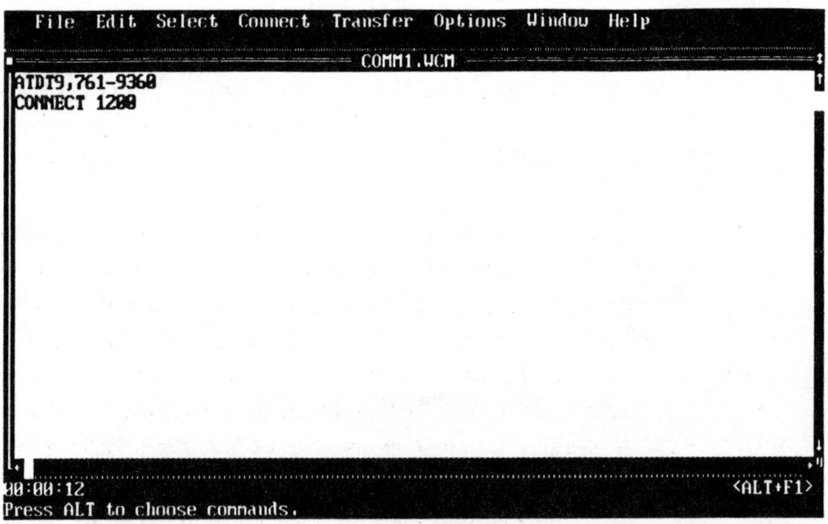

Figure 9.5. Communications screen during connection

mation, will appear if the initial connection has been successful. If the telephone number is incorrect or the computer was unable to make contact for other reasons, the message *NO CARRIER* will appear.

2. When the *CONNECT* message appears, enter the commands required by your information system to **Sign-On** (begin communications). The sign-on procedure may involve use of key combinations and responses to prompts (which appear in the Work Area) sent by the information service. A user identification number and password issued by the information service are usually entered at this time.
3. Continue interacting with the information service until you are finished.
4. End the communication by typing the command used by your information service to indicate that you are done.
5. Select **Connect/Connect** again to discontinue the connection. The Status Line message should return to *OFFLINE*.

Using the Dial This Number Feature

A separate, but related, activity using a modem utilizes the Works ability to dial a phone number. This will establish a normal telephone connection so that you can talk over the phone, not a connection to an information service. Typically, you might have a Works database of telephone numbers (similar to a rolodex), look up the desired number so that it is displayed on the screen, place the cursor on it, and choose **Options/Dial This Number**. Works will instruct the modem to dial each digit. Either now or when you hear the other party answer, pick up your telephone receiver, press **ENTER** to confirm the Works message *Pick up phone and press OK to answer*, and you may converse.

Dial This Number can be used while working with the word processing, spreadsheet, or database tools, but not in communications since that tool completes connections to other computers. Selecting the desired telephone number is slightly different in each of the three tools. In the spreadsheet and database tools, move the cursor into the field or cell containing the number. The entire telephone number in that field or cell is automatically selected. In the word processing tool you must begin selecting the phone number either through **Select/Text** in the menu or with **F8**, the **EXTEND** key, and then highlight the entire number with the arrow keys.

A Dial This Number Example

Whether or not you have a modem installed, you can do this exercise. Of course, you cannot actually complete a telephone call unless you have a modem installed, yet Works will appear to perform the connection and then hang up immediately.

Although a telephone number may be dialed from any of the three major tools, we will enter it into a spreadsheet cell. Although you enter only one phone number to test the **Dial This Number** menu choice, typically a telephone number would be one in a list of phone numbers, probably with names and addresses as well. For example, you might keep your personal telephone book in a Works database. Then, when you look up a number, simply place the cursor on it and let Works dial the number.

1. Open a new spreadsheet by selecting **File/Create New File/New Spreadsheet**. A blank spreadsheet will appear with the familiar spreadsheet menu. The pointer will be in cell *A1*.
2. In cell *A1*, type: **123-4567** (or an actual telephone number) and press **ENTER**.
3. Be certain the cursor is in cell *A1* and select **Options/Dial This Number**. The left-hand side of the Message Line will change to *Working...* as Works dials the number (Figure 9.6).

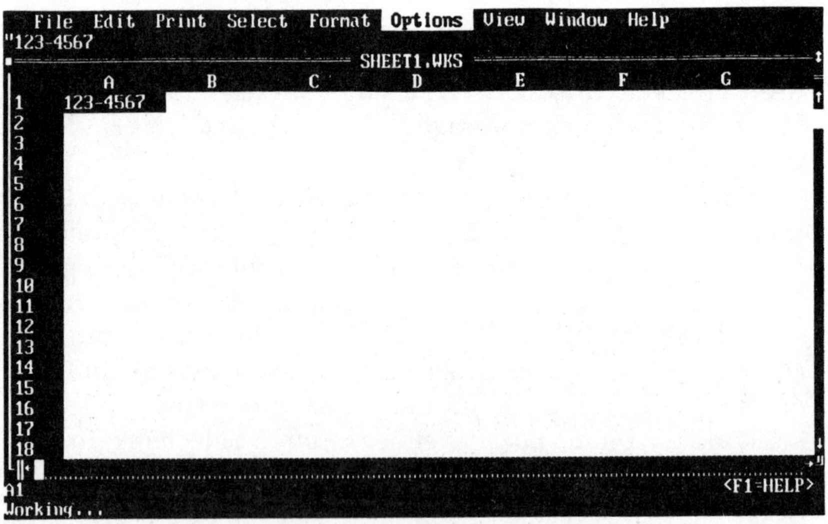

Figure 9.6. Dial This Number screen

4. Once the connection has been made, or after a few seconds if you do not have a modem, a Dialog Box will appear with the message *Pick up phone and press OK to answer*. You may pick up the receiver at any time, but you can converse only after you select **OK**. Press **ENTER** to select **OK**.

If you do not have a modem, the call will end immediately. If you actually completed a call with a modem, the connection is maintained until you hang up. You may continue with whatever you were doing in Works prior to dialing the phone number as soon as the connection is made and you select **OK**, even if you are still talking on the telephone.

---

1. Type another phone number into a different cell in the spreadsheet and use **Dial This Number** to call it.
2. Open a new word processing file and enter the following memo:

   TO: All Faculty

   FROM: Office of the Dean

   On September 9 there will be a meeting concerning the new academic year. If for any reason you cannot attend, please call 897-4619.

3. Use **Dial This Number** to call the number included in the letter.

Note If you have a modem, change the suggested telephone number to an actual number.

---

1. *a. Use the **ARROW** keys to select another cell in the spreadsheet.*
   b. Type in a phone number.
   *c. Be sure that the cursor is still in that cell and select **Options/Dial This Number**. The Message Line changes to* Working... *as Works dials the number.*
   *d. A Dialog Box appears. Press **ENTER** to answer.*
   *e. Select **File/Close** to continue.*
2. *a. Choose **File/Create New File/New Word Processor**. A blank word processor document will apppear with the already familiar menu.*
   b. Type the text of the memo.
3. *a. Placse the cursor on the 8 in the phone number.*
   *b. Press the **F8 Extend** key and the **RIGHT ARROW** to highlight the entire phone number.*

c. *Select **Options/Dial This Number**.*
d. *The Message Line changes to Working... and a Dialog Box appears. Press **ENTER** to answer.*
e. *Select **File/Close**.*

The Communications tool is fairly simple with far fewer commands than any of the other Works tools, but it adds an entirely different dimension to the use of a personal computer. With a modem and the Communications tool, your computer becomes the access line to a vast range of information and services. This chapter described the preparations for communications, which should be carried out only once for each communications partner. Future connections can be made in seconds. Even if you do not currently have the hardware necessary to actually communicate with another computer, it is important to be aware of this aspect of computing. The use of computers linked by modems or connected in various types of networks is dramatically changing the availability of information in the workplace and the way information is used by businesses.

Appendix

A

Solutions to Chapter Exercises

This Appendix provides the answer key for the Exercises at the end of each chapter.

Answer Key for Chapter 1

1. To start Works:
   a. If you are using Works from a floppy disk, insert the disk in the A drive and type: **Works**
   b. If you are using Works from a hard drive:

   - Type: **cd\(directory)** where directory is the name of the subdirectory containing the Works program.
   - Type: **works**

2. a. The File Menu should already be displayed; therefore to select the **File/Open Existing File** command, it is only necessary to select **Open Existing File**. There are two ways to do this:

- Use the **DOWN ARROW** to move the cursor to **Open Existing File** and press **ENTER**; or
- Type the highlighted letter in **O**pen Existing File: **O** (the letter "oh," not zero)

  The Open Existing File Dialog Box should be displayed, listing several word processor, spreadsheet, and database files.

b. Move the cursor to the Files List Box by pressing **TAB**, or by holding down the **ALT** key and pressing **F**. Press the **DOWN ARROW** to view the names of the files on your disk.

c. Move the cursor to the filename you want to select and press **ENTER**. You may choose any of the files listed under the headings *Word Processor, Spreadsheet* or *Database.* Do **not** choose files listed under *Other Files*. These are program files and are not readable in Works.

d. To save the file to your exercise disk:

- Press **ALT**. The File Menu should be opened.
- Type **A** to select **Save As**, or use the **DOWN ARROW** to highlight **Save As** and then press **ENTER** .
- Insert your exercise diskette in Drive A or B, if it is not already there.
- Change the directory to the drive containing your exercise disk by pressing **TAB** until the first entry in the Directories List Box is highlighted **or** by pressing **ALT-I**.
- Press the **DOWN ARROW** until the drive containing your exercise disk is highlighted. This should be -A- or -B-.
- Press **ENTER**. The cursor will automatically return to the Save File As Text Box.
- If you want to save the file using a new name, type the new filename. Remember to use only one to eight letters in your filename.
- Press **ENTER**. The new file name should appear in the Title Bar at the top of the screen.

e. To close the file:

- Press **Alt** to open the File Menu.
- Use the **DOWN ARROW** to move the cursor to **Close** and press **ENTER** or type **C**.

3. The File Menu should be displayed and the **Create New File** command highlighted. Therefore, to create a new word processing file:
   a. Press **ENTER**. The New Word Processor button should be enclosed in highlighted brackets.
   b. Press **ENTER** to select the New Word Processor button.
4. Type a few words.
5. Select the **File/Save** or **File/Save As** command. Since this is the first time you are saving the file, Works assumes that you want to give it a new name and displays the File Save As Dialog Box.
   a. If the directory listed on the second line of the screen is not the drive containing your exercise disk, follow the directions listed under 2d beginning with the third step.
   b. If the directory listed on the second line of the screen is the drive containing your exercise disk, type a new file name and press **ENTER**.
6. Select the **File/Close** command. Follow the directions in 2e if you are not sure how to do this.
7. The File Menu should be displayed on the screen. To exit from Works, type **x**, the highlighted letter in **Exit Works**, or use the **DOWN ARROW** to move the highlight to *Exit Works* and press **ENTER**.

Answer Key for Chapter 2

1. To copy the block of information for the *Green Room*:
   a. Place the cursor on the *R* of *Room*.
   b. Press **F8**.
   c. Extend the highlight to the end of the Fee line.
   d. Select **Edit/Copy**.
   e. Move the cursor directly below the Fee line.
   f. Press **ENTER**.
2. To spell check the document:
   a. Move the cursor to the beginning of the document.
   b. Select **Options/Check Spelling**.
   c. Make the appropriate selections if any words are flagged.
3. To save the document:
   a. Select **File/Save.**
   b. Enter an appropriate filename and the correct directory.
4. To print the document:
   a. Select **Print/Print.**

b. Press **ENTER.**

5. To close the file, select **File/Close.**

Answer Key for Chapter 3

Here are some helpful steps to assist you in solving your first spreadsheet independent exercise.

1. To widen columns, choose **Format/Column Width** and then specify the width of the column. This will only widen one column at a time. To widen all the columns, first press **F8** and **EXTEND** your cursor from the A column through the E column. Then choose **Format/Column Width.**
2. The formula to be placed in *D8* should be:

   =C8-B8

   After placing the formula in *D8,* use **F8** to **EXTEND** your cursor through *D13*. Then choose **Edit/Fill Down.** This will copy your formula and relatively adjust the results.
3. To format the values in the B, C, and D columns, again use **F8** to **EXTEND** the entire range. Then, choose **Format/Comma** and specify the number of decimal places as 0.
4. Repeat the above process for the E column, but the format you will choose is **Percent**.
5. To save your results, choose **File/Save As** and specify the filename as **INDPROJ1.WKS**.

To print your results, move your cursor to *A1*. Press **F8** to cover the cells you want printed. Select **Print/Set Print Area** to send a signal to Works to print only the range you specified. Then select **Print/Print** to print the area selected.

Answer Key for Chapter 4

1. To create a new file, choose **File/Create New File/New Database**.
2. Remember to place a colon **(:)** after each field name.
3. You may enter data on either the FORM or LIST View Screens. Type in the data, press **TAB** key to move from field to field, and press the **TAB** key at the end of the record to move to the next record.

4. To save the file, choose **File/Save As**. Choose a name for your database.
5. To change field widths, choose **Format/Field Width.** Be sure your cursor is in the column before you attempt to change the width.
6. The second time you save your file, you can choose **File/Save.**
7. To print out the database, choose **Print/Print.**
8. To search for students taking lessons on Thursday, choose **Select/Search,** type in the criteria, and press **ENTER**. To repeat the search to look for the next record, press **F7**.
9. To select all records of the instructor Zash, choose **Select/Search**; the criteria is Zash, but this time choose *All Records*. Print using the same instructions as in step 7.
10. To display all records, choose **Select/Show All Records.**
11. To sort the database, choose **Select/Sort Records.** Type in the field name, Instructor. Press **ENTER.**

Answer Key for Chapter 5

1. First add the enhancements to the cover letter.
   a. To right justify the date:

   - Place the cursor on the date line
   - Select **Format/Right**, type the date, and press **ENTER**
   - Select **Format/Normal.**
   - In order to format the date after it has been entered, move to the date line and select **Format/Right**; move the cursor to the next line and select **Format/Normal**

   b. To bold the address lines:

   - Place the cursor on the *M* of *Ms*
   - Press **F8**
   - Extend the highlight to the end of the address
   - Select **Format/Bold** or press **CTRL-B**

   c. To underline *Computer Analyst*:

   - Place the cursor on the C of *Computer*
   - Press **F8**

- Extend the highlight to the end of *Analyst*.
- Select **Format/Underline** or press **CTRL-U**

d. To double space the paragraph:

- Place the cursor anywhere on the paragraph
- Select **Format/Double Space**

2. To insert the page break, press **CTRL-ENTER**.
3. Next enhance the list on the second page.

a. To change the tab settings:

- Select **Format/Tabs**
- Type: **2** in the Position Text Box
- Press **ENTER**
- Type: **4** in the Position Text Box
- Press **ENTER**
- Select **<Done>** by pressing **ALT-D**

b. To center the top line:

- Type the text: **Candidates for Computer Analyst**
- With the cursor still on this line:
- Select **Format/Center**
- Press **ENTER**
- Select **Format/Normal Paragraph**
- Press **ENTER** to insert a blank line

c. To underline *Name, Yrs. Experience,* and *Salary Requirements*:

- Place the cursor on *N* of *Name*
- Press **F8**
- Extend the highlight to the end of *Name*
- Select **Format/Underline** or press **CTRL-U**
- Repeat the above steps for *Yrs. Experience* and *Salary Requirements*

d. To search for each occurrence of *years* and replace it with *yrs.*:

- Move the cursor to the beginning of page 2
- Select **Select/Replace**

- Enter **years** in the **Search for** Text Box
- Enter **yrs.** in the **Replace with** Text Box
- Select **<Replace All>** by pressing **ALT-A**

e. To add a header and footer:

- Select **Print/Headers & Footers**
- Select the **Use header & footer paragraphs** Check Box
- Press **ENTER**
- Move the cursor to the Header line on the top of the document
- Type: Purdy Personnel Agency

Answer Key for Chapter 6

1. Choose **Create New File/New Spreadsheet.**
2. To type in the labels, just move to the cell and type. To type in the values, do the same. Do not worry about cosmetics now.
3. To change the width of the column A, place the cursor anywhere in column A and choose **Format/Column Width/15.**
4. To change the width of columns B through G, first use **F8** to **EXTEND** the range; then choose **Format/Column Width/7**.
5. The formula in *I6* should be: **=SUM(C6:H6)**
6. To copy the formula, first use **F8** to **EXTEND** the range, then choose **Edit/Fill Down.**
7. The formula in *B15* should be: **=SUM(B6:B13)**
8. To format the data:
    - Use **F8** to **EXTEND** the range
    - Then choose **Format/Comma/2.** Press **ENTER**
9. To copy the titles, use **F8** to **EXTEND** the range; then choose **Edit/Copy.** Then move your cursor to cell *A19*.
10. The formulas for the high, low and average expenditures are:
    - High **=MAX(C9:G9)**
    - Low **=MIN(C9:G9)**
    - Average **=AVG(C9:G9)**
11. To create a chart, first use **F8** to highlight **A19** through **D23**. Choose **View/New Chart.**

12. To add titles, choose **Data/Titles**. Type in the appropriate titles and press **ENTER.**
13. To add legends, choose **Data/Legend.** The *1st Y* should be **High**, the *2nd Y* should be **Low,** and the *3rd Y* should be **Average**.
14. To print the graph, choose **Print/Print.**
15. To print the spreadsheet, choose **View/Spreadsheet.** Use **F8** to **EXTEND** the range you want to print. Choose **Print/Set Print Area.** Then choose **Print/Print**.
16. To save the file, choose **File/Save As**.

Answer Key for Chapter 7

1. The new field can be added in either LIST or FORM View. To add it in LIST View:
   a. Move the cursor to the right of the last field.
   b. Select **Edit/Field Name** and type: **Contract**
2. With the cursor on the first record in the Contract field, type: **y** and press the **DOWN ARROW**. Continue entering the data for the rest of the column.
3. Select **View/New Report** and press **ENTER** until the Report Definition screen is displayed.
4. To delete the extra fields:
   a. Move to the first row in the address field.
   b. Press **F8** to begin extending. Use the **RIGHT ARROW** to highlight one entry in the City, State, and Zip fields.
   c. Select **Edit/Delete Row/Column**. When the Dialog Box appears, select **Column**.
5. Type a title of your choice in the first *Intr Report* row. The column you choose to enter it in will depend on how long your title is. Enter it in a column so that it will be approximately centered on the page.
6. a. Select **Select/Sort Records**.

   - Type **Contract** in the 1st Field Title Box. Make this a break field by pressing **ALT-G**
   - Enter **last name** in the 2nd Field Title Box and **first name** in the 3rd Field Title Box

   b. Move the cursor to **=COUNT(Las** in the *Summ Contract* row. Use **F8** to highlight the entries before **=sum(estim.** Select **Edit/Clear**. Use the same procedure to remove the remaining COUNT statistics.

c. To enter the sum for the total database:

- Move to the Estimate field in the second report summary row(or wherever you want the sum to appear)
- Select **Edit/Field Summary**
- Highlight the Estimate field. If Sum is not already selected, select it and then press **ENTER**

To add the Count field for the Report summary, repeat the first three steps for part c, only use First Name as the field and Count as the summary statistic.

d. Move the cursor to the columns in the *Summ Contract* and *Summ Report* rows adjacent to the summary statistics and type the text you want included.

7. Select **Print/Print** to print the report.
8. To name the report:
   a. Select **View/Reports**.
   b. Type a new name for the report in the Name Text Box and press **ENTER**.
   c. Select the **<Done>** button.
9. Select **View/List**. If you entered REPORT View from FORM View, first select **View/Form** and then press **F9** to display LIST View.
10. Select **Select/Sort Records**. The field on which the records were previously sorted should appear in the 1st field Text Box. Press **ENTER** to re-sort the fields.
11. Select **Select/Search.** Enter **NY** in the Text Box and select the **Select All Records** option. Press **ENTER**. Only the records for clients in the state of ny should appear on the screen.

Note

In a larger database, this search could select extraneous incorrect data, since names or street addresses including the letters "ny" would be found. To prevent this, move the cursor to the state field, select **Select/Field** and repeat the search, this time limited to the State field.

12. Select **View/(name of report that you created in this exercise).** Press **ESC** to display the REPORT Screen and then select **Print/Print** from the menu.

13. Select **File/Save** to save the database using the same name, or **File/Save As** if you prefer to save the database using a different name.

Answer Key for Chapter 8

1. To open the source file, choose **File/Open Existing File.** The filename is **BUDGET1.WKS.**
2. To open the destination file, choose **File/Create New File/New Word Processor**.
3. Type in the information in Figure 8.12. To save the word processor file, choose **File/Save As.** The filename is **LEE.**
4. In order to select the spreadsheet as the active window, you should choose **Window/BUDGET1.**
5. To copy the data from the spreadsheet to the letter, you must be in the spreadsheet. Choose **Edit/Copy**. When prompted *to select the new location and press ENTER*, choose **Window/LEE** and press **ENTER.**

Note If the data are being placed incorrectly into the letter, check where the cursor is located in the letter. You might have positioned your cursor incorrectly.

6. Save the file using **File/Save.**
7. To print out your letter, choose **Print/Print**. Press **ENTER.**
8. Close the file using **File/Close.**

Appendix

B

System Requirements

The system requirements for running of *Microsoft Works* are listed here. Although some of the terminology will be familiar to you from explanations incuded throughtout the nine chapters of this book, many of the terms are technical ones with which you may not be acquainted.

System Component	Requirement
Computer	An IBM Personal Computer or IBM Personal System/2 or Compatible
Memory	512 kilobytes
Monitor	CGA, EGA, MCGA, VGA, or Hercules graphics adapter
Disk Drives	Two 360 kilobyte drives or one 720 kilobyte drive
Diskettes	5.25 or 3.5 inch disks (whichever is appropriate)
Disk Operating System	Version 2.0 or higher

Appendix

C

Microsoft Works Menu Commands

The following table lists the menu commands used in the Word Processor, Spreadsheet, Database, and Communications tools and describes the function of the specific commands. Most of the tools have File, Edit, Print, Select, Format, Options, and Window selections; however, some of the specific commands in each are different. There are additional menu commands in each tool depending on the specific capabilities of that tool. The menu commands listed in the following table are organized as they appear on the menu, integrating options from the various tools.

Note The Database uses four different screens and the Spreadsheet uses two different screens, which are listed in the explanation of abbreviations.

Explanation of abbreviations

WP = Word Processor
SS = Spreadsheet
Ch = Spreadsheet CHART Screen
DB = Database
F = FORM Screen
L = LIST Screen

R = REPORT Screen
Q = QUERY Screen
C = Communications

File

Create New File...	WP,SS,DB(All),C	Creates new *Works* file
Open Existing File...	WP,SS,DB(All),C	Opens existing *Works* file
Save	WP,SS,DB(All),C	Saves active file on disk
Save As...	WP,SS,DB(All),C	Saves active file on disk with a new name
Close	WP,SS,DB(All),C	Removes active file from RAM
File Management...	WP,SS,DB(All),C	Copies, deletes files; creates, removes directories; copies, formats disks
Run Other Programs...	WP,SS,DB(All),C	Runs programs other than *Works*
Convert...	WP,SS,DB(All),C	Converts Word Processor file from one format to another
Exit	WP,SS,DB(All),C	Exits Works and returns to DOS

Edit

Undo	WP	Reverses the last editing or formatting action
Move	WP,SS	Moves selection to another location
Move Field	DB(F,L,R)	Moves selection to another location
Move Record	DB(F,L,R)	Moves selection to another location
Copy	WP,SS	Copies selection to another location
Copy	DB	Must select label
Copy Record	DB	Copies selection to another location
Copy Special	WP,SS	Copies selection to another location using special options
Clear	SS,DB(F,L,R,Q)	Erases selection
Delete	WP	Deletes selection
Delete row/column	SS,DB(R)	Deletes rows or column
Delete record/field/label	DB	Deletes this record/field/label
Insert row/column	SS	Inserts rows or columns
Insert record/field/line	DB	Inserts blank record/field
Insert Field Name	DB(R)	Inserts field name
Insert Field Contents	DB(R)	Inserts field contents

Insert Field Summary	DB(R)	Inserts specified summary statistic
Fill Right	SS,DB(L)	Copies left-most cell(s) to rest of selection
Fill Down	SS,DB(L)	Copies top-most cell(s) to rest of selection
Fill Series...	SS,DB(L)	Fills selection with numbers or dates
Field Name	DB(L)	Creates or changes a field name
Range Name...	SS	Marks and names selection or deletes marks
Insert Special	WP	Inserts special characters for date, time, and filename
Insert Field	WP	Inserts database field for printing form letters or labels
Insert Chart	WP	Inserts spreadsheet chart
Footnote...	WP	Inserts footnote, or edits selected footnote mark
Bookmark Name...	WP	Marks and names selection, or deletes marks

Print

Print...	WP,SS,Ch,DB(F,L,R)	Prints active file
Set Print Area	SS	TellsWorks to print just the area selected
Insert Page Break	WP,SS,DB(L,R)	Inserts page break mark
Delete Page Break	SS,DB,(L,R)	Deletes page break before selected row or column
Page Setup & Margins...	WP,SS,DB,Ch	Specifies page size, margins, and first page number
Preview...	WP,SS,DB,Ch	Shows printed page on screen
Print Form Letters...	WP	Prints one letter for each database record
Headers & Footers...	WP,SS,DB	Adds headers or footers to file
Printer Setup...	WP,SS,DB,Ch	Specifies printer and port
Print Labels...	WP	Prints one mailing label for each selected database record

Select

Go To...	WP	Selects specified page or bookmark
Go To...	SS	Selects specified cell range or named range
Go To...	DB	Selects specified record or field
Search...	WP,SS,DB(F,L)	Selects next occurrence of specified text
Replace...	WP	Selects and replaces specified text
Row	SS	Extends selection to entire row
Column	SS	Extends selection to entire column
Text	WP	Selects range of text
All	WP,SS	Selects file
Cells	SS	Selects range of cells
Sort Rows...	SS	Sorts selected rows
Apply Query	DB	Applies query to all records
Hide Record	DB	Hides selected records
Show All Records	DB	Displays all records
Switch Hidden Records	DB	Displays hidden records and hides visible records
Sorts Records	DB	Sorts records

Format

Plain Text	WP	Removes all character styles from selection
Bold	WP	Applies this character style to selection
Underline	WP	Applies this character style to selection
Italic	WP	Applies this character style to selection
Font & Style...	WP	Applies character font and style to selection
Normal Paragraph	WP	Removes all paragraph formatting from selection
Left	WP	Applies this alignment to selection
Center	WP	Applies this alignment to selection
Right	WP	Applies this alignment to selection
Justified	WP	Applies this alignment to selection

Single Space	WP	Applies this line spacing to selection
Double Space	WP	Applies this line spacing to selection
Indents & Spacing	WP	Applies indents, line spacing, and alignment to selection
Tabs...	WP	Sets and removes tabs in selection
Borders...	WP	Applies borders to selection
General	SS,DB(F,L,R)	Applies this number format to selection
Fixed...	SS,DB(F,L,R)	Applies this number format to selection
Currency...	SS,DB(F,L,R)	Applies this number format to selection
Comma...	SS,DB(F,L,R)	Applies this number format to selection
Percent...	SS,DB(F,L,R)	Applies this number format to selection
Exponential...	SS,DB(F,L,R)	Applies this number format to selection
True/False	SS,DB(F,L,R)	Applies this number format to selection
Time/Date	SS,DB(F,L,R)	Applies this number format to selection
Font...	SS,DB(F,L,R)	Specifies font for entire file
Style...	SS,DB(F,L,R)	Applies alignment, character style, and locks to selection
Column/Field Width...	SS,DB(F,L,R)	Specifies width of columns fields in selection
Field Size...	DB(F)	Specifies field width and height
Show Field Name	DB(F)	Displays or hides field name
Bar	Ch	Applies this chart format to current chart
Stacked Bar	Ch	Applies this chart format to current chart
100% Bar	Ch	Applies this chart format to current chart
Line	Ch	Applies this chart format to current chart
Area Line	Ch	Applies this chart format to current chart

Hi-Lo-Close	Ch	Applies this chart format to current chart
Pie	Ch	Applies this chart format to current chart
X-Y	Ch	Applies this chart format to current chart
Title Font...	Ch	Specifies font for title chart
Other Font...	Ch	Specifies font for chart subtitle, labels, and legends.
Data Format...	Ch	Specifies colors, patterns, and markers for data series

Options

Works Settings...	WP,SS,Ch,DB(All),C	Sets screen colors, lines, and other Works settings
Calculator...	WP,SS,Ch,DB(All),C	Shows calculator
Alarm Clock...	WP,SS,Ch,DB(All),C	Shows alarm clock
Dial This Number...	WP,SS,Ch,DB(All),C	Dials selected number
Show Ruler	WP	Displays or hides ruler
Show All Characters	WP	Displays or hides special characters
Show Footnotes	WP	Displays footnote pane
Wrap For Screen	WP	Wrap text at margins for screen only
Typing Replaces Selection	WP	Turns on or off overtype
Check Spelling...	WP	Selects next misspelled or incorrect word
Thesaurus...	WP	Finds synonym for selected word or phrase
Paginate Now	WP	Updates page breaks now
Freeze Titles	SS	Freezes rows and columns before selection, or unfreezes them
Show Formulas	SS	Displays either formulas or values
Protect Data	SS,DB(F,L)	Turns on or off locks specified in Style command
Protect Form	DB	Protects form layout from accidental changes
Manual Calculation	SS	Turns automatic calculation on or off
Calculate Now	SS	Calculates spreadsheet when Manual Calculation on
X-Axis...	Ch	Specifies axis scale and format

Y-Axis	Ch	Specifies axis scale and format
Right Y-Axis	Ch	Specifies axis scale and format
Two Y-Axes	Ch	Assigns Y-series to left or right Y-axis
Mixed Line & Bar	Ch	Creates chart with both line and bar series
Format for B&W	Ch	Displays chart in either B&W or color
List Printer Formats	Ch	Lists either printer or screen formats in Data Format Dialog Box
Show Printer Fonts	Ch	Shows either printer or screen fonts in Chart View
Show Legends	Ch	Displays or hides legends
Shows Border	Ch	Turns on or off chart border
Terminal...	C	Specifies terminal type, terminal settings, and buffer size
Communication...	C	Specifies communications and port settings
Phone...	C	Specifies phone number and modem settings

Window

Move	WP,SS,Ch,DB(All),C	Moves window to new location
Size	WP,SS,Ch,DB(All),C	Changes window size
Maximize	WP,SS,Ch,DB(All),C	Makes window full-screen
Arrange All	WP,SS,Ch,DB(All),C	Arranges windows so all are visible
Split	WP,SS,Ch,DB(All),C	Creates panes to display different parts of file
(filename)	WP,SS,Ch,DB(All),C	Changes the active file

View

Spreadsheet	SS,Ch	Displays the spreadsheet
New Chart	SS,Ch	Creates a chart from the highlighted data
Charts...	SS,Ch	Renames, deletes, or duplicates a chart
(chart name)	SS,Ch	Displays the named chart
Form	DB(All)	Displays the database, one record at a time
List	DB(All)	Displays the database in columns and rows

Query	DB(All)	Displays the form for entering Query formulas
New Report	DB	Creates a new report
Reports...	DB	Renames, deletes, or duplicates a report
(report name)	DB	Displays the named report

Data

1st Y-Series	Ch	Specifies selection as this series
2nd Y-Series	Ch	Specifies selection as this series
3rd Y-Series	Ch	Specifies selection as this series
4th Y-Series	Ch	Specifies selection as this series
5th Y-Series	Ch	Specifies selection as this series
6th Y-Series	Ch	Specifies selection as this series
X-Series	Ch	Specifies selection as this series
Series...	Ch	Selects and deletes existing series
Titles...	Ch	Specifies chart titles
Legends...	Ch	Specifies Y-series legends
Data Labels...	Ch	Specifies Y-series data point labels

Connect

Connect	C	Connects to or disconnects from other computer
Dial Again	C	Redials if host busy or connection fails
Pause	C	Sends either pause or continue signals
Break	C	Sends break signal
Sign-On	C	Plays back recorded sign-on sequence
Record Sign-On	C	Starts or stops recording of sign-on sequence

Transfer

Capture Text...	C	Captures incoming text in specified file
Send Text...	C	Sends text file
Receive File...	C	Receives file
Send File...	C	Sends file

Appendix

D

Microsoft Works Function Keys

This table is a summary of the function keys used in Microsoft Works.

Key	Word Processor	Spread Sheet	Data Base	Communi-cations	Purpose
F1	Help	Help	Help		Access Help
Alt-F1				Help	Access Help
Shift-F1	Lesson	Lesson	Lesson		Access tutorials
Alt-Shift-F1				Lesson	Access tutorials
F2		Edit	Edit		Changes data already entered
F3	Move	Move	Move		Moves selected data to new location

Key	Word Processor	Spread Sheet	Data Base	Communi-cations	Purpose
Shift-F3	Copy	Copy	Copy	Copy	Copies selected data to new location
F4		Reference			Makes cell reference absolute
F5	Go To	Go To	Go To		Moves cursor to specified location
Shift-F5	Next Bookmark	Next Range			Moves cursor to next bookmark or named range
F6	Next Pane				Moves cursor between panes (e.g., footnote pane)
Shift-F6	Previous Pane				Moves cursor between panes
Ctrl-F6	Next Window	Next Window	Next Window	Next Window	Moves cursor to next split-screen window
Ctrl-Shft-F6	Previous Window	Previous Window	Previous Window	Previous Window	Moves cursor to previous split-screen windows
F7	Repeat Search	Repeat Search	Repeat Search		Finds and selects next instance of the search data
Shift-F7	Repeat Copy	Repeat Copy	Repeat Copy		Makes multiple copies of selected data or format

Key	Word Processor	Spread Sheet	Data Base	Communi-cations	Purpose
F8	Extend	Extend	Extend	Extend	Highlights data
Shift-F8	Shrink Selection				Cancels a selection made with **F8**
Shift-F8		Select Column	Select Column/Field		Extends selection to entire columns/ fields
Ctrl-F8		Select Row	Select Row/Record		Extends selection to entire row(s)/ record(s)
Ctrl-Shft-F8		Select all cells	Select all cells		Extends selection to the entire spreadsheet
F9	Paginate Now				Paginates file when manual pagina-tion is turned on
F9		Calculate Now			Calculates formulas when manual calculation is turned on
F9			View List/Form		Switches between view and form screens
F10		Exit Chart	Exit		Exits report, chart, or query screen
Shift-F10		View Chart	View Report		Displays chart or report

Index

G

H

N

O

P

T

U

V

W

X

Y

Z